T0338075

IT Best Practices for
Financial Managers

IT Best Practices for Financial Managers

JANICE ROEHL-ANDERSON

John Wiley & Sons, Inc.

Library of Congress Cataloging-in-Publication Data:

Roehl-Anderson, Janice M.
  IT best practices for financial managers/Janice Roehl-Anderson.
    p. cm.
  Includes bibliographical references and index.
  ISBN 978-0-470-50828-2 (cloth)
  1. Information technology–Management.   2. Business enterprises–Finance.
3. Finance.   I. Title.
  HD30.2.R643 2010
  658.150285–dc22
                                                                2009035914

Printed in the United States of America

10 9 8 7 6 5 4 3 2 1

Contents

Preface

One of the most important aspects of a financial executive's job is helping to ensure that financially related systems are implemented on time and on budget and that the systems are secure and reliable. Additionally, the financial executive needs to be aware of other key system-related topics, including the systems planning and software selection processes, ways to effectively implement systems using a well-established methodology, ways shared service centers can enhance the investments in systems, the impact of International Financial Reporting Standards (IFRS) on systems projects, trends related to e-commerce and software as a service (SaaS), and the impact mergers, acquisitions, and divestitures can have on the finance area.

There has been a tremendous amount of change in the systems world over the past several years. As a result, it is very hard to stay abreast of the latest system trends and best practices[1] for finance. This book is focused on providing the financial executive with an understanding of some of the most important system-related areas that can impact the finance function. It also contains best practices for selecting, implementing, and maintaining systems.

---

[1]The term *best practices* represents the authors' collective experience of what works in the real world and the hundreds of years of their combined time facilitating the successful delivery of information systems projects.

The book is divided into three parts:

- **Part I: The Basics (Chapters 1 through 6).** Many organizations fail to effectively implement and manage their financial systems. This part includes a detailed discussion of the strategic systems planning and software selection process and the best practices associated with them. It also contains a detailed overview of an approach to successfully implementing financial systems, ways to address the "people aspects" of implementations, and an overview of key financial applications. Part I concludes with a detailed overview of shared services and best practices associated with them, some of the trends related to outsourcing that financial executives need to understand, and the next wave for financial systems.

- **Part II: IT Hot Topics (Chapters 7 through 14).** Since the passage of the Sarbanes-Oxley Act, the importance of strong security and controls has risen dramatically. Part II discusses some of the best practices associated with automated security and controls and provides an overview of system privacy and why the financial executive needs to be aware of this aspect of system implementations. This part of the text also contains a detailed discussion of IFRS, one of the hottest topics in the financial and systems world. International Financial Reporting Standards are a single set of accounting principles that are rapidly gaining acceptance by the financial reporting bodies of countries around the world, including the United States. IFRS is focused on the objectives of transparency, reduced complexity, and market-versus-accrual valuation. Part II describes the impact of IFRS on financial organizations and contains a best practices–based approach to implementing IFRS-based systems.

  The only thing constant about information technology is that it is constantly changing. This part of the book also discusses some of the latest trends and related best practices that are impacting the marketplace and financial organizations, including software as a service (SaaS), e-commerce and the impact it is having on financial systems, and the importance of managing product information.

- **Part III: Mergers, Acquisitions, Divestitures, and IT (Chapters 15 through 21).** Over the past several years, a significant number of companies have been involved in mergers, acquisitions, and/or divestitures (MA&D). As a result, it is imperative for financial executives to understand the systems-related aspects of these deals, whether they are the buyer or the seller. This part of the book contains overviews of and best practices related to the following aspects of these deals: key questions financial executives should ask during a deal, ways to conduct IT due diligence prior to closing a deal, methods for capturing IT-related synergies and reducing IT costs, ways an MA&D event can be used to build value, approaches to managing the IT function during a deal, and ways of facilitating data integrity during a deal.

This book is designed to be a practical guide to IT for the financial executive. It is written in nontechnical terms and is focused on helping you add value to your organization via the IT function. In short, it is a guide to IT best practices for the financial executive.

Acknowledgments

Information technology is constantly changing. Therefore, it was essential for the material in this book to be timely, accurate, and relevant. Accordingly, I selected contributing authors known for their expertise and hands-on knowledge of information technology and how it impacts the finance function. Listed below, in alphabetical order, are these authors. They all have done a superb job of developing a book that is practical and informative.

- Ajay Bhatia
- Peter Blatman
- Colleen Chan
- David Deckter
- Robert Fabiszak
- Sheri Fedokovitz
- Nancie Fernandez
- Jeff Fisher
- Indira Gillingham
- Jessica Golden
- Brenda Haroian
- Colin Hartnett
- Susan Hogan
- Hilary Horn
- Ryan Jones
- Varun Joshi

- Joseph Joy
- Pavel Krumkachev
- Anna Lea Doyle
- Angela Mattix
- Jason McClain
- Deborah Metzger
- Krista Mondschein
- Shalva Nolen
- Brandon Patterson
- Sharon Piech
- Johannes Raedeker
- Asish Ramchandran
- Karl Rupilius
- Kalyana Sundaram
- James J. (Jeff) Taylor II
- Michael Vowles
- Franscisca Wahjudi
- Mark Walsh
- Amy Wolbeck

Additionally, I would like to thank the following individuals from John Wiley & Sons who made this book possible:

- Sheck Cho, Executive Editor
- Helen Cho, Senior Editorial Assistant
- Stacey Rivera, Development Editor
- Lisa Vuoncino, Production Editor
- Todd Tedesco, Senior Production Editor

Dave Lewis and Jen Webster of Deloitte should also be acknowledged for their outstanding editorial skills. Their expertise was greatly appreciated.

I'd also like to thank my husband, Fritz Anderson, for his unending patience and support as I worked on this book over weekends and during vacations.

Finally, I'd like to thank my Lord and Savior, Jesus Christ, for making this all possible and for His unending blessings.

Janice M. Roehl-Anderson
Cherry Hills Village, Colorado

About the Contributors

Ajay Bhatia is a senior manager in Deloitte's Enterprise Application practice. He joined Deloitte after spending time at KPMG, Andersen Consulting, and Oracle Corporation focusing on high-technology, manufacturing, automotive, consumer business, and public sector organizations. His consulting experience includes strategic assessments, service delivery models, business transformation, supply chain optimization, and enterprise system implementation management. Additionally, he has a wide breadth of experience with business and IT strategy alignment, business process reengineering, program management, and change management. Ajay received his MBA from Ashland University in Ohio and a master's degree in Information Systems from Eastern Michigan University.

Peter J. Blatman, MS, Computer Science, and MBA, is a senior partner and leads Deloitte's National Technology Strategy practice, which focuses on driving business performance through effective use of information and enabling technologies. With more than 28 years of experience, Peter has consulted nationally and internationally at major corporate financial services, retail, healthcare, high-tech, energy, transportation, and telecommunications industry clients regarding the application of advanced technology to business systems development and business transformation. Peter's focus in his consulting practice is the intersection of business strategy, information, and technology—particularly the shaping/enabling impact of new and emerging technologies on business strategy. He has deep experience in IT strategy development, IT governance, IT organization design, pre-merger IT due diligence, and post-merger IT integration.

Colleen Chan is a senior manager with Deloitte Consulting LLP, with over 15 years of consulting experience. She specializes in large-scale system implementation and pre-deal planning for merger and acquisition–related IT activities as well as customer relationship management system design and implementation. She has served some of the largest Fortune 500 companies in high-tech manufacturing and life sciences. Colleen received her MBA in Information Systems and MS in Industrial Engineering from Rensselaer Polytechnic Institute, and a BS in Computer Science from the University of Wisconsin.

David Deckter, CISSP and ISSMP, is a senior manager with Deloitte & Touche LLP with over 11 years of extensive international experience helping clients solve business problems as they relate to risk management, privacy, and security. His hands-on experience developing integrated risk and compliance programs and implementing large-scale security and privacy solutions across industries allows him to quickly roll out practical solutions tailored for his clients. He received his Bachelor of Science in Economics from Purdue University, located in West Lafayette, Indiana. He has contributed to numerous papers, presentations, and publications, including the *Information Security Management Handbook*, Volume 4, edited by Harold F. Tipton and Micki Krause.

Robert F. Fabiszak, MBA, is a director with Deloitte Consulting LLP, with over 10 years of consulting experience. He specializes in helping companies transform their finance functions, particularly with respect to performance management processes and technology. Prior to joining Deloitte, Robert held several roles in the Finance group at Alexander and Alexander, and he began his consulting career with PeopleSoft. He received his MBA from the University of North Carolina at Chapel Hill, and he also has a degree in Economics from Loyola College and a degree in English from Towson University.

Sheri Fedokovitz is a partner within Deloitte & Touche LLP's Audit and Enterprise Risk Services practice, where she specializes in data analysis, statistical analysis, continuous monitoring/auditing and data quality and integrity techniques and solutions. She has over 19 years of experience and is the firm's national leader of the Data Quality and Integrity service line. Sheri graduated from Eastern Michigan University with a BBA in Accounting Information Systems. She is a Certified Public Accountant and a Certified Information Systems Auditor.

Nancie W. Fernandez is a principal with Deloitte Consulting LLP, with over 20 years of business and consulting experience. Nancie has extensive experience managing the people-related issues on large-scale, complex projects, including large technology implementations, merger integration, divestiture, HR, shared services, and organizational transformation engagements. Prior to joining Deloitte in 1997, Nancie worked for 15 years in the insurance industry, where her focus was primarily on IT and business process reengineering.

Jeffrey Fisher is a senior manager with Deloitte & Touche LLP. He has been with the firm for over 11 years and serves as the project manager and technical quality assurance role for one of Deloitte's largest clients. Jeff specializes in helping companies assess and improve their processes designed to mitigate financial statement, business, and technology risk. He has assisted several Deloitte's clients in preparing for and successfully implementing Sarbanes-Oxley assessment processes on a global basis. Jeff received his Bachelor of Science in Accounting and Computer

Information Systems from Ferris State University. He is a Certified Information Systems Security Professional (CISSP) and a Certified Information Systems Auditor (CISA). Jeff served as a contributing editor for the Institute of Internal Auditors's *Global Technology Audit Guide on Management of IT Auditing* and has presented at several audit conferences and association meetings on technology- and controls-related topics.

Indira Gillingham is a senior manager in Deloitte Consulting LLP's Technology Integration practice, focusing in technology strategy and M&A services. She has ten years of professional consulting experience servicing a variety of clients in the technology, media, and telecommunications industries. Her specialty is in helping clients with strategy and execution of large complex business transformation initiatives across all phases, including planning, development, and implementation of technology solutions. She is also experienced in complex merger integration and divestitures, including planning, blueprinting, and post-merger integration execution. Indira has a bachelor's degree in Business Administration (BBA), concentrating on information systems, from the University of Washington.

Jessica Golden, a principal at Deloitte Consulting LLP, specializes in performance improvement and cost reduction strategies through global shared services and technology implementations. Jessica's experience includes optimization strategies for finance and accounting, information technology, and human resources at Fortune 500 companies in consumer business, life sciences, high-technology and media, and financial services industry verticals. She also is actively involved in merger-and-acquisition back-office synergy strategies for public companies and private equity. Jessica is a frequent speaker at industry conferences and author of shared services publications.

Brenda S. Haroian, MBA, is a manager with Deloitte Consulting LLP, with over nine years of consulting experience.

She specializes in the design, planning, and implementation of financial systems for global organizations and for merger and divestiture implementations. Brenda received her MBA with concentrations in information management and operations from the University of Texas at Austin, McCombs School of Business, and received a BA in Business Administration/Accounting from Washington State University.

Colin M. Hartnett is a principal with Deloitte Consulting LLP. He has 24 years of experience focusing on finance transformation design as well as systems design and implementation of global financial and ERP systems for Fortune 500 clients. He received a Bachelor of Science in Computer and Information Science from Ohio State University. Colin has led several global implementations of multi-GAAP and IFRS reporting financial systems.

Susan C. Hogan, MBA, is a principal with Deloitte Consulting LLP and has over 15 years of consulting experience at Deloitte Consulting and 5 years of manufacturing and retail experience. Susan, who leads Deloitte's U.S. Infrastructure Operations and Comprehensive Shared Services Practices, specializes in leading organizations through the shared services journey from the initial strategy, through the design, implementation, and optimization of their service centers. Susan earned her MBA from Harvard Business School and her BS in Industrial Engineering from North Carolina State University. She frequently speaks at conferences regarding the latest shared services trends and leads Deloitte's biennial global studies of shared services operations.

Hilary Horn is a senior manager in Deloitte's Human Capital, Organization and Talent practice. She has experience leading and driving change and learning programs for Fortune 500 clients undergoing large-scale technology and change transformation efforts. Hilary's areas of experience include: global strategic change leadership programs, technology adoption, communication strategies, program/project leadership, executive leadership development, organization transformation, and learning programs. Hilary has consulted with a number of Silicon Valley's software and hardware technology companies as well as financial services and oil and gas companies.

Ryan C. Jones, MBA, is a principal with Deloitte Consulting LLP with over 12 years of consulting experience. He specializes in e-commerce strategy, implementation, and customer and channel transformation initiatives. He received his MBA and BS from Bradley University, and attended the MS program at the University of Chicago. Ryan has served as the chief editor and contributing author for the *Deloitte Consulting Web Channel Solutions Journal*, and has spoken at several conferences on the topic of e-commerce.

Varun Joshi, MBA, is a manager with Deloitte Consulting LLP with over 11 years of consulting experience. He specializes in mergers, acquisitions and divestitures with a focus on IT strategy, IT governance, IT demand and portfolio management, and M&A technology. Varun received his MBA in Finance and Information Systems from the Indian Institute of Management, Ahmadabad (India), and a BS in Electrical Engineering from Delhi College of Engineering, University of Delhi (India).

Joseph Joy, MS Computer Science, is a specialist leader with Deloitte Consulting LLP, with over 16 years of consulting experience. He has extensive experience in IT strategy development, pre-merger IT due diligence, and post-merger IT integration. Joseph focuses on risk analysis, planning, quality control, developing frameworks, methodologies, data center strategy, and best practices. Joseph has consulted nationally and internationally at major financial services, retail, high-tech, energy, and telecommunications corporations. Joseph's experience also includes implementing OLTP, ERP, CRM, and package-based applications, high-availability infrastructure, and architecture design.

Pavel Krumkachev is a principal with Deloitte Consulting LLP with over 14 years of consulting experience. He specializes in enterprise application architecture, application integration, and merger and acquisition–related IT integration. Pavel received a BA in Business Administration from Lewis & Clark College. He has published a number of whitepapers and delivered presentations on the topics of M&A, service-oriented architecture, and enterprise application implementation.

Anna Y. Lea Doyle is a principal at Deloitte Consulting LLP focusing on mergers, acquisitions, and divestitures. She has led more than 15 integration and carve-out engagements. Her expertise is in the areas of program management, MA&D capability development, integration diagnostics, Day 1 planning and readiness assessment, IT synergy, IT blueprinting and implementation, and large ERP selection and business case initiatives.

Angela Mattix, CPA, PMP, MBA, is currently a senior manager with Deloitte Consulting LLP, with over 13 years of consulting experience. Prior to joining Deloitte, she was a senior manager with Cap Gemini–Ernst & Young. She specializes in project management, system analysis, design, and implementation for enterprise resource planning packages. Prior to consulting, she spent 10 years working in finance departments of various industries. She received her Certified Public Accountant of Texas license in 1997 and her Project Management Professional certification in 2006. She received her MBA at Webster University and a BBA in Accounting from Midwestern State University.

Jason McClain is a senior manager within Deloitte & Touche LLP's Audit and Enterprise Risk Services practice, with over 12 years of consulting experience. He specializes in assisting organizations with improving the quality of their data through the use of data analysis and process improvement techniques. Jason graduated from Baldwin-Wallace College with a BA in Business Administration. He is a Certified Information Systems Auditor.

Deborah Metzger is a senior manager with Deloitte Consulting LLP. She specializes in ERP system design and implementation, including master data management and overall system solution design. Deborah has worked in information technology consulting for the past 13 years. Prior to becoming a consultant, Deborah worked in the manufacturing and defense industries. She has an MS in Software Engineering and a BA in Quantitative Methods from the University of St. Thomas in Minnesota.

Krista D. Mondschein, MPP, a senior manager at Deloitte Consulting LLP with close to ten years of consulting experience, earned her MPP from the University of Chicago. Krista has worked across the public and private sectors, maintaining a focus on performance and process improvement, especially as related to shared services in finance, human resources, and technology.

Shalva Nolen is a senior consultant with Deloitte Consulting LLP with over five years of consulting experience. She specializes in advising companies on their next-generation data center and IT-related merger, acquisition, and divestiture projects. She attended Harvard University, where she received an AB in History and Science, and the University of Notre Dame, where she received her PhD in Physics. She has co-authored several papers in scientific journals and trade publications.

Brandon P. Patterson is a manager with Deloitte Consulting LLP and has over 14 years of consulting experience. He specializes in technical strategy, planning, and implementation for ERP applications and merger and acquisition–related IT integration. Brandon was a manager with KPMG Consulting's Information, Communication and Entertainment practice prior to joining Deloitte Consulting LLP. He received his BS in Computer Engineering from Case Western Reserve University and an AAS in Computer Systems Electronics Technology from Westmoreland CC. Brandon has successfully completed his Oracle Database Administration Master's Certification and presented twice at the North Central Oracle Applications Users Group Conference.

Sharon F. Piech, MBA, is a senior manager with Deloitte Consulting LLP with over 10 years of consulting experience. She specializes in building communication between different groups, such as bridging the communication barriers between business and technology users or U.S. and global users. She has also worked in the nonprofit industry and enjoys volunteering on nonprofit boards and events. She received her MBA from Duke University and her BS in Computer Science from the University of Notre Dame.

Johannes Raedeker, MBA, is a senior manager with Deloitte Consulting LLP with over 15 years of consulting experience. He specializes in ERP strategic planning, business cases, and software selection and has led a number of large-scale ERP implementations. He received an MBA from the University of California at Berkeley (Haas School of Business) with emphasis in high-tech marketing and management of technology, and a master's degree in Computer Science and Organizational Behavior from the University of Mannheim, Germany.

Asish Ramchandran, MBA, is a principal with Deloitte Consulting LLP with over 10 years of consulting experience. He specializes in merger, acquisition, and divestiture–related transactions, spanning extensive cost transformation, integration, divestiture, carve-out, restructuring, and cost realignment leadership experience. Asish has provided senior advisory services to drive the planning and realization of over $1B in synergy-related savings and participated in IT portfolio realignment of application suites at clients ranging from $150 million to over $30 billion. He has written articles on various topics, including "A CIO's Look in the Rearview Mirror," "Managing Integrated Data in a Diverging Environment," and "A House Begins with a Blueprint."

Karl Rupilius is a senior manager with Deloitte Consulting LLP with over 13 years of experience in implementation of ERP solutions. Karl has a comprehensive background in the full implementation lifecycle, including delivery and support of complex information systems. Throughout his consulting career, Karl has successfully implemented business solutions across North America, Latin America, and Europe. Karl holds a Master of Sciences degree from the University of Mannheim, Germany.

Kalyana Sundaram, MBA, is a director with Deloitte Consulting LLP with over 20 years of consulting experience. He specializes in supply chain and implementation of enterprise applications with a focus on distributed delivery. He is currently focused on building and deploying intellectual capital for the firm to facilitate global delivery. Kal's prior experience includes consulting work in three other countries and operations manager in the high-tech manufacturing industry. He received his MBA in Marketing and Information Systems from the Indian Institute of Management and a Bachelor of Engineering in Mechanical Engineering. Kal has contributed to *The Controller's Function: The Work of the Managerial Accountant*.

James J. (Jeff) Taylor II is a senior manager with Deloitte Consulting LLP with over 18 years of combined industry and consulting experience. He specializes in enterprise resource planning systems with a focus on financial accounting system design and implementation. Jeff has designed and implemented more than 13 full lifecycle implementations during his career, including solutions for multi-GAAP and IFRS-based systems in Canada, Serbia, and Slovakia. He received his BSBA in Accounting from Ohio State University.

Michael S. Vowles, MA, is a senior manager with Deloitte Consulting LLP with over 15 years of consulting experience. Michael specializes in financial accounting system analysis, design, and implementation. He completed his master's degree in Public Administration and BA in Political Science and Economics at Carleton University in Ottawa, Canada. Michael was a manager in the Federal Government of Canada in Ottawa prior to joining Deloitte Consulting.

Franscisca Wahjudi, BA, English, is a manager within the Technology practice of Deloitte Consulting LLP with over 13 years of consulting experience. Prior to joining the U.S. firm, Franscisca worked for the Deloitte Australia practice and for a large New Zealand energy company. She specializes in customer relationship management process design and implementation with a focus on software as a service. Franscisca is able to complement her technical background with her business expertise in leading different phases of the implementation lifecycle.

Mark Walsh is a principal in Deloitte Consulting's Mergers & Acquisitions Practice. He is the national lead for Deloitte's M&A IT Practice and has over 20 years of professional experience leading due diligence, divestiture, carve-out, integration, joint venture, and portfolio swap engagements in the consumer business, manufacturing, high-technology, and healthcare industries. He has written several articles on various merger IT topics, including "The Missing Piece of the M&A Puzzle," "Walking the M&A Tightrope (with a Safety Net)," "Simple Ideas to

Determine Your M&A IT Intelligence Quotient (Your M&A IT IQ)," and "Virtual M&A: Event Driven IT Transformation." Mark has a BS in Electrical Engineering from Northeastern University, a CSS from Harvard Extension School, and an MBA from Columbia University.

Amy Wolbeck is a principal with Deloitte Consulting LLP with over 13 years of system implementation experience. She specializes in finance transformation and large-scale finance ERP system implementations. She received her bachelor's degree in Business Administration from North Dakota State University.

PART I

The Basics

CHAPTER 1

The Information Technology Planning Process

Robert Fabiszak

Accurate and timely financial information is essential to managing a modern corporation. Investors and regulators require periodic disclosures, while managers and executives rely on financial data for decision making and strategy. Businesses have no shortage of such information—in fact, the very volume and complexity of their financial data often presents a significant challenge to their ability to use it wisely. This financial data is maintained in a wide variety of information systems, ranging from sophisticated *enterprise resource planning* (ERP) systems, to single-purpose tools such as financial consolidation systems, to the individual database on someone's personal computer that generates an important journal entry each quarter.

In most companies, this array of financial systems and databases has been built up over time, sometimes with great foresight and planning and other times as an expedient reaction to a specific business need. As a business grows and becomes more complex, the difficulty in managing its financial information can also grow, often disproportionately. It can become more difficult to provide appropriate financial controls as transactions become more complex and new business models evolve.

Duplicate systems can arise due to mergers, which often leads to inefficient operations and inconsistent data between systems. Responding to management requests for information can become more difficult as reporting databases and spreadsheets proliferate.

The task of managing these complexities largely falls on the *information technology* (IT) department. However, the chief financial officer (CFO) and the *Finance* function also play an important role in this process. They are not just passive users and producers of financial information. They must also be actively involved in financial system planning and decisions. This chapter will discuss some of Finance's roles and responsibilities with respect to information systems—in particular its role in information technology planning.

Finance and Information Systems

The role of the CFO and the Finance function has evolved over time. From mere bookkeepers who played a purely supporting role, Finance has evolved to become an integral part of the strategy and management of most companies. Regulations adopted in the shadow of Enron's collapse, such as Sarbanes-Oxley, require CFOs to exert more control over financial data and to take responsibility for its accuracy. In order to assume that responsibility, which includes personally attesting to the accuracy of publicly reported financial results, CFOs have realized that they cannot simply accept financial data that they do not control. As a result, CFOs generally "own" their companies' numbers: They have the primary responsibility for the data in financial systems, if not responsibility for the financial systems themselves. More important, Finance has become a strategic player in most companies, requiring it to analyze and understand the financial data to provide insights and strategic recommendations. This, of course, means that the appropriate data must be available, accurate, and accessible.

Every part of a company's business processes ultimately impacts Finance. Certain processes, such as order-to-cash and procure-to-pay, are primarily the domain of Finance. But other processes, like procurement, customer management, manufacturing, and so on, also impact Finance, because it either uses or generates financial data. Thus, the systems that these processes use are at least indirectly financial systems as well. As the primary stewards and important consumers of the company's numbers, the CFO and the Finance function are key stakeholders in the vast majority of a company's information systems.

To better understand the linkages between Finance and information systems, it is useful to look at a conceptual model of a company's systems and information environment. In this way, we can examine the role that Finance plays as both steward and consumer of information. Figure 1.1 shows a simple systems and information model.

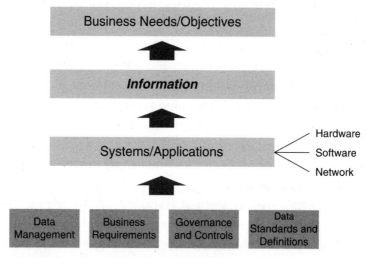

FIGURE 1.1 Systems and Information Model

In this model, *information* takes its rightful place as the central focus. This collection of financial data consists of three major components:

1. **Master data.** This is the set of codes and structures that identify and organize the data. Data elements such as customer codes, customer names, general ledger account numbers, employee IDs, and business unit codes and names are part of master data. All transactions and other business processes use this master data to identify the business entities impacted by the transactions. Most transactions use several different master data elements. For example, taking an order from a customer will involve (or create) such master data elements as customer number, address, order number, stock-keeping unit, salesperson ID, and so on. Master data elements can be arranged into hierarchies, such as a legal entity structure showing the ownership of each legal entity within a corporation, which is used for financial consolidation and external reporting.

2. **Transactional data.** This is the set of records of individual business activities or events. Transactions are associated with specific business entities (defined by the master data) and record the economic impact or value of the activity. A single activity may create a number of transactions or accounting records. Continuing the customer order example, taking an order will generate records in the order system and, upon shipment, will record revenue and a receivable as well. This transactional data is the heart of any financial system, and maintaining its accuracy and timeliness is a key Finance responsibility.

3. **Reporting and analytical data.** While the transactional data contains all of the financial records of a company, it is often difficult to use that data for reporting. A large company may have millions of transactions, which could make

filtering and aggregating the data very time-consuming (not to mention slowing down the transactional systems). In addition, some reports or analyses will likely require data from multiple systems, which often have differing sets of master data, making it difficult to link data from one system to another. As a result, most companies have a data warehouse, or possibly a series of data marts, or some other type of reporting database to facilitate reporting and analysis. These reporting databases extract and, in some cases, transform data from the source (transactional) systems, and store it in a way that permits easier reporting. Data in these reporting systems can be aggregated using master data hierarchies to allow reports on rollup data to process more quickly. In addition, these databases can further support reporting and analysis by calculating and storing key performance indicators or other metrics, as well as by aggregating the data across a variety of *dimensions*, or slices of data (e.g., by legal entity, business unit, and geography).

In this model, the term *information* is preferred to *data*, because in addition to the transactional data, the model allows for the reporting and analytical data, to which some degree of financial intelligence and business rules have been applied. Just as Finance is the main steward of transactional data, it is a major consumer of financial data as well, and much of the value it adds to the strategic and management functions of the business derives from its ability to use this reporting and analytical data transformed into information.

All of this financial information is maintained and managed by a variety of systems. The systems and applications layer of the model includes all of the hardware, software, and network infrastructure that support business operations. The primary financial systems are generally part of an ERP system, and would include the general ledger, the receivables and payables modules, procurement, order entry, payroll, and others. However, most companies have other financial systems beyond their primary ERP, such as legacy systems from acquired companies and homegrown systems written to support specialized business situations. In addition, most companies have *best-of-breed* applications to support specific business processes, such as financial consolidation, budgeting and planning, reporting and analysis, and treasury management. Finally, in an uncomfortably large number of cases, companies maintain important financial information in desktop databases and spreadsheets. In fact, it is likely that most companies use spreadsheets to perform at least part of some key business processes, such as budgeting and planning.

The systems and applications are used to define and implement a number of important elements that go into maintaining financial information. These *foundational elements* are shown in the bottom row of Figure 1.1 and include:

- **Data management.** This represents the maintenance and management of master data, including the definition of links between systems. Master data management has become an area of emphasis for IT departments in recent years, and it is particularly valuable in environments with multiple inter-related systems. It also includes the mappings and interface rules required for one system to feed data to another or to a reporting database or data warehouse.
- **Business requirements.** This represents the rules implemented within the financial systems to process transactions and implement business logic. Business requirements can include implementation of accounting rules (such as elimination of intercompany transactions at the lowest common parent), definitions of business processes (such as the approval routing before a payment is issued), and specifications for outputs (such as regulatory or management

reports). These business requirements are implemented through the configuration of the ERP or other financial system and through system and database code.

- **Governance and controls.** With the increased scrutiny of financial results and the need for greater transparency and governance in the wake of Sarbanes-Oxley, companies have built more automated controls into their financial processes. In some cases, these controls are implemented within the financial systems, such as requiring different individuals to enter and approve journal vouchers. Financial system governance and controls are an important part of a company's larger risk management efforts.

- **Data definitions and standards.** As noted earlier, despite their best efforts, most companies have a somewhat fragmented financial system environment, due to legacy systems from mergers, one-off solutions, and desktop applications. In order to effectively manage and use financial information, consistent data definitions and data standards are required. This is particularly an issue with desktop reporting and analysis, where it is not uncommon for two analysts to walk into a meeting with two completely different sets of numbers for what is supposed to be the same report. Similarly, financial systems in separate divisions or business units may have been implemented differently, leading to inconsistencies in transaction processing and reporting. For example, one large payment-processing company conducted a worldwide ERP implementation with minimal corporate guidelines for data definitions and standards. As a result, it ended up with different and irreconcilable charts of accounts in each business unit, requiring a costly and time-consuming process to map business unit data to another, separate *consolidating* instance of the general ledger. More explicit and well-enforced data standards would have eliminated the need for this effort.

These foundational elements, along with the system and application environment and the information that they support, must serve the broader business needs and objectives. Many executives complain that despite an array of financial and business systems, they do not have the information they need to run their businesses. Well-managed enterprises, however, generally have a system environment that can support their strategic and operational objectives.

To further the objective of developing financial systems that provide timely and accurate information to support the business, most companies periodically develop an information systems strategy. This strategy then supports an *Information Technology Plan* that guides the company along the path of developing the appropriate system environment. The sections that follow describe the *information technology planning process* and Finance's role in that process.

Information Technology Planning Process

Despite the best efforts of information technology departments, most companies' information system environments are anything but stable and predictable. Business needs change. New companies are acquired and integrated. Laws and regulations change. Disruptive technologies (such as the Internet) or external forces (such as the "Year 2000" problem) mandate changes. Through it all, the need for business and financial data remains unchanged—or grows.

Managing this complex environment and trying to accommodate future needs is an ongoing process. Each technology decision, whether it is a new system, an upgrade, or a change in the hardware environment, is made with an eye toward compatibility with the existing environment, meeting business needs, and providing a path for future growth. Unfortunately, a series of such decisions made individually and in isolation will rarely result in an optimal technology environment, just as a series of isolated business decisions related to pricing, markets, product development, and acquisitions cannot be expected to maximize the value of the business. Executives generally rely on a strategic planning process to set a direction for the company and to coordinate tactical business decisions and investments. In much the same way, a strategic Information Technology Plan can be used to establish a technology vision for a company and to coordinate system development efforts and investments. Developing an IT plan is one way to break down the various silos and provide a more coordinated approach to information systems. More important, it provides an opportunity to engage the business side, to make sure that the key business needs can be met, and to gain consensus for the systems approach across the organization.

Systems planning should be a regular process, not unlike the annual business planning process. A large-scale strategic Information Technology Plan could be undertaken periodically or in response to some triggering event. There are many events that might provide a good opportunity for a systems plan, such as a need to replace a core business system (such as an ERP system), a large merger and the corresponding need to standardize the IT environment, or even the presence of a new chief information officer (CIO) who wants to take a fresh look at the company's IT strategy.

Developing an Information Technology Plan

An Information Technology Plan is the result of a comprehensive review of an organization's systems and technical architecture, the business processes that they support, and a desired future state. It includes a description of where the company is with respect to its IT environment and where it needs to be. It also includes a strategy for achieving these *future-state goals*.

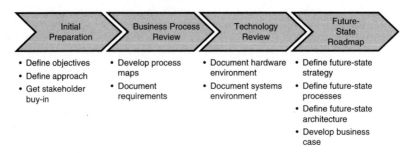

FIGURE 1.2 Information Technology Plan Approach

Developing an IT plan is necessarily a collaborative exercise. Gaining participation from both the IT and business sides of the organization is crucial to developing a good plan that is accepted across the organization: All of the key stakeholders must feel that they have skin in the game. Many companies use an outside consulting firm to help them drive the development of the plan, to gain an outside perspective, and also to help gain participation and cooperation from both business and IT.

There are generally four phases to the development of a plan: initial preparation, review of business processes, inventory and review of the technology environment, and development of the future-state goals and roadmap. These phases are shown in Figure 1.2.

Depending on the size of the organization and the depth at which the processes and technology are reviewed, developing the plan would generally be expected to take from one to three months. This assumes part-time involvement for those developing the plan. Assigning full-time staff to the project or using outside resources could reduce the time to develop the plan or allow greater depth of analysis.

During the initial preparation stage of the plan process, the company will define its objectives for the plan and lay out its approach, which could include a formal project plan. The most important activity in this phase is to get buy-in from both senior management and the key business and IT stakeholders to undertake the activity. Management buy-in is needed to get the necessary stakeholders engaged and to lay the groundwork for eventually gaining their authorization to implement the plan. Stakeholder buy-in is needed for them to invest the time and effort to participate in the planning activity.

The first major activity in developing the plan is to review the company's key business processes. This may sound somewhat counterintuitive: There is a natural tendency when doing an IT plan to dive immediately into an analysis of the company's systems. However, that approach ignores the most important context that must be considered in the plan. After all, the primary purpose of most information systems is to manage some part of an operational business process. Therefore, in order to assess a company's IT environment and plan for the future, a thorough understanding of the major business processes is needed. One common cause of issues in business processes and technology is designing (or forcing) the business processes to accommodate the supporting technology, rather than designing and implementing the technology to support optimized business processes. So, a review of business processes and business-side requirements must be a component of the IT plan. The planning team will develop (or utilize existing) process maps, highlighting the systems involved and touch points with other processes and systems. Business requirements and issues with the current processes and technology would be documented through interviews and small-group workshops.

Following the business process review, or roughly in parallel with it, is the documentation of the company's technology environment. This will include both the hardware and applications used to operate the company. Most companies have system architecture documents, but these become outdated quickly as new systems come online or acquired companies add their own systems to the environment. In addition, most existing system architecture documents concentrate on enterprise-level systems like ERP systems. They often omit department-level systems and desktop applications and databases. These systems can be troublesome, since they do not necessarily adhere to corporate IT standards and some of them, especially any desktop applications, may lack proper controls, security, or data standards. The IT plan should go out of its way to document such systems, not only to understand potential sources of risk, but more important to identify potential opportunities for improvement. These departmental and desktop systems are obviously addressing some previously unmet business need; if that need is sufficiently important, the company should consider an enterprise-class solution as part of the future-state environment.

After the business processes and technology environment have been reviewed and documented, the planning team can turn its attention to the future state. They should start by developing a set of high-level goals and objectives for the future state to provide direction to the future-state design. They can then assess how well the current environment meets those objectives. The prior review activities will most likely have identified issues or improvement opportunities with either business processes or technology, which is a good starting point for the future-state gap analysis. From there, the team can begin to explore different approaches to the major business processes and the technology required to support them. Achieving alignment between the business processes and the supporting systems should be a primary goal of the future state. The planning team should also give attention to future-state systems or applications to support reporting, especially across the various systems and processes. At this point, the team should be able to develop a high-level system architecture to meet the future-state goals and objectives.

The final step is to develop an implementation roadmap and develop a business case.

Once the IT plan is complete, the hard work of gaining a consensus among all of the stakeholders and getting the approval of management can begin. Having participation from all of the stakeholder groups during the development of the plan will go a long way toward having them sign off on the plan. Developing a realistic business case will greatly enhance the chances of management approval.

Components of an Information Technology Plan

The prior section outlined the major steps in developing an Information Technology Plan. In this section, we will look in a little more detail at what should be included in such a plan.

It is essential that the company's IT strategy complements its business strategy. Similarly, changes in a company's business strategy or environment must be reflected in an updated IT strategy and environment. Therefore, the IT plan must incorporate elements from both the business (functional) side of the organization as well as the technology side of the organization. The contents of the IT plan reflect these dual requirements, which are then brought together in the final strategy and future-state roadmap.

BUSINESS PROCESS REVIEW   The initial component of the business process review is the documentation of a company's core business processes. These could include operational processes, such as order fulfillment, as well as financial processes. The most common way to document business processes is to develop *process maps*, which are relatively high-level flowcharts showing the major steps in a process, who is responsible for them, and what information is collected or handed off. Many companies already have some level of business process documentation, often as the result of some prior reengineering effort or process documentation projects to support Sarbanes-Oxley requirements or similar needs. These process maps can then be reviewed to identify potential bottlenecks, manual processes, inadequate controls, and other opportunities for improvement.

The other major component of the business process review is an assessment of the current processes and identification of additional process requirements. The assessment would identify issues, report on stakeholder satisfaction with the process, identify additional steps or controls required by the process, and identify any data issues (such as missing or invalid data). During the future-state design efforts, this assessment will be useful in identifying needed improvements.

SYSTEMS AND ARCHITECTURE REVIEW   The systems and architecture review will identify and assess the major elements of the company's technology environment. Two main elements of this section include diagrams of the company's application architecture and of the hardware/network architecture. The application architecture is an inventory of the company's systems, including all of the ERP modules and other business systems. The architecture diagram would also identify data interfaces between systems. There also should be supporting detail to identify the purpose of each system, the data it collects or generates, and the data it feeds to (or is fcd by) other systems. The application architecture also should include any data marts, data warehouses, or other repositories used for reporting and analysis, even if they are not a part of any specific business system—and cvcn if they are not managed by the corporate IT department.

The hardware and network architecture diagrams would show the underlying technical architecture, including servers and communication hardware. The software running on each server, including operating systems and applications, should be identified as well.

16

The interfaces between systems can be very complex, so these should also be documented in the systems and architecture review. The inbound and outbound systems should be identified, along with the type of data being interfaced and the frequency of update. Supporting technologies, such as extract, transform, and load (ETL) tools, should also be indicated.

Since most IT functions are constantly developing or deploying new software or hardware, the systems plan must take into account ongoing projects and other initiatives. These should be summarized and their impact on the existing technology environment should be identified.

The final part of the systems and architecture review is an assessment of the current systems and hardware environment. This assessment would identify system issues, such as performance or reliability, and identify opportunities to retire obsolete systems or otherwise optimize the technology environment.

FUTURE-STATE ROADMAP The business process and technology environment assessments are only preludes to the main attraction of the Information Technology Plan, which is the development of a *future-state vision* and a roadmap for achieving that vision. This future-state vision should represent a stretch goal for the organization, but it must also be practical and achievable.

The first element of the future-state vision is a statement of the company's high-level information strategy and objectives. In other words, the company must outline the context in which decisions on the future-state direction will be made. These objectives could include goals such as increased standardization of applications and processes, cost efficiencies, or greater availability of specific financial data to support business decisions. It is important, when outlining information systems strategies and objectives, to take into account potential changes in the business strategy and potential changes in the technology landscape.

17

With the information strategy and objectives in place, a high-level future-state process and application architecture can be developed. This would include identifying optimized business processes and the required systems and infrastructure to support them. The future-state environment would be necessarily somewhat high level or directional, but it must be detailed enough to provide a useful guidepost for future development.

The achievement of the future-state environment will likely require several years to achieve, and it will be built out in a series of individual initiatives. As a result, there must be a roadmap that lays out an approach to building out the future-state environment and achieving the overall objectives. The roadmap would likely outline a series of programs and individual initiatives within these programs. The roadmap must take into account the potential availability of resources (both people and funding), especially when any of the initiatives overlap and compete for resources. In addition, there should be specific deliverables or milestones identified to be able to track progress.

In order to even get approval of the future-state vision and to be able to proceed with the implementation, there will need to be some type of business case or justification for the investment. Business cases can vary in terms of detail and rigor. At a minimum, they must identify the anticipated benefits to be derived from the future-state environment. These benefits can be hard-dollar savings from efficiencies and improvements in business processes as well as "softer" yet no less important benefits such as better information for decision making, reduced risk, and greater employee satisfaction. The other side of the equation is the identification of estimated costs for building the future-state environment. The costs should be broken down by major program or system, as in many cases approval can be obtained for only a partial achievement of the future-state vision. Ideally, some level of benefit can be quantified and a payback period and return on investment can be calculated. Most companies will not approve significant system investments without a business case showing an adequate return on investment.

The Role of Finance in the Systems Planning Process

As one of the key consumers of a company's information technology, Finance will be one of the key stakeholders in developing the Information Technology Plan. In addition, its role as steward and "owner" of the numbers further reinforces the need for Finance to be central to the planning efforts. Nevertheless, it would be very easy for Finance to abdicate its role, thinking that an IT plan is solely concerned with hardware and software. Similarly, the IT shop could operate in its own silo and neglect the perspectives and potential contributions of Finance.

At the very minimum, Finance would be a key constituency in supporting the adoption of the IT plan and socializing it within the organization. But Finance must play a larger role in developing the plan, not merely be a stakeholder in the final result.

In reality, Finance and IT should operate largely as partners in the information technology planning effort. While there are some areas that are logically the sole domain of IT, such as the hardware and software inventory and the data interface mappings, developing the rest of the plan would be largely impossible—or at least very inadequate—without the active participation of the Finance staff. This section will outline some of the main contributions that Finance can make to the IT planning process.

The fundamental contribution of Finance is its knowledge of the business, the company's major business processes, and the specific requirements of financial management and reporting. The individual business units or other operating entities obviously have the most detailed knowledge of their own processes.

Finance, however, as it takes on a larger, more strategic role in most organizations, is the one unit that has some functional understanding of processes across the organization. Finance has to understand the organization's business models and functional processes in order to account for business activity and establish the appropriate controls. In addition, it must understand the interrelationships among business units and between the business units and corporate. In addition, Finance, as a consumer of financial data from across the organization, is well positioned to understand the data and reporting needs across the organization, identify differences in data definitions or business rules, and identify opportunities for standardization. For example, the Finance group in one large consumer business company was able to identify differences among the ERP implementations at its various business units as it struggled to standardize the data-gathering process for its periodic financial consolidations. Since the company's operations—including IT—were very decentralized, the corporate IT group was unaware that local variations had been introduced to the standard ERP template, potentially making support and upgrades more complicated.

The areas of the Information Technology Plan that would most concern Finance are those outside the detailed analysis of hardware and software. If we refer back to the information model from Figure 1.1, the areas of interest to Finance would be the business goals and objectives, the quality of the information itself, and the foundational elements that support the technology environment.

As a major consumer of information, Finance has a major stake in the quality and timeliness of financial information and, to a lesser extent, other operational information as well. It would be a significant source for functional requirements for data to support reporting and analysis. This would include all information required for a number of reporting processes:

- **Financial statement preparation.** This includes the standard profit and loss (P&L) and balance sheet, but also the cash flow statement and footnotes, which often require data not usually recorded in the ledger or other ERP modules.
- **Management reporting.** This includes business unit or product-level P&Ls, operational reports, and key performance indicators.
- **Planning, budgeting, and forecasting.** In addition to the standard financial statements, these processes often require data related to specific planning drivers, such as commodity prices, interest rates, or other internal and external data.

One of the most frequent complaints heard in Finance departments is that they do not have the information that they need to help managers and executives run the business. It is important to note that *information* in this sense is not just data from the financial systems. Good, useful financial information often requires some level of transformation, aggregation, or manipulation by some set of business rules to meet end-user needs. A crucial element of any IT plan must be to understand the organization's information needs and to incorporate the means to meet these needs in the future-state design.

While on the topic of reporting, it is important to understand the different perspectives that Finance and IT bring to the question of what constitutes an effective reporting environment. Finance is primarily concerned with the availability, accuracy, timeliness, and ease of access to financial and business information. While it understands the need for a sound technical environment and it appreciates the role of IT in developing and maintaining its reporting capabilities, Finance is mainly interested in what the end results are. The IT department, however, is responsible for maintaining what is likely a hodgepodge of reporting tools, databases, and source systems. It is

21

primarily concerned with maintaining a scalable environment with appropriate data integrity and proper design (such as properly normalized data and conformed dimensions in the data marts). The IT department is not always aware of what business questions are being asked; it primarily provides a means to ask them.

Clearly, each of these perspectives is limited and incomplete. Finance brings the business perspective and the reporting requirements, but has limited understanding of the technology environment. The IT organization brings the deep expertise in the technology, but cannot really be sure if its design is providing the needed answers. A collaboration between both of these organizations can provide the most complete picture of the company's reporting needs and capabilities, and facilitate the most effective design of a future-state environment.

Finance also has a considerable stake in the foundational elements of the information model: data management, business requirements, governance and controls, and data definitions and standards. While Finance is not primarily concerned with the mechanics of data management, such as maintaining master data, it is very interested in the quality of the master data. For example, Finance usually has an interest in standardizing, to the extent possible, master data such as customer codes and the chart of accounts. For example, in order to perform customer-level reporting from multiple business units or multiple systems, either customer IDs must be standardized or there must be some type of central customer master with mappings from the various feeder systems. Similarly, in order to consolidate financial data, a standard corporate chart of accounts must be available with mappings from local ledgers. Maintaining these mappings and ensuring the consistency of these mappings across business units is very important to Finance. Thus, Finance is a stakeholder whose data management needs must be accounted for in the IT plan. Similarly, while Finance is not very interested in the technical details of how specific controls are implemented in the ERP system, it is very concerned that the proper controls are in place and are effective. To the extent that the IT plan will incorporate strategies for controls and other governance features, Finance will have an important say in those requirements. In addition, having consistent definitions for data elements is important for reporting and control functions. The future-state design must ensure that standardized data definitions and business rules are enabled.

Another role that Finance would play in the development of the IT plan is to help to ensure that it is aligned with the company's overall strategy. We noted earlier that the Information Technology Plan must complement the company's business strategy. Given Finance's strategic role, and its centrality in the planning and budgeting process, Finance would be expected to have considerable insights into the future direction of the organization and thus its potential future information systems needs.

Finally, much of the IT plan will be impacted by future-state processes. We indicated earlier that a prerequisite to developing the future-state systems architecture is an understanding of the future-state business and financial processes. Ideally, the plan will not envision applying improved technology to existing, often suboptimal, processes. As part of its involvement in developing the IT plan, Finance should be responsible for identifying process improvements and driving improved performance of both the individual processes and the organization as a whole.

Conclusion

The information technology planning process is an opportunity for the organization to take the first steps to optimize both its technology environment and the processes that the technology supports. Finance has a unique position in the organization, with its increasingly strategic role and its involvement with processes and business units across the company. It should have a central role in working with IT to develop the IT plan and to ensure that optimized processes and information are delivered along with an enhanced technology environment.

CHAPTER 2

ERP Software Selection

Johannes Raedeker

Enterprise resource planning (ERP) software offers comprehensive functionality that encompasses virtually all aspects
of an organization's operations. Understanding this pervasive coverage is important to realize the full potential of
the software and its impact on the success of the organization. This requires a complete and informed decision process
that should help identify the best-suited ERP software as well
as an effective implementation approach. It also necessitates
a significant investment in time and resources involving all
parts of the organization to position the organization to best
achieve targeted results. And it is not just the final result
that matters, but the process through which the organization
derives the answer to the selection, as it manifests organizational understanding of and buy-in to the benefits and changes
associated with the new application. Conversely, not understanding the importance of this process can pose a significant
risk to the organization, as has been demonstrated through
many failed implementations, often with devastating financial
impacts.

ERP software selection should be a structured process in
which a wide field of vendor offerings is systematically nar-
rowed down to a few options through a process of elimination.

FIGURE 2.1 Steps in the ERP Software Selection Process

Project Preparation Scope Definition Approach	Vendor Identification and Short-Listing	RFI/RFP Vendor Demos References	Preliminary Vendor Recommendation and Negotiation	Final Vendor Decision and Procurement

Deliverables

• Kickoff presentation	• Vendor short list	• Request for Information/Request for Proposal	• Completed scorecard	• Final recommendation
• Project charter	• Refined evaluation criteria	• Vendor demonstration scripts	• High-level software gap analysis	• Selection decision documentation
• Selection project plan	• Refined high-level requirements	• Reference evaluations	• Final price comparison	• Final signed contract
• High-level requirements				
• Balanced scorecard				

As shown in Figure 2.1, this is usually accomplished in a formalized approach encompassing five phases. It is critical for financial executives to be involved in all phases of the selection process.

Project Preparation, Scope Definition, and Approach

In this phase of the selection process, the initial functional and organizational scope of the selection is defined and the executive sponsors, which should include financial executives, stakeholders, and selection team members, are identified. Also, the approach for the project is established by defining the selection methodology and laying out the timing for the different activities.

Usual deliverables during this phase are a *project charter*, a supporting *project plan*, *high-level requirements*, and a *balanced scorecard*. The charter should include strategic objectives, desired business value and process improvements for the project, the agreed-upon scope, the involved resources and responsibilities, the overall time frame, as well as the evaluation criteria and respective weighting of these. It is important that the charter be developed and reviewed by key stakeholders and agreed to by the executive sponsors to create buy-in and direction for the project and establish a commitment to the budget. The charter should be supported by a detailed project plan listing the individual tasks as well as the resources identified to perform these tasks. The high-level requirements document should list the identified functional, process, organizational, and geographic scope areas as well as the desired technology foundation, including database, middleware, tools, and interoperability standards. The requirements should be gathered through interviews with key business users and ranked to determine areas of high impact. The balanced scorecard should contain all criteria that will be used during the evaluation, identifying their relative weighting. It usually contains the following topics:

- Application Functionality (fit to requirements)
- Technology Stack and Technical Fit
- Implementation Considerations, Support, and Service
- Vendor Strength, Industry Alignment, and Risk
- Future Flexibility
- Total Cost of Ownership

It is important to establish this evaluation framework early to avoid later disagreement and potential manipulation within the selection team.

This is also the time to reach agreement on the selection approach, which can be a full-suite review, a "Why not vendor X?" review, or a fast-track review focused on a few areas. Each approach will vary in terms of the number of vendors evaluated, the effort and resources put into the process, and the overall duration and cost:

- **Full-suite review.** This process entails doing a complete evaluation of all potential vendors. A thorough evaluation includes determining criteria to be used for scoring, identifying the in-scope business processes, defining and developing scripts, and scoring each vendor's demonstrations and capabilities based on the predetermined criteria. Complete cost analyses are performed and future integration and scope are considered.
- **Vendor validation: "Why not X?"** This process is used to validate the hypothesis that a single preselected vendor can meet the unique requirements of the business. The evaluation will not be a thorough review of all the business processes, but rather a condensed review of only the

signature and unique processes that are addressed in great detail and serve as a proxy.

- **Fast-track review.** This process is an accelerated approach that includes an evaluation of only two or three vendors. Rather than including future scope and integration points in the review, this approach involves reviewing only the current scope. Also, since only a short list of processes is usually reviewed, it is important to select the unique or major processes of the business.

These approaches can be adopted either individually or in combination; the chosen alternative depends on the organization's decision-making style and preferences.

This phase should start with a kickoff meeting to bring the selection team together, provide general background on the objectives, and lay out expectations and timeframes. It should include initial requirements gathering and prioritization interviews with key stakeholders and educational sessions to bring ERP background and technical foundation knowledge to all team members. Guidance on the process and background education is often provided by third parties specializing in ERP evaluation projects.

During this initial phase, it is critical that the organizational structure and participation level of the selection team members are identified, including participation of potential external parties.

Vendor Candidate Identification and Short-Listing

The identified high-level functional and technical requirements should be used to condense the wide field of vendor choices down to a select few whose software is most likely to address the most important requirements. There are many sources of analyst or research service briefings that should be used to initially reduce the list of potential candidates to a short list of three to five vendors. Some good sources of this market research are Internet searches, vendor websites, industry associations, conferences, information technology (IT) and business publications, and consultants specializing in this field. In addition, team members who have joined from organizations in the same industry might bring a perspective as to how specific ERP packages have worked in their prior environment, further narrowing the field.

Other factors playing into this process might be existing investments into other products from a vendor or internal compatibility or skills with a certain technology. Since ERP systems are a longer-term investment, it also can be helpful to evaluate the strategic viability and continued level of research and development (R&D) investment of the ERP vendor specific to the industry, so that the package will be likely to be supported through its expected lifecycle.

This process will probably result in a refinement of the requirements, as additional information about features and functions of the different packages might open new areas to consider or indicate a level of similarity that would not result in any further differentiation between the packages. It can also serve as a good initial education for the internal team and help establish the right focus.

Deliverables created during this phase are a vendor short list, refined evaluation criteria, and refined requirements.

Request for Information/Request for Proposal Analysis, Vendor Demonstrations, and References

Whereas the previous phases were primarily executed without direct vendor involvement, this phase will move into the interaction with ERP vendors and their sales force.

Based on the chosen approach, a single or multiple vendors might receive a *request for information (RFI)/request for proposal (RFP)* that communicates process scope as well as functional and technical requirements desired from the application and provides the vendor with such details as the number of users, locations, and geographies. It is advisable to structure requirements along the future processes that would be executed in the new ERP. This process orientation can ease the development of scenarios that demonstrate how the software will support the way the organization intends to run its operation. The short-listed vendors will receive the RFI/RFP and should be required to respond in a predefined way so that the responses can be quickly evaluated, but they also need to describe how the software functionality addresses the requirements in more detail. Vendors will naturally have the tendency to respond that their software can address 99 percent of the listed requirements, so the validity of this step is sometimes questionable. It will, however, provide a written response to specific requirements that can inform the selection team. At a minimum, this step should provide initial information about how the software and support are licensed and priced and what commercial terms the vendor proposes.

Detailed, scripted vendor demonstrations are a key component of every selection process. These scenarios are the most effective way to showcase the vendor software in the context of the future end-to-end processes of the evaluating organization. The processes demonstrated should be unique and meaningful to the organization, so that they can see a true differentiation between the software offerings. The request should be very specific as to what part of the process needs to be executed and give the vendor terminology and data that allow the software to come to life for the software demonstration attendees.

Vendors should be given enough time to prepare and execute the demos well, as they serve both as data points for the overall evaluation and as education for the organization participants. Participation should be opened to a wider internal audience, but scoring input should be restricted to the core team members of the evaluation team. Some vendors showcase sleek functionality and highlight their application's ease of use as well as the nice touch and feel.

While these features can give additional impressions about the software, the software should primarily be evaluated against the original prioritized requirements. Vendors should be closely directed to stay on the prescribed script, so that the software functionality can be evaluated and compared. Participants evaluating the software should be given clear criteria, so that their evaluation of the different vendor demonstrations can be compared. The evaluation should be documented immediately following the demonstration as otherwise the scoring tends to blur over time. The team should specifically identify any gaps the software has in meeting the requirements and share this information immediately during debriefings.

If there is consulting support for the evaluation process, their software-knowledgeable but vendor-independent resources should attend the demonstrations, so they can give some direct, unbiased feedback behind closed doors after each demonstration. This can provide additional clarity and help determine whether the demonstration contained any "vaporware." The focus of the evaluation should be on what was demonstrated and not on how it was demonstrated, as the latter speaks more to the capabilities of the presenter. Finally, it is also informative to provide each presenting vendor a limited amount of time to present its differentiating functionality for your organization.

One important note: Through the discovery in the demonstrations, it might be necessary to refine the software scope as well as user counts, transactions volumes, and required hardware and operating system standards, which all drive vendor pricing.

Another important activity in this step is checking the software vendor references. They should be specific to the release level of the software as well as the industry of the evaluating organization. Also, they should be provided by people who have direct insight into how the software is supporting their processes and operations.

Deliverables created during this phase are the RFI/RFP, the vendor demonstration scripts, the script evaluation criteria and worksheets, the software scope document, and the reference evaluations.

Preliminary Vendor Recommendation and Negotiations

Through tabulation of the market research, the RFI/RFP evaluation (if applicable), and vendor demonstration, the core selection team will populate the balanced scorecard and arrive at a vendor recommendation. This includes an assessment of potential software customizations necessary to address the requirement gaps.

Frequently, organizations enter into preliminary contract negotiations with two software vendors. The initial software contract negotiation process often requires the involvement of procurement and legal professionals with deeper negotiation and contracting skills. Vendors should be asked to provide their best and final offer, which will flow into the recommendation.

Deliverables created during this phase are the completed scorecard, software gap analysis, and final price comparison.

Final Vendor Decision and Procurement

The recommendation from the selection team and stakeholder group should be taken to the steering committee for a final vendor decision. Once it is approved, the final contract negotiations can proceed.

Deliverables created during this phase include the final recommendation presentation, the documents of the final selection decision, and the final signed contract.

By this time, there is often significant momentum and motivation on the part of the organization to move from the selection to an implementation. This should include wider internal involvement and, in many cases, requires the selection of an implementation consultant to build the implementation team and start readiness activities, which include the definition of the project structure, the governance model, the implementation approach, the project plan, and the technical architecture and infrastructure plans.

Conclusion

Selecting ERP software has far-reaching impact and is one of the most critical systems-related activities an organization can perform. Therefore, it is important for the financial executive to be deeply involved with the process and to ensure the right team and approach are deployed.

CHAPTER 3

The Software Implementation Process

Karl Rupilius

The next step after the software selection process is the software implementation. Financial systems implementations can be either a stand-alone implementation (i.e., only the financial system is implemented) or they can be part of a larger enterprise resource planning (ERP) implementation. This may include other areas, such as logistics, operations, and manufacturing. The scope of the implementation will depend on many factors, such as the size of the company, measured in annual revenue, number of employees, business areas, and geographic reach.

The long-term success of the financial system implemented is dependent on a successful implementation. In this context, success can be defined as follows:

- Implementation is on time.
- Implementation is within budget.
- Compliance with legal financial requirements is achieved.
- Key financial processes are standardized.
- The financial system can be rapidly audited.
- The system can scale.

If these key success criteria are met, the financial system will be well positioned to support ongoing business operations with a reasonable amount of support. Implementations that do not meet these success criteria can be hampered by ongoing expensive system enhancements and changes to key business procedures.

Independent of the scale of the implementation, there are typically at least three different parties involved in a financial systems implementation: the software vendor, the systems integrator, and the organization itself. The implementation of a financial system will typically follow a structured methodology. There are many implementation methodologies that are being used in the market, and frequently the different parties involved in an implementation will have their own methodologies. The project will follow either the implementation methodology of one of these parties or a hybrid among the different methodologies.

Key Implementation Concepts

In order to describe the implementation process, it is necessary to agree on the naming of some key concepts that are relevant to the software implementation.

A *project phase* describes a grouping of different activities that are performed during a major stage of the project. An implementation is composed of a number of different phases, starting with project scoping and planning and ending with project deployment. The project phases we will review in this chapter are:

- Scoping and Planning
- Design
- Build

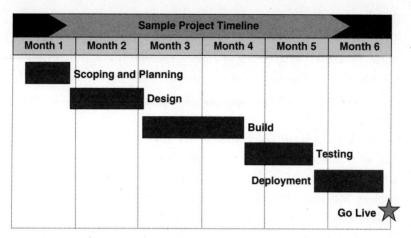

FIGURE 3.1 Sample Project Timeline

- Testing
- Deployment

The project phases and their sequencing are illustrated in Figure 3.1.

A *project thread* refers to a common theme of functional areas and a team that performs related activities during each project phase. Project threads include the following:

- Project Management Office (PMO)
- Process and Applications
- Technology
- Change Management
- Data

A *deliverable* is a work product completed within a project phase by members of a project thread. When defining the project approach, a set of deliverables will be determined to be completed within each project phase by a specific project thread.

As mentioned earlier, a *project methodology* (i.e., a structured approach) is used to complete the implementation of a financial system. Software vendors use and promote their own methodology, and system integrators will usually use variations of these methodologies that incorporate other concepts.

Project methodologies differ in how they organize work across phases and threads and what the specific deliverables are during the course of the project. In the description of the project lifecycle in this book, we will not refer to a specific project methodology but instead use common concepts that are applicable to multiple software packages.

The Implementation Phases in Detail

The following sections describe each of the project phases in further detail. For each project phase, key activities and deliverables within each of the different threads are described.

The Scoping and Planning Phase

During the scoping and planning phase, the project team will perform initial planning and preparation activities, including the following:

- Defining the project goals.
- Confirming the project scope.
- Deciding on project standards to be used.
- Finalizing the project schedule, project plan, staffing, and budgeting.
- Staffing the project and determining the project organization.
- Establishing a governance model for the project.

The different project threads will perform very specific activities during the scoping and planning phase.

The PMO thread will initiate the project, prepare logistics, and establish the overall project management structure. Project initiation includes holding a kickoff meeting for the extended project team and establishing key project logistics. The PMO will also prepare a detailed project plan with input from all other threads. The project plan may include detailed activities through the design phase and then be on a higher level for refinement at a later time. The PMO will also start executing against the project, overseeing and tracking activities from the other threads. It will also put in place key project control mechanisms, such as a project budget with actual and forecasted numbers. The PMO will also start the creation of a deployment plan. The deployment plan contains the sequence in which individual processes will be rolled out within the organization. Common deployment methods include deployment by geography, by business area, and by process area.

The Process and Applications thread will confirm the project scope based on previous high-level scope and relate it to business processes and system components. It will also create a vision for each of the high-level process groups that are in scope of the project. The vision will be the foundation for the design of the business processes and ensure that the designed processes are in alignment with the overall company strategy. The definition of the scope will cut across several dimensions, such as business area, geography, and application component.

The Technology thread will review the current system infrastructure and prepare the project infrastructure. As part of this work, the current technology will be assessed and the future technology needs will be determined. A technology infrastructure for the project will be created and the *to-be* infrastructure will be planned. As part of this work, the Technology thread will define detailed technical infrastructure requirements and define a conceptual technical architecture. To establish the project infrastructure, nonproduction hardware, software, and third-party tools must be purchased.

The Change Management thread will initiate alignment with the key project stakeholders and confirm the commitment to the project by the company organization. As part of these initial activities, the thread will create a change management strategy that will serve as a guideline throughout the project. The thread will assess leadership alignment and establish actions that need to be taken to strengthen leadership alignment with the project. Another key task of the Change Management thread is to develop a change readiness approach that will be used to gauge the overall organization's readiness for the upcoming changes. The Change Management thread will also establish a communication strategy and work on completing an overall training strategy.

The Data thread will determine the *as-is* data standards and confirm data objects that will be impacted by the implementation. The thread will complete the master data scope in alignment with the process scope. The thread will also determine the master data-conversion scope and create a conversion strategy.

Some of the key deliverables of the scoping and planning phase are illustrated in Table 3.1.

The Design Phase

The purpose of the design phase of the project is to create a to-be business model with sign-off from all key stakeholders. Along with the business process design, the project team will create a functional design of the system to support these business processes.

TABLE 3.1 Key Deliverables in the Scoping and Planning Phase

Thread	Key Deliverables
PMO	Project Plan
	Project Governance Model
	Project Standards and Templates
	Project Budget and Budget Tracking Mechanisms
	Project Organization and Staffing
Process and Applications	Process Scope
	Application Scope
	Process Vision
	High-Level Conceptual Design
	Process Design Approach and Work Plan
Technology	As-Is Technology Infrastructure Assessment
	To-Be Technology Infrastructure Approach
	Nonproduction System Procurement
	Conceptual Technology Architecture
	Technology Standard Definition
Change Management	Change Management Strategy
	Leadership Alignment Strategy
	Change Readiness Approach
	Communication Approach
	Training Strategy
Data	As-Is Data Standards
	Data Object Scope
	Data-Conversion Scope
	Data-Conversion Approach and Strategy
	Data Vision

Some of the key activities during the design phase are:

- Ratification of business requirements
- Confirmation of current business pain points
- Definition of to-be business processes
- Fit/gap analysis with application software

- System application design
- Creation of functional specifications to close application gaps

The project threads will perform a number of important activities to complete the design phase of the implementation project.

The PMO thread will continue to monitor the project progress against the project plan and ensure the project is executed against the established timeline with the agreed-upon resources and budget. The thread members will also ensure the deliverables are completed on time and within the established quality parameters. The PMO thread will also establish mechanisms to track business issues and facilitate resolution of key issues. These issues can cross different threads. In this context, an integration team may be established as part of the PMO thread to ensure that all integration issues are addressed and resolved.

The Process and Applications thread will execute a series of workshops to document the business requirements and to define the to-be business processes. The thread will also define the future organizational structure to support these business processes. In order to organize the processes against future testing plans, key business scenarios will be identified that cut across all functional areas. These business processes will later be a foundation for integration testing. Based on the business requirements and processes, the thread will also conduct a *fit/gap analysis.* As part of this activity, the team will document what requirements can be met by the software application through configuration and what requirements can be met only through additional development. The team will start creating a *RICEF catalog. (RICEF* stands for *reports, interfaces, conversions, enhancements, and forms.)* This catalog will be the foundation for ongoing technical activities throughout the project. Based on this catalog, the thread will start creating functional specifications, where the business logic of the identified developments is described, so that the technical team can translate these into technical specifications.

The Process and Applications thread will also define a functional test approach that describes how implemented functionality will be unit tested. In this context, unit testing refers to the testing of individually contained business activities, which are either configured in the system or implemented through custom development. The team will also establish a configuration approach to document the activities that will be completed to configure the system. As part of this approach, configuration activities will be listed in their correct sequence and dependencies between the configuration activities established. The configuration activities will be linked to the business requirements to build a foundation for a traceability matrix.

The Technology thread will focus on creating a software development plan and use the RICEF catalog to create effort estimates. These estimates will allow planning for appropriate staffing during the build phase. The thread will also create a design of the technical architecture to support the to-be business processes. It will build the nonproduction system environments and test these thoroughly. This includes installation of the main application software as well as bolt-on applications or third-party software. Depending on the timing of the functional specification documents created by the Process and Application thread, the team may also start the creation of technical specification documents. The team will create a technical testing approach that complements the functional testing approach created by the Process and Applications thread. This testing approach focuses on technical activities, such as performance testing. Finally, the team will complete the sizing of the production environment and start procurement procedures for this environment.

The Change Management thread will develop a learning strategy for end users. This learning strategy will be aligned with the business process design developed by the Process and Applications thread. As part of this activity, the organization leadership will be involved in the project to provide guidance and to start evangelizing throughout the organization. The Change Management thread will start executing on their communication strategy and monitor the organization readiness. Key stakeholders will start executing on their action plan to drive change within the organization. Finally, the Change Management team will also develop a knowledge-transfer approach that will allow the organization to take over support of the application upon completion of the implementation.

The Data thread will focus on executing on the data-conversion strategy and develop a data-cleansing approach. They will assist the technical team in developing data architecture and establish a data governance model.

Table 3.2 shows some of the key deliverables that are completed in the design phase.

The Build Phase

As part of this phase, the project team will build the system based on the agreed-upon design. This is accomplished by system configuration and development of functionality that is not configurable in the software package. Within the build phase, the project team will unit test the functionality and may also complete testing of several process steps. This type of testing is called *string testing* and is an effective method to prepare for integration testing.

Key activities within the phase include:

- System configuration
- Completion of functional specifications

TABLE 3.2 Key Deliverables in the Design Phase

Thread	Key Deliverables
PMO	Project Charter
	Detailed Project Plan for the Build Phase
	Financial Plan
	Risk Plan
	Issues Plan
Process and Applications	Organizational Model
	Process Design
	Functional Design
	RICEF Catalog
	Functional Specifications
Technology	Nonproduction System Installation
	Production System Procurement
	Detailed Technology Architecture
	Technical Test Approach
	Technical Specifications
Change Management	Learning Strategy for End Users
	Stakeholder Alignment Plan
	Detailed Communication Plan
	Organization Readiness Plan
	Knowledge-Transfer Approach
Data	To-Be Data Standards
	Data Object Design
	Data Conversion Detailed Work Plan
	Data-Cleansing Approach
	Data Quality Assessment

- Creation of technical specifications
- System unit and string testing
- Completion of a detailed integration test plan
- Creation of integration test scripts
- Implementation of security profiles
- Creation of reports

During the build phase of the implementation, the PMO thread will continue to monitor the progress of the project, specifically the completion of system configuration and system development. This is typically done with a number of different trackers that allow tracking of actual progress against planned weekly progress. This information can be updated in the project plan to help assess overall project status. The PMO will also focus on assisting in resolution of any key issues, specifically integration issues. Another key activity of the PMO in this phase is to assess and evaluate any required changes to the agreed-upon design. The PMO will also hold regular risk-review meetings to review significant project risks and mitigation steps. Toward the end of the build phase, the PMO thread will focus on creating the project plan for the testing phase and drive the preparation of the testing phase.

The Process and Applications thread of the implementation team will be focused on completing all outstanding development functional specifications and configuring the system. The team will also complete unit testing of configured functionality and of developed RICEF objects. The Process and Applications thread will be involved in string-testing activities throughout this phase. String tests are a concatenation of several individual unit tests and are used to ensure that a specific system function works as intended within a broader business context. The Process and Applications thread will also assist the Change Management thread in finalizing the learning plan and learning materials. Finally, the team will assist the development team with the implementation of development objects, reporting functionality, and security roles. Toward the end of this phase, the Process and Applications thread will either drive or assist with creation of integration test scripts. These test scripts describe the steps required to execute end-to-end business scenarios that cover different functional areas.

The Technology thread will be heavily interacting with the Process and Applications thread, especially in the area of system development. The team will create technical specifications and complete development of RICEF objects, including technical unit testing of the development objects. The Technology thread will also develop reports using different reporting or data warehousing technologies. Within the application, the Technology thread will also implement security profiles that support a role-based user concept. In this context, it will be important to consider segregation of duty concepts to comply with Sarbanes-Oxley regulations. The Technology thread will also support the development environment and complete establishing a *quality assurance* (QA) environment that will be used in the next phase of the project.

The Change Management thread will finalize the learning plan and develop learning materials. The team will implement its readiness change approach and deliver ongoing communications within the project team and the overall organization. The Change Management thread will assist the project teams in the creation of knowledge-transfer agreements that formalize the knowledge-sharing activities between the system integrator and the client organization.

The Data thread will implement master data management functionality to support master data business processes. The functionality will be based on the data governance model that was designed in the previous phase. The team will also support the Technology thread to build reporting and data-mining functionality. The Data thread will heavily interact with the Process and Applications thread to ensure that all data requirements of the business are considered and implemented. The Data thread will unit and string test the functionality it has built. Throughout this phase, the Data thread will continue implementing data-cleansing and data-conversion routines. It is important to start testing these procedures early in this phase to enable an iterative process of data validation by the business owners. In order to obtain clean, consistent, and accurate data during the final system go-live, it is typically required to go through several mock conversions with data validation by the business groups.

Table 3.3 shows some key deliverables that are completed in the build phase.

TABLE 3.3 Key Deliverables in the Build Phase

Thread	Key Deliverables
PMO	Detailed Project Plan for the Testing Phase
	Risk-Mitigation Strategies
	Detailed Integration Test Plan
	Business Continuity Plan
	Updated Financial Plan
Process and Applications	System Configuration and Documentation
	Tested RICEF Objects with Documentation
	Business Process Procedures
	Documented Unit and Strings Tests
	Integration Test Scenarios
Technology	QA System Installation
	Production System Preparation
	Security Roles
	Implemented RICEF Objects with Documentation
	Implemented Reports
Change Management	Final Learning Plan
	Training Curriculum
	Implemented Readiness Approach
	Client Satisfaction Report
	Knowledge-Transfer Agreements
Data	Master Data Management Configuration
	Unit and String Tests with Documentation
	Data-Cleansing Programs
	Data-Conversion Programs
	Mock Data Cleansing and Conversions

The Testing Phase

During the testing phase of the project, the system will go through a series of tests. In typical ERP implementation projects, the following tests are executed during this phase:

- Integration test
- Performance test
- User-acceptance test
- Cutover rehearsal

Integration testing is based on a number of test scripts that comprise all business processes in scope. The project team will execute several cycles of integration tests with increased complexity. The purpose of executing multiple cycles is to ensure that the final integration test cycle is performed without any critical defects.

The purpose of the performance test is to confirm that the production system will be able handle the anticipated volume of users and transactions. It will also test whether the system can handle planned batch processes within defined parameters.

The focus during the user-acceptance testing activities will be to confirm that the users can perform their business functions with the application that has been created and that all business requirements are met. The project team will perform a series of cutover rehearsals to test the go-live procedures that have been put in place. This includes any data-conversion activities and switching on the new environment with all converted data.

During this phase, the PMO team will be focused on executing and monitoring the progress of the different tests. For this purpose, this thread will closely interact with the Technology and Process and Applications threads. The PMO will organize regular status meetings and defect meetings to review the progress of the testing phase. The PMO will also continue monitoring project issues and project risks. Finally, the PMO thread will complete building a cutover plan that contains all steps that are required to cut over to the new system.

The Process and Applications thread will dedicate some of its members to executing the integration test cases. Other members will be focused on analyzing and resolving defects. This thread will also assist the Technology thread in its tests and work closely with the Change Management thread on completing the training activities. Finally, the Process and Applications thread will interact with the Data thread to confirm the accuracy of the data-cleansing and data-conversion procedures.

The Technology thread will be part of all the testing activities to ensure that the system infrastructure works properly and to resolve any defects that are detected in custom-developed objects. The Technology thread will also be part of confirming the cutover plan in preparation for system go-live.

The Change Management thread will complete all training documentation and prepare for end-user training. The thread will also ensure that the organization is prepared for the changes resulting from the system implementation and that business roles are correctly mapped to the new system.

The Data thread will complete its data-cleansing and data-conversion tests and obtain final confirmation from the business community on the accuracy of the converted data.

Table 3.4 shows some key deliverables that are completed during the testing phase.

The Deployment Phase

During the deployment phase of the project, the team will perform all activities to cut over to the new system and start monitoring the system operations. This phase is the culmination

TABLE 3.4 Key Deliverables in the Testing Phase

Thread	Key Deliverables
PMO	Detailed Project Plan for the Deployment Phase
	Deployment Plan
	Detailed Cutover Plan
	Cutover Test with Documentation
	Updated Financial Plan
Process and Applications	Integration Tests with Documentation
	User-Acceptance Tests with Documentation
	User-Role Tests with Documentation
	Verified End-User Training Documents
	Tested Reports
Technology	Production System Installation
	Batch Program Schedule
	Performance Tests with Documentation
	Tested Security Roles
	Backup Plan for Production System
Change Management	Learning Environment Implemented
	Stakeholder Buy-in Completed
	Ongoing Project Communication
Data	Master Data Management System Tested
	Integration Tests with Documentation
	Mock Data Cleansing and Conversions Completed

of meticulous planning during the previous phases. Some of the key activities in this phase include:

- Training delivery
- Execution of system cutover
- Knowledge transfer
- Implementation of the support organization

The PMO thread will focus on executing and monitoring the cutover plan. Once the new system is operational, the PMO will ensure the new support organization is executing against established service-level agreements.

The Process and Applications thread will assist in cutover activities and help key users with execution of transactions in the new system. Members of the Process and Applications thread will become part of the new support organization and address any defects that are being identified.

The Technology thread will be focused on assisting with the cutover activities and ensuring the production system is available at all times and performing as expected. This thread will also schedule all batch programs that need to be executed in the production environment.

The Change Management thread will complete the training with the end users and communicate with the larger organization about the system go-live. It will then monitor the impact of the new system on the user community and work with key stakeholders to obtain acceptance of the new system within the organization.

The Data thread will execute the data-cleansing and conversion processes as part of the cutover plan. As with all other activities executed in this phase, the success of this activity is largely dependent on proper testing in the previous phases.

Table 3.5 shows some key deliverables completed during the deployment phase.

Common Risks and Mitigation Strategies

ERP implementation projects are complex by nature and require an experienced and dedicated team. There are a number of common risks that need to be managed properly. Some of these risks are:

TABLE 3.5 Key Deliverables in the Deployment Phase

Thread	Key Deliverables
PMO	Established Support Organization
	Cutover Plan Executed
	Organization Acceptance of the System
	Updated Financial Plan with Project Closeout
Process and	System Cutover
Applications	Knowledge Transfer Completed
Technology	Production System Live
	Batch Programs Scheduled
	System Backups Scheduled
	Knowledge Transfer Completed
Change	End-User Documentation
Management	Final Project Communications
Data	Master Data Management System Implemented
	Data Cleansing and Conversions Completed

- Scope creep
- Lack of user buy-in
- Insufficient executive alignment
- Missed business requirements

Scope creep can occur when different members of the organization include specific functionality in the new system. This can be the result of a belief that if certain functionality is not implemented in the initial project deployment, it will never be implemented. The chief financial officer (CFO) can assist in mitigating this risk by ensuring the project is part of a larger roadmap and the business community understands that the system will go through several iterations of ongoing improvements. The CFO can also assist by buying into the agreed-upon scope and assist the project team in adhering to this project scope. For this purpose, the CFO can participate in regular scope-review meetings and be a member of the Change Control Board throughout the project.

A lack of user buy-in can be a serious risk to the success of the project. This can be the result of insufficient communication and missing incentives for the user community to accept the new system. The CFO can assist in mitigating this risk by incentivizing employees based on project success and linking their goals to their participation and the success of the project. Frequently, end users do not see the immediate benefits of the new system and are concerned about changes to the job functions they perform. It will be important for the CFO to communicate the criticality of the success of the project within the financial organization.

Overall executive alignment is key to the success of the project. Any financial systems implementation will go through difficult times. It is in those times that executives must be committed to the success of the project and help in the decision-making process to resolve any issues that are causing difficulties. The completion of a business case prior to the project can be a very useful instrument to drive executive alignment and commitment to the project. The CFO can drive the completion of this business case.

It is important to ensure that no critical business requirements are missed during the system implementation. For this purpose, the project team can create a *traceability matrix* that enables linking all integration test scenarios to the original business requirements. With this traceability matrix it will be possible to see whether any business requirements have not been considered in the integration test phase. Additionally, the financial organization should carefully review the ratified business requirements and the system design. The CFO can be the ultimate approver of the proposed system design and rely on his or her organization to ensure that all business requirements are met in the proposed design.

Areas that Require Special Attention from the CFO

There are a number of items that require special attention within the financial organization and ultimately from the CFO. We will focus on the following key items:

- Segregation of duties
- Compliance with accounting rules
- Payroll and commission processing
- Security and audit trails
- Period closing

It is important that the new financial system complies with segregation-of-duties rules. A simple example of such a rule is that an employee who creates vendors in the system should not be allowed to create payments for this vendor. In order to comply with segregation-of-duties rules, it is important that controls-experienced resources are part of the project. The CFO can also commit members of the internal audit group to the project. The CFO can participate in regular meetings by the internal audit group that focus on compliance of the new system with segregation-of-duties rules.

The new system must comply with accounting rules. However, if the project is not appropriately staffed, the project may end up with team members who are experienced in setting up system functionality but not with the accounting rules the new system must follow. As an example, revenue-recognition accounting rules can be very complex and require experienced resources as part of the project. It will be important for the CFO to ensure that the project team includes experienced financial resources who understand the accounting rules the company must follow. In this context, regular review meetings can be held in which the CFO is updated on some of these complex accounting topics and how they are implemented in the new system.

Payroll and commission processing will require special testing procedures, as they follow a set of complicated calculations. A well-established testing method is parallel processing. As part of parallel processing, the new system and the legacy system will perform these calculations in parallel until it has been confirmed that the new system performs correct calculations.

The new system must provide security concepts that provide users with access to transactions they need to execute and precludes them from executing transactions that are not part of their job function. In addition, the new system should provide an audit trail of all activities performed in the system, including user name as well as date and time stamp. As an example, it should be possible to review who changed the payment terms on a vendor master record. The internal audit group can be part of regular meetings to review these security concepts and report back to the CFO.

Most ERP systems provide the advantage that they are integrated by nature. As an example, a sales transaction and its invoice are automatically reflected in the financial module of the application. The integrated nature of ERP systems can help in reducing the duration of closing periods at month- or quarter-end. However, it will be important that the period-closing process is thoroughly tested as part of integration testing. Therefore, one of the scenarios during integration testing should be the closing of a month and the closing of a period. The results of these tests should be communicated to the CFO.

Conclusion

As described in this chapter, a financial system implementation must follow a very structured approach to help position the system to meet its long-term objectives. A number of different project methodologies exist to organize the project into phases and threads, with specific deliverables assigned to each of these phases and threads.

When executing the project, it will be important to find the right balance between following such a structure and remaining flexible enough to address any unforeseen challenges. Defining exit criteria for each phase and confirming these criteria at the end of each phase can help in keeping the project on track.

The CFO can be of great support to the implementation by providing executive sponsorship and leadership, for example, by being an active member in regular steering committee meetings. By engaging during the entire project lifecycle, the CFO can help create enthusiasm and commitment from the entire financial organization, which will go a long way during the course of the project.

CHAPTER 4

Critical Success Factors for IT Implementations

Ajay Bhatia

Angela Mattix

Have you ever been involved in an information technology (IT) implementation project for your organization that has been considered less than successful? If so, you are not alone. When embarking on an IT implementation project, many organizations achieve less than the expected results.

Why is this the case? Well, there are numerous factors that contribute to the perceived, as well as actual, success or failure of a project. In this chapter, we will explore some of the key *critical success factors* (CSFs) and why they are important. Critical success factors are the essential areas of activity that must be performed well if you are to achieve the mission, objectives, or goals for your business or implementation. The advantages of identifying CSFs are that they are simple to understand, help focus attention on major issues, are easy to monitor, and can be used in concert with application implementation methodologies.

Identifying and monitoring CSFs is important, as they allow the implementation team to focus their efforts on building their capabilities to meet these CSFs and allow the team to decide whether it has the capability to build the requirements necessary to be successful.

By identifying your implementation-critical success factors prior to launching a project, you can create a common point of reference to help you direct and measure the success of your implementation.

Our top-ten critical success factors are:

1. Provide effective sponsorship.
2. Select a dedicated and experienced project team.
3. Establish project infrastructure.
4. Utilize a well-established approach.
5. Address people issues.
6. Communicate within and outside of the project team.
7. Manage scope.
8. Establish a supportive culture.
9. Conduct periodic quality assurance (QA) reviews.
10. Provide a stable technical environment.

These CSFs are not listed in any particular order, because we believe they all play a key role in helping an organization execute a successful project. Following is a discussion of our top-ten CSFs.

Provide Effective Sponsorship

The sponsor(s) should be identified and engaged as early in the project planning phase as possible. Ideally, you should have a key sponsor for each area of the business that will be impacted. This should provide full representation from all areas of the organization at the highest level of the project.

Sponsors have two vital functions within a project. The first function is to provide strategic direction and business insight on a project to ensure the project is delivering the value that was anticipated based on the business case. The second function is to promote the project and to ensure that the contractual obligations and deliverables of the project are realized. In order to have effective sponsorship, the sponsors must be engaged and kept informed of the project's progress. Depending on the size, complexity, and duration of the project, the sponsors should meet with the project management team at least monthly; this is typically known as the *steering committee* meeting. If a project is of shorter duration or is in a critical phase where issues need to be escalated and addressed quickly, the steering committee should meet more frequently.

To be an effective sponsor, the individual must be engaged and supportive of the project and its goals and objectives. The sponsor should be open and willing to listen to all opinions and then help drive decision making. An effective sponsor must also model the way for the project team and support the long-term vision and objectives. One key aspect of a sponsor's job is to help resolve issues for projects that have cross-functional impacts where the decisions across teams cannot be made internally. Good sponsors look at the big picture and long-term strategy and vision of the company to help the project teams make the correct long-term business decisions. Without effective sponsorship, a project can veer off track and end up not meeting its original goals and objectives, resulting in an unsuccessful project.

Select a Dedicated and Experienced Project Team

Why is selecting a dedicated and experienced project team a critical success factor? Let us take a look at why a dedicated team is important. When you do not assign key resources to a project full time, other day-to-day activities end up taking away valuable time from the resource, which can significantly impact the project timeline and budget. When other job-related activities or responsibilities interfere, the resource may lose focus or become engaged in decisions or behavior that can be counter-productive to the goals of the project. Ideally, key project team members should be 100 percent dedicated to project activities with no other assignments.

Organizations also tend to fall short in the assignment of experienced resources to projects. It is difficult for organizations to reconcile pulling strong, experienced resources from their daily business, but this is a vital component for a successful project. A successful project requires a project team that has a strong understanding of the business's needs and resources and that can assist in making and driving the right process decisions for the organization. In too many projects, organizations attempt to assign less experienced or more junior resources to these roles. This is fine if done on a limited basis, but it is extremely important to have strong, experienced resources in key positions of the project to significantly increase the likelihood that the organization's long-term goals are achieved.

Establish Project Infrastructure

There are several key elements of the project infrastructure that need to be established early in the scoping and planning phase of a project. These include the development of a project charter, work plan, issue management system, change management system, and status reporting mechanism.

The development of a project charter is an effective project management practice. It is developed as a guide for the project team to help them understand the scope and objectives of the project. A good charter should:

- Outline the project's goals and objectives and constraints.
- Define the project scope.
- Define the roles and responsibilities between the vendor assisting with the implementation and the internal project team.
- Identify the primary stakeholders.
- Provide guidance on issue management, change management, and status reporting.
- Establish the authority and boundaries of the internal project manager.

The project charter should be shared with every steering committee and project team member. Most organizations do not want to share the contracts related to the project since they sometimes contain confidential data. However, the project charter should be developed and widely distributed in order to facilitate a better understanding of the project scope and governance guidelines.

The work plan, issue management system, change management system, and status reporting are all key interrelated components of the project governance structure. The project work plan is used to communicate and track progress against the key milestones of your project so the team has visibility into whether the project is on track or at risk of not meeting any of the key dates. Using the work plan with key dependencies, you can monitor the potential impact a missed or delayed milestone would have on downstream milestones.

Issue management is an essential process that all team members should understand. The most successful projects encourage team members to document potential issues as early as possible so that project management has visibility into these items and can start determining how to address them. As for the change management system, it is tightly integrated with managing scope, which we will discuss in more detail shortly. It is imperative to have the change management system documented so the team understands what the process will be to both add and remove scope. Change management is critical since it could have an impact on resources, timeline, or budget of a project. Any time the scope of a project is changed, all parties should understand the overall project impact. The other governance component that is important to have defined is the status reporting process. The general process is to have weekly status reporting by the key process streams to provide project management visibility into the overall project status, how each team is tracking against the project work plan and the key milestones, any issues that need to be resolved, and any decisions that have been made.

Utilize a Well-Established Approach

Why is utilizing a well-established approach an important component to achieving a successful project? Leveraging a well-established approach should provide the project team with guidelines and a standard structure to follow. This helps a project to be planned and managed appropriately. Implementing systems is a very complex process. Therefore, it is critical to use a well-established approach that addresses the people, processes, and technical aspects of the initiative. (See Chapter 3 for a detailed description of a well-established implementation methodology.)

Address People Issues

How does addressing people issues impact the project? A significant component of any project is how the organization's employees will be affected by the impending changes a project brings to an organization and how well the people are prepared for these changes. When an organization ignores or does not address the people issues, employees can become negative, and some even go so far as to attempt to undermine the project. It is inevitable that rumors will start to circulate when employees become concerned about what the future may hold for them. This ties in nicely with one of the other critical success factors, communication, which is discussed in more detail in the next section and in Chapter 5.

When project leadership and sponsors address people issues, there are multiple areas that end up being positively influenced, such as overall team morale, resource interest in the project, and the project teams' support of the project. See Chapter 5 for a complete discussion of effective practices related to addressing the people aspects of a systems implementation.

Communicate

There are multiple types of communication that should be considered when you are developing a communication strategy. There are project-level communication, organizational communication, as well as external communication requirements for suppliers and customers.

Communication is essential to keep everyone involved in the project informed of what is going on and for the team to be able to coordinate and take appropriate action. Communication is also fundamental to the organization to start building awareness of and buy-in to the impending organizational changes.

When communication is not thought through and executed properly, it can lead to disgruntled employees. This can then cause resources to have the perception that the project will not be successful, which can unfortunately turn into reality.

When structuring the overall communication strategy, it is important to remember that not everyone retains and absorbs information in the same way; therefore, you should always plan on communicating critical messages via multiple formats and/or media, such as e-mail, phone messages, or even town hall–type meetings.

Manage Scope

As you may already be aware, managing scope can make or break a project and is essential to control throughout the entire project lifecycle. Many times, organizations find it relatively easy to just keep adding in some seemingly small, but potentially important, functionality to a project. These small additions can add up and tend to have a harmful effect on both the project timeline and the budget.

One of the main activities in scope management is ensuring the entire project team is aware of the defined scope of the project. This scope needs to be continually reinforced and part of the onboarding process for any new team member. (Managing scope is a good application for the project charter we discussed earlier.)

The second concept all project team members need to understand is how scope management ties in with the change control process. In many projects, you will find that some scope items and their impact may need to be escalated to the sponsors of the project due to the budget or timeline impact of the scope change.

Establish a Supportive Culture

A supportive culture encourages the team to discuss or raise potential issues early in the project lifecycle. When team members feel comfortable bringing up potential risks or issues, project management can take corrective action or escalate the issue to the steering committee. When there is not a supportive culture on the project, then the team may feel uncomfortable raising issues to the project management group early enough to allow time to resolve the issue before the project timeline or budget would be impacted.

Conduct Periodic Quality Assurance Reviews

Conducting periodic quality assurance reviews can help you uncover potential issues early in the project lifecycle. A quality assurance review should be conducted by someone not actively involved with the project to provide an independent perspective. A good review should include interviews not only with the project leadership, but also with various dedicated project team members to discover potential risk areas and challenges that might need to be addressed and to ascertain what risk mitigations might need to be put in place. Sometimes issues are at the project leadership level; an effective way to identify this is for the individual performing the quality assurance review to talk with the team members.

Quality assurance reviews should be scheduled at regular intervals for the duration of the project. At a minimum, they should be scheduled no less than once every three months. However, depending on the stage and complexity of the project, you might consider doing quality assurance reviews more frequently.

Provide a Stable Technical Environment

When it comes to providing a stable technical environment, there are a couple of questions you should consider before you embark on an IT project:

- Is the technology you are implementing right for the maturity of your IT organization?
- Is the technology supported in house, or do you use a hosting provider?

Why are these important questions to answer?

The following is an example of a project where these questions were not thought through properly and the project ended up being stopped after 14 months. The investment of long hours by the project team and millions of dollars had to be written off.

The organization was doing a package selection and then ultimately the implementation of the package. Although the organization included business process selection criteria and technology criteria, the business criteria were given a much heavier percentage of the ratings than the technology criteria since the tool was to be used by over 1,000 business users. The package that ended up being selected had the best business process rating but had the lowest technological rating. As a result, the package was rated the best of its competitors and was selected for implementation.

The implementation of the product was planned for 12 months, and the package was to be integrated with the organization's back-office financial system to maintain master data such as customers, vendors, and items, and for transactional processing. Although the extent of the integration points was known at the time of the package selection, it was not specifically addressed in the package selection criteria. When the team began the testing phase of the project, it was quickly discovered that the technical architecture would not support the volume or number of transactions the company was attempting to integrate between it and the back-office product. After 14 months of trying to resolve the issue, the IT organization did an in-depth study and analysis of the application and determined it was unable to support the organization's needs.

There are other factors you should consider related to the technology component:

- Have at least one database administrator on site as part of your project.
- If your environments are hosted by third parties, ensure that your on-site development team has the required access to the database and the applications.
- If your environment is hosted, make sure your service-level agreements with the outsourcer are sufficient for the project.

Many organizations fail to take these points into consideration during the planning phase of the project. Outsourcers frequently leverage the same production support resources to support a new project. As a result, production issues can take away resources from project-related issues. This has been known to cause significant delays to a project that end up impacting the project timeline and budget.

Conclusion

As mentioned at the beginning of the chapter, all these criteria form an integral part of a successful project. Failing to incorporate even one of these components into the structure of your project could lead to a less than successful implementation.

CHAPTER 5

Steering Clear of a "Crisis in Confidence" and Other People Pitfalls

Sharon F. Piech
Hilary Horn
Nancie W. Fernandez

A *crisis in confidence* will cause a financial system implementation to halt or fall significantly off schedule. A crisis in confidence is not a technology or financial issue; it is a people issue that can strike at any time during a project. Examples of crises include a severe project team morale crash due to a significant number of bugs uncovered during testing, a change of leadership within the company or project team that causes uncertainty around the project, a loss of momentum resulting from a delayed timeline, or a strident rejection of the new system by end users immediately after go-live.

To mitigate the risk of having a crisis in confidence occur, the financial executive needs to control five things:

1. **Project team effectiveness.** The project team must consist of the *right* people working in a supportive environment. In

almost every case, the right people for the project are not the people easily available at the time of the project. In addition, the project environment needs to facilitate the team working together to get their jobs, and the project, done.

2. **Leadership engagement.** The leadership of the company must be actively engaged in leading the project, supporting the project team, and managing the changes necessary for realization of business benefits.

3. **Stakeholder management.** All internal and external stakeholders must be aware of and prepared for the changes resulting from the new system and processes.

4. **Training.** Employees must be taught how to perform their jobs in the new environment.

5. **Workforce transition and adoption.** A plan must be developed and executed to implement necessary changes to the organizational structure, jobs, operating model, policies, and metrics to enable realization of business benefits.

With only five things to control, why is it that projects commonly have a crisis in confidence related to one of these items? We believe it is because *people* are the most difficult factor to predict and influence over every other factor of an implementation. The impacts people have on a project are the single most underestimated aspect of an implementation. That is why we also believe the five-facet framework and the time-tested approaches described in this chapter could help you in your efforts to have a successful project and limit the havoc that might have otherwise resulted from a crisis in confidence.

Think of your project in three phases: *before, during,* and *after* the implementation. Table 5.1 describes the critical activities for the five facets during each phase. Although there are many other people-related activities you can engage in, we believe these are the most important ones.

TABLE 5.1 Critical Activities for Each Focus Area by Project Phase

Focus Area	Before the Project	During the Project	After the Project
Project Team Effectiveness	Assemble the team.	Motivate the team.	Recognize the team.
Leadership Engagement	Prepare executives and leaders.	Support executives and leaders.	Support executives and leaders.
Stakeholder Management	Define success.	Communicate.	Communicate.
Training	Understand your critical audience.	Deliver training.	Deliver additional training.
Workforce Transition and Adoption	Understand risk areas.	Modify organization, jobs, policies, operational model and metrics.	Track benefits.

Phase 1: Before the Project

Prior to launching the project, you should assemble the team, prepare executives and leaders, define success, and understand risk areas.

Focus Area: Project Team Effectiveness

TASK: ASSEMBLE TEAM Nothing blows up a project faster than not having the right people on your team. The project team can include employees and external third parties, such as software and hardware vendors, outsourcing vendors, and consultants.

Projects that do not have the necessary talent, skills, experience, and resources that a results-oriented organization needs to make smart decisions and deliver forward-thinking results are very likely to experience at least one crisis in confidence. When selecting the project team members, you may be tempted to staff the team with available resources, such as those holding expendable roles in the business. However, nothing is worse than paying for a brand-new system that is a replica of the dinosaur system or does not do what the business requires. This is what will likely happen if the team is not staffed with top-performing resources. It should be no surprise that a "C" team will deliver "C" results; do not settle for anything less than the "A" team.

Focus Area: Leadership Engagement

TASK: PREPARE EXECUTIVES AND LEADERS In many cases, financial executives are responsible for the success of the implementation. However, one person cannot bear the burden alone. You should engage other executives and leaders to help support and lead the project, and this group should include business and organizational executives currently responsible for leading and managing the business. You will want these people to be your allies. They will need to forgo personal pet projects, communicate the imperative of this project, give up their best resources for the project, and accept responsibility for the success of this project as part of their own performance objectives.

By talking and listening to these executives and leaders, you will know what the business and organizational leaders think of your vision and assess who will be the most critical to making your project successful. Some leaders may be resistant to change; that is expected. We have discovered that most of these people are not actively *opposed* to changing; rather, they have competing priorities, or they simply do not have enough time to fully understand and commit. To overcome their resistance to change, you need to understand their concerns and help them shift their priorities. This means that you have to help them understand *what is in it for them.*

You, along with this group of executives and leaders, will need to actively lead the change, visibly support the project, and make tough decisions to resolve competing priorities within the company. Support from them needs to be more than head nodding. It is imperative to win their support prior to the start of the project. It will be much more difficult to gain their commitment once the project is under way. Neglecting to gain their support significantly increases the likelihood that your project will fail. A common theme among successful projects is that financial executives spend more time gaining and sustaining leadership commitment and selling the project than actually delivering the project.

Focus Area: Stakeholder Management

TASK: DEFINE SUCCESS A standard definition of a successful implementation is "on time, on budget, and meets business objectives." This fact-based definition can be unsatisfactory and devoid of meaning to stakeholders, and looking to the business case to provide a clear explanation can be too complicated for certain audience groups. Stakeholders want a clear, compelling reason to be excited about the project—preferably a reason that is impressive! Being able to persuasively explain why people should care about a project and tying that message back to a company's business strategy can make an enormous difference in the quality and overall success of the project.

The financial executive must portray the project imperative in an inspiring way and talk about the future after the project as impressive and inevitable. Stating a mediocre project imperative is simple; creating an inspirational message is genius. Next we present an example of a company that blended emotion with the fact-based vision.

EXAMPLE: "INDEPENDENCE FROM THE OLD WAYS"   A child company completed spinning off from its parent company. Although the company was free of its parent in many aspects, the parent continued to house all the information technology (IT) aspects of its business. The parent had graciously agreed to support the child's IT for 12 months for a nominal fee but then would substantially increase those fees. The child could not afford these high costs, so the timeline for the child's own financial systems was established based on the concept of a platform that was "burning" in 12 months. People were outraged when they learned of the exorbitant costs that the parent would put into effect. The chief financial officer (CFO) underscored the magnitude of the project (it was the largest enterprise resource planning implementation at the time) and the complexity of doing such a large project under the imposed time constraints. The executive leaders, stakeholders, and project team members felt that they were part of something historic and knew they each played a role in breaking the final ties with the parent. This compelling and impressive message, personally and regularly reinforced by the CFO, motivated the team to meet the immovable timelines and achieve independence.

Once the project imperative is finalized, it should be communicated as tenaciously as a marketing campaign. A single voicemail or e-mail will achieve very little in today's noisy world; you need to rise above this through in-person dialogues, messages tailored to audience segments, and listening to feedback from your interactions.

Stakeholders beyond the project team and company employees include customers, suppliers, partners, investors, and analysts. These groups might wonder why the company is doing the project, how their interface with the company might change as a result of the project, and perhaps whether they will have a relationship with the company after the project. It is helpful to list your stakeholders, assess what each stakeholder cares about, anticipate how they might perceive the implementation, and describe what benefits they might gain from the project. This will help you and the other executive leaders to tailor your message to each group of stakeholders.

Share the vision of the project with each stakeholder group and listen to their feedback. Align executives and leaders with each stakeholder group and hold them accountable for developing and following through on a communication plan with their assigned stakeholders. Communicate in a way that is relevant to each of your stakeholders, because this builds their trust in your organization and momentum for achieving your vision. Ultimately, it can help make your organization stand out in a crowded marketplace.

Focus Area: Training

TASK: UNDERSTAND YOUR CRITICAL AUDIENCE GROUPS   When thinking about training, a grand ambition is to train every user on every process and all functionality. This is both expensive and unrealistic. By establishing a clear understanding of who will be affected by the new system and to what degree they will need to perform their job differently, your training plans can hone in on those audience groups that are critical to business operations. Many training programs are unsuccessful not because the training was bad but rather because the training was not relevant to the end users. A successful training plan effectively teaches the end users what they need to know right before they need to know it.

The first step in putting together a training plan is to identify the top-ten user groups and the top-ten things that they need to know about the new system. Each of these top-ten lists should be ranked from highest to lowest, resulting in a focused list of end-user groups and what they must know prior to go-live.

Prioritizing audience groups before the project is under way should provide a clear list of who the most important users will be. The time spent understanding the different end-user groups can save time and money not only on training but on all other change and transition activities. The project team can more efficiently manage scope when they have a clear understanding of high-priority end-user groups, because they are now equipped to prevent requests from noncritical end users from being piled onto the system.

Focus Area: Workforce Transition and Adoption

TASK: UNDERSTAND RISK AREAS   Prior to launching a project, it is smart to compile risks and develop mitigation plans, especially around the people aspects of the project. It may not be your responsibility to know the specific skills and capabilities of your entire workforce, but it is important to assess whether your workforce will be able to operate adeptly in the future state. Your Human Resources (HR) function can conduct a workforce assessment to measure the skills of your workforce and make risks visible. Using tools such as manager/employee talent surveys, workforce analytics, and predictive modeling, HR can provide you with a perspective of your talent landscape and gaps. This perspective will enable you to accelerate the company's overall adoption of the change.

We recommend conducting a change-readiness assessment with each stakeholder group. This can provide objective data concerning which stakeholder groups are most resistant to change and what their specific concerns are. It produces a quantitative and qualitative measure for a nebulous area (i.e., "how people feel"), which allows for tracking readiness and alignment over time. The assessment should pinpoint hazards such as:

- A weak project imperative or vision
- Uncertainty about the roadmap or steps involved in making the transition
- A perceived lack of leadership competency
- Change fatigue due to multiple or conflicting projects
- A rigid organizational structure that will reinforce old behaviors versus new behaviors
- A deficiency of key skill sets required for users of the new system

The results from the change-readiness assessment can help you prioritize the areas that require more leadership and support to make the change stick.

It is also the time to start defining end-user adoption and determining how you will measure end-user adoption. The adoption metrics should be grounded in the same metrics used to define project success. When end-user adoption is as important as budget or time, the focus shifts to being about people and business realization. Start with the end in mind: What type of results do you expect to see? Then it becomes easy to see what people need to do differently to achieve these results. Now the important dialogue around defining expectations and behavior changes necessary to achieve business results can begin.

Recap: What to Do Before a Project Begins

Here is a checklist of activities to complete prior to launching a project:

- Assemble the A-players for your project team.
- Engage executives and leaders as passionate allies.
- Create an impressive and inspirational project imperative. Share this with each of your stakeholders, and take the time to explain what is in it for them.

- Identify and prioritize the top-ten audience groups and the indisputable things that they must know about the system.
- Conduct a change-readiness assessment of your stakeholders to understand where risks exist and where you need to prioritize.
- Begin defining end-user adoption and business realization.

Phase 2: During the Project

Focus Area: Project Team Effectiveness

TASK: MOTIVATE TEAM Whether you believe that people are your biggest asset or not, it is indisputable that people make the largest contribution to successful implementations. Some pundits have erroneously believed that large technology implementations could focus solely on technology to achieve business benefits. Today, from our experience, we know that it is essential to engage people quickly and effectively to attain the desired business adjustments.

The project team needs to hear from you, directly and regularly. They need to see you. Without leadership, the project team will struggle to remain committed to the project. There will be worriers and resisters, but you have the influence to push them to become believers.

One meticulous financial executive we know tracked the number of communications he made during the first month of a project. He had talked about the project more than 1,000 times and estimated with mortification that he was only 1 percent complete in communicating the message. It will undoubtedly feel like a second full-time job to keep your project top of mind.

It is critical to explain what the project means to people and how they and their colleagues will be impacted in the future. If you do not tell people what the project means to them, they will be inclined to make up their own answer. Their answer probably will not be an answer you would like.

Focus Area: Leadership Engagement

TASK: SUPPORT EXECUTIVES AND LEADERS   Implementing a financial system will test your people skills. You need to provide constant communication with business and organizational leaders to discuss their activities to support and lead the project. It is likely that, during the implementation, you might see resistance even from your previously formed allies of other executives and leaders. Some former supporters may defect to focus on other projects, which might even be in direct conflict with your project.

Regularly meeting and engaging with leaders is critical throughout the implementation. A good tool is a leadership engagement plan. First, develop a list of all of the leaders and key influencers within the company. Then assess their level of influence on and support for this project. Be honest; if you do not know someone's level of support, note it as low or zero. Prioritize actions with leaders rated as high influencers but low supporters. Track their engagement and note when you see their support moving in any direction.

As the project progresses, you will also want to develop action plans for these leaders. The action plan can include having them talk to other leaders, send communications to their direct reports, or talk about the project at their next staff meeting. You should monitor and measure their support to help keep your project a priority with them.

Focus Area: Stakeholder Management

TASK: COMMUNICATE   To keep employees informed of the status of the project, one financial executive we know set up a blog to articulate the imperative of the project, describe its expected benefits, and respond to inquiries and feedback. This allowed the employees to be instantly plugged in and kept actively engaged.

A good *communication plan* greatly increases the likelihood of a project's success. A communication plan is used to organize and track your activities, help you tailor your messages to the recipients, and demonstrate visible leadership. The details of the plan should include all recipients who should receive communications, including the owner of the communication, the frequency of the communication, the method of the communication, the intended message of the communication, and the method of measuring the effectiveness of the communication.

To reach down into your organization, be sure to include middle management in your communication plan. Middle managers possess firsthand knowledge of operations, and they can make the adoption of the system easy or painful. While executive leaders are excited to announce a new project, many fail to realize that it takes middle management to bring the banner home. Engaging managers in discussions allows you to push information about the project throughout your organization, and, more important, can provide advanced understanding of anticipated impacts to operations and other real or perceived obstacles.

Focus Area: Training

TASK: DELIVER TRAINING   New systems almost always require that employees learn how to do their jobs differently. This learning begins with communications from you and their managers to first help them understand what is changing. Then hands-on training should be used to teach them the new system and processes.

It is ironic that companies spend a massive amount of money on implementation but then often try to cut corners on training. Beyond the chance of completely derailing the implementation, poorly trained users can severely limit the realization of benefits since they will not know how to use the system. As a financial executive, you must commit to a high standard for training. The training budget should including end-user training, ongoing events for leadership, team members, super-users, training-the-trainers, and operations. When resistance comes to devoting time and resources to training, the previously communicated definition of success can be used to remind leaders of the imperative of the project and the link between training and successfully performing the project.

Here are the key questions to address as part of the training effort:

- How will information be shared across the project team members? Is there an existing library of material about the system or business processes that can be a used as a starting point for training content?
- What software tools will be used to accelerate training documentation? This can help reduce the amount of effort and cost associated with training development.
- When should the training be conducted? The best time for training is *just in time*, which means that training should be done as close to the time of the go-live as possible. This is usually inconvenient for the project team. However, retention rates can be dramatically impacted as the length of time between the training and the go-live increases.
- Can training development be accelerated using offshore resources? Using offshore resources can be an incredible accelerator and cost saver, provided careful analysis is completed and development requirements are established. The

appropriateness of offshoring depends on project-specific requirements.

- Can alternative channels be used to supplement classroom training? Classroom training is certainly a key component, but other channels can be effective as well. Training is a social experience, where people carry back knowledge to enable the smooth adoption of the new system. Community learning channels, such as wikis or blogs, mobile learning, and game technologies, can be extremely effective at augmenting formal classroom sessions.
- How will training be available outside of the classroom? It is very important for users to be able to access the training while they are using the system. This can help them recall complex steps and allow them to adjust and learn on the fly.

A key to successful training is knowing who needs to be trained and on what topics, using offshore resources to accelerate development, and creating a training model with both traditional and new methods of learning.

Focus Area: Workforce Transition and Adoption

TASK: MODIFY ORGANIZATION, POLICIES, AND OPERATIONAL MODEL

Many companies do not thoroughly assess and align the organizational structure prior to go-live. This can result in a severe lack of integration between processes and technology, making it frustrating and cumbersome for users to use the system as it was designed. The operating model and organizational structure must support the changes being introduced. This may require reorganizing an entire department or function, changing staff to new jobs, and modifying performance metrics. Since these organizational changes can have a significant impact on people's jobs and overall company morale, careful planning is required to communicate the changes and maintain a productive workforce.

Designing the organization to implement the new system effectively must go further than "sticks and boxes." Here are some items to consider in building your future operating model:

- **Start with the business strategy and objectives.** These are very important drivers of organization design.
- **Get key stakeholders involved.** Stakeholders, such as senior executives, should have a personal interest in providing input to the organization model, since it directly impacts their teams and reporting relationships. Excluding them from the process will create problems in the future.
- **Design organizations with pencil, not pen.** Evolve your organizational structure as needed to match changes in the strategy, organization, and marketplace.
- **Develop an implementation plan.** A new operating and interaction model must clearly define roles and responsibilities. Change can have a significant impact on people's jobs and requires careful planning to avoid a backlash. HR can help in assessing and aligning the organizational structures, operating models, and performance metrics to support the strategy and reinforce the change.

Although there is no single correct answer for how an organization should be designed, an effective model must put the right people with the right competencies in the right places.

Recap: What to Do During a Project

Here is a checklist of activities for project leadership to do during a project:

- Make yourself visible to the project team with regular frequency.

- Nurture your relationships with your allies, including other executives and leaders, and ensure they remain committed to the success of the project.
- Communicate with everyone, all of the time.
- Set a high standard for training and employ multiple training channels to reach your key audience groups.
- Design and implement the new organization to support the achievement of business benefits.

Phase 3: After the Project

Focus Area: Project Team Effectiveness

TASK: RECOGNIZE TEAM   The financial and project executives should recognize the contributions of the project team. Rewarding team members with a financial bonus is common. It can be very meaningful to give team members inexpensive mementos related to the imperative of the project. These are often displayed on team members' desks for years.

It should be a top priority to help team members transition back into the organization. Many individuals stepped away from their prior jobs for a significant period of time, and they will need guidance to determine the best fit for them in the new organizational structure. It can be a time of uncertainty for them, especially if there were significant organizational changes as a result of the project. If you used A-team people for your project, they likely should be part of the future of your company.

Focus Area: Leadership Engagement

TASK: SUPPORT EXECUTIVES AND LEADERS   After a large effort to get the system implemented, it can be disheartening if end users, business leaders, or organizational leaders are not immediately complimentary of the system. However, do not hold your breath waiting for their applause! It is normal that end users do not immediately express their undying love for the new system, due to the amount of change that everyone is processing. Backlash can occur no matter how intricate the system is or how much input was provided by stakeholders. Let things settle down before you thoroughly evaluate the results.

Based on the end-user adoption metrics defined before your project was launched, we recommend conducting 30-, 60-, and 90-day end-user adoption assessments. You can analyze these results to determine whether new policies, behaviors, and performance metrics should be adjusted or introduced to drive business results.

Focus Area: Stakeholder Management

TASK: COMMUNICATE   Now is not the time to throttle back your communication efforts. Your stakeholders need to hear from you now more than ever. It is during this time that they will be really paying attention to your messages and how you will be addressing their concerns. The change is real for them now.

As a financial executive, you will hear comments and complaints from stakeholders about how the system does not meet their needs. If you implemented everything that everyone wanted, you would never be able implement anything at all. Communication with them is critical, because they need to be assured that this will work and this is important.

Focus Area: Training

TASK: DELIVER ADDITIONAL TRAINING   Ongoing education and programs to align behaviors with business objectives need to be established. The training used during the project deployment should be refreshed, made available to all employees, and expanded to include known pitfalls and uncommon transactions.

If at all possible, super-users and project champions should deliver planned classroom training. Support should be available to employees through portals or other methods.

We talked with a CFO who said that his project provided significant and varied training for users prior to go-live. Unfortunately, no one showed up for the training because they were tied up in their current jobs. Once the system went live, end users had to scramble to learn how to use the system. In this case, training was needed *after* go-live to teach the users how to perform their jobs. They were ready to learn when they had no choice.

EXAMPLE: POST–GO-LIVE ON-THE-JOB TRAINING   One company we know had locations in 15 cities in the United States that were using a new system. Even though there were super-users in each city, there were inconsistencies in data quality and varying levels of system adaptation in each location. The project sent a five-person team to each city for one week to watch the system users, provide real-time feedback to correct data entry errors, and suggest tips and tricks to make the system a more enjoyable experience for the users. Each week, the five-person team visited another city, until, at the end of 15 weeks, the data-quality problems were virtually eliminated. Not only were the users much happier with the system, the five-person team came back with several easy ideas for improving the system.

Focus Area: Workforce Transition and Adoption

TASK: TRACK BENEFITS   Consider whether your new system lives up to your definition of success. After an implementation, the focus should be relentless on constant improvement of the financial system and your workforce. True success is ongoing, with the initial go-live viewed as one of many. Each subsequent go-live should focus on hammering out the undesirable aspects of the system. Gaps in business intelligence and dysfunction on dashboards are examples of functionality that can be created, enhanced, or fixed. To determine what functionality should be improved, analyze the type and volume of questions logged at the support desk, the remaining manual processes or newly created workarounds that support the system, and the job-related performance improvements and behavioral changes.

Additionally, now that employees have new roles and responsibilities, it is a great time to roll out rewards, incentives, and programs that align with the business objectives. Employees should know what they are being measured on, and these performance measures should include things that help keep them from going back to their old way of doing things. When motivated properly, employees can also have brilliant ideas for future improvements.

Recap: What to Do after a Project

Here is a checklist of activities for project leadership to do after project go-live:

- Recognize the project team and help members transition into the new organization.
- Continue relationships with your allies of executives and leaders, and remember not to expect positive feedback immediately after the go-live.
- Communicate with your stakeholders and respond to their feedback.
- Make additional training available to end users and create new training opportunities as they are needed.
- Improve the system with functionality that matters, and track the benefits that are resulting from the system.
- Keep an eye on your workforce and establish or refine performance measures.

Conclusion

Before, during, or after your financial system implementation, you might experience one or multiple crisis-in-confidence moments. This chapter provides a five-facet framework and related tools that can help you navigate through these moments and ultimately deliver a successful project. Focus on these five items to sidestep people pitfalls:

1. **Project team effectiveness.** Have the *right* people on the project who understand the business and command the necessary influence to make decisions.
2. **Leadership engagement.** Ensure the leadership of the company is actively engaged and committed to the project.
3. **Stakeholder management.** Engage with internal and external stakeholders to make them aware of the changes resulting from the new system.
4. **Training.** Train employees before and after go-live.
5. **Workforce transition and adoption.** Align the organizational structure and operating model to achieve high value from the system and enable realization of business benefits.

Remember that change does not just happen; *people* make change happen. Dedicating sufficient time and attention to the people aspects of implementations is critical to the success of any systems-related project.

CHAPTER 6

Objectives and Scope of Implementing Automated Financial Systems

Michael S. Vowles

Brenda S. Haroian

Organizations have several motivations for implementing financial systems, from streamlining existing process to synchronizing with a corporation's overall business strategy. Whatever the motivation, organizations implementing automated financial systems should focus on achieving process and control simplification and standardization across the organization, efficiency gains resulting in lower costs, globalization, regulatory, compliance, and effective use of end-to-end electronic processes, real-time information delivery, and business performance management.

Objectives

It is important for an organization to understand both the impacts and the benefits that financial systems can provide in order to effectively plan for their efficient implementation. The following are objectives an organization should keep in mind when implementing financial systems.

Changes to Financial Processes and Financial Strategies

Implementing financial systems provides an opportunity to review and transform an organization's existing financial processes and strategies. Since most financial systems are built based on effective practices, these systems can provide an appropriate foundation for future financial growth and change.

Inefficient Processes

When implementing financial systems, organizations should take the opportunity to review, redesign, and streamline financial processes. This is a perfect opportunity to transform existing processes to increase efficiency and reduce costs. Organizations with broken or outdated processes may exhibit one or more of the following inefficiencies:

- Lengthy close timelines (more than five days to final consolidation and financial statement review)
- Processes riddled with manual workarounds, causing lack of transparency and control
- Financial organizations dependent on offline spreadsheet analysis (as opposed to standard reports and streamlined data)
- Lack of a shared services model for repetitive back-office processes such as accounts payable processing (see Chapter 7)
- Shared services models working with multiple processes (e.g., local statutory models per country), multiple systems, and manual work steps
- Dependence on manual approvals and paper workflow

Redesign, Readdress, and Streamline Processes

Financial processes and financial transaction flows should be evaluated not from a "continuous improvement" perspective but from a clean-sheet, *ground-up* approach in order to gain the greatest possible benefit from a new financial environment and system features.

Clear, simple, and efficient processes, supported by standard finance system functionality, can enable close time *best practices* (i.e., one to five days) through evaluating the consolidation close logic and the flow of accounting data. Ideally, transactions should be created with the appropriate accounting data (and approval) at the source, as opposed to being manually adjusted in the general ledger due to legacy system or transactional process limitations. Automated workflow, approvals, and online data inquiry and analysis can enable faster processing, evaluation of key performance metrics (as data will be available to measure), and greater automated Sarbanes-Oxley (SOX) controls.

The financial system needs to support a global standard financial policy and process to enable either virtual or physical shared services for repetitive and required nonanalytical back-office processes. Financial systems implementations should take into consideration (if not be in lockstep with) any shared services initiatives (e.g., new shared services organizations or shared services process improvement initiatives).

Overall, a financial systems implementation cannot be successful without considering how financial processes and transaction flows can be improved. Many implementations have been considered marginally successful when the system is implemented with new features, but the old processes limit the ability of the organization to take advantage of them.

Scalability

New financial systems implementations should be designed for future scalability as the organization grows. Over time, financial function will likely need to address the impact of new product lines, new business models, or new advantageous legal entity or tax structure changes. Ideally, the addition of a business or the purchase of another entity through mergers and acquisitions should be relatively seamless and have low overhead in being integrated into one financial system and process. Keeping processes and financial systems implementations simple and noncustomized can aid in achieving this goal. This can allow the organization to focus on realizing the benefits behind the acquisition and not solely on integration issues.

If systems and processes are so complex that customization and "hard-coding" are required, the addition of new structures or, more important, the modification of current business models and legal entity structures, may become extremely difficult. Organizations that cannot effectively consider future business models with their financial systems may find themselves faced with the question of whether to invest in reworking or the reimplementation of a system.

Another major objective of a new financial systems implementation is ensuring that as the business grows, the growth of required resources to maintain the financial processing is at a lower rate. Addressing common global and streamlined (noncustomized and uncomplicated) financial processes is key to achieving the objective of a slower rate of headcount growth to revenue growth over time.

Finally, thinking about and designing *key performance indicators* (KPIs) into the financial systems and understanding how data can be pulled for regular checkups on transactional efficiency can allow financial organizations to find and track candidate processes for continuous improvement. It is important to identify the bottlenecks, process limitations, and system limitations early, when addressing and fixing them are small efforts and scalability is not yet impacted. Waiting to address KPIs in the later phases of an implementation may result in custom reports and special processes to access the information.

Accounting Principles, Statutory Requirements, and Governance

Financial systems should be designed to enable the latest accounting principles and facilitate compliance with statutory and governance requirements in today's financial environment. More important, the system should be designed for flexibility to handle the ever-changing financial environment and statutory requirements in corporate generally accepted accounting principles (GAAP), local GAAP, and International Financial Reporting Standards (IFRS) (see Chapter 10).

GLOBAL ACCOUNTING POLICIES AND GOVERNANCE   Financial organizations should take advantage of financial systems implementations to revisit their global accounting policies. Ideally, financial systems implementations should drive new accounting policies as new processes are created, and accounting organizations should review their existing financial accounting policies to find areas of improvement and simplification for the global organization. Transactional systems can be on one centralized system, with one centralized GAAP policy. Local variations in the transactional books should be limited to the requirements that must be handled in this manner; other requirements should be moved to local reporting ledgers.

MANAGING ACCOUNTING CONTROLS   A key objective of financial systems implementations is to help manage, streamline, and automate accounting controls. As financial organizations entered into the SOX-regulated environment, many organizations put a large number of controls in place without implementing

95

new financial systems. These large lists of controls (many of which may be manual) can be inefficient by being repetitive, unnecessary, or manually intensive. SOX control matrixes should be evaluated for completeness, reduction, and automation. Using new financial systems functionality provided by the major software vendors in newer releases can enable businesses to cut down on manual controls and use workflow and online approvals to document and manage SOX controls to help reduce paper workflow, spreadsheets, and unnecessary levels of duplicate control.

REVIEW SECURITY AND PRIVACY   Financial organizations should use the financial systems implementation to evaluate their systems and data for security levels and privacy issues. As processes are defined, the security levels are determined; data should be evaluated for access and appropriate use (or availability in the system). Although not directly a financial application, data contained in human resource management systems is often utilized throughout the financial applications, such as in accounts payable, for employee expense reimbursement. Privacy concerns surrounding the disclosure of employee information, such as home address and Social Security number, must be taken into account.

ACCOUNTING POLICIES AND STATUTORY REQUIREMENTS CHANGES
Another key objective of financial systems implementations is to plan for changes in the statutory accounting environment in both the transactional books and the reporting books for local GAAP. A relevant example for U.S. corporations is planning for a transition to the new system of International Financial Reporting Standards. As discussed in Chapter 10, IFRS provides standards, interpretations, and the framework for the preparation and presentation of financial statements adopted by the International Accounting Standards Board (IASB).

Financial systems implementations should plan for scalability for future accounting changes by simplifying processes and enabling reporting books (through either financial systems or financial reporting solutions). It is key for financial systems to consider initiatives evaluating the impact of new accounting statutory and transactional GAAP requirements and, if possible, align financial systems implementations with these initiatives.

Technical Strategies

Financial organizations are dependent on and must be major players in technology strategies that support simplification, standardization, and efficiencies in the technical environment of the business. Technology can be a major driver and influence in deciding to go forward with a new financial system, and can support the business case to justify the cost.

END-OF-LIFE OR UNSUPPORTED FINANCIAL SOFTWARE Accounting organizations should be aware of the risk involved in using financial systems that are so outdated that technical support has been discontinued or the system is not being updated with new features to meet new requirements. A key objective of a financial systems implementation is to engage a software vendor that is keeping current with the latest technology challenges (e.g., security and SOX automated processes) and is offering new features for making the accounting process environment more efficient. A new financial system, despite a large up-front cost, can save the organization overall through operational efficiencies and a reduction in internal customization when it uses a software vendor that regularly updates its software to handle new accounting challenges for its client base as a whole.

CONSOLIDATION OF SYSTEMS (ERP) Financial systems have a part to play in the overall consolidation of business software, reducing integration complexity and duplication of data. A key objective of financial systems implementations is to ensure that the financial accounting data comes from one single "source of truth." Information technology organizations can benefit (and become more efficient support for accounting organizations) from the reduction of complicated layers of skill sets resulting from managing multiple systems and streamlining their service offerings to the business as a whole.

Master Data Management

Finally, a financial systems implementation should have as an objective to simplify and streamline business data to reduce data duplication, data reconciliation, data mapping, and different definitions of the same data that make analysis difficult and confusing. Financial systems implementations should assist in ensuring *data stewards*. These resources are subject-matter experts and are nominated to help define, refine, and manage accounting data in a system-wide manner. Consistent data management and a single source of truth or *system of record* will make accounting data more flexible for financial analysis and reconcilable for financial validation.

Core (First-Tier) Applications

The applications required to support the previously mentioned objectives are discussed next. The basic or *core* functions of an accounting system are:

- Maintain a single or multiple sets of books.
- Maintain and execute disbursements.
- Maintain and execute revenue collection.

- Manage cash and fixed assets.
- Generate financial and management reports.

These processes form the *first tier* of any financial automated system. The applications listed next support these core functions and are required as the foundation to all financial systems.

General Ledger

The general ledger is the *primary key* to the financial system linking the entire financial application together. As such, the general ledger forms the basis or foundation of the solution; it is difficult to find an application in the solution that does not have a direct connection to the general ledger through either the chart of accounts or which transactions are controlled through an accounting period.

The general ledger will be used to consolidate financial activities across the subledgers and also across the various sets of books. The legal entity structure and corresponding set (or sets) of books not only must be planned for today's requirements, but must be flexible enough to meet future needs. Finally, the general ledger forms the basis of all financial and management reporting.

Accounts Payable

The disbursement function of an organization needs to be tightly controlled and, as such, qualifies as a tier-one financial application. To be highly efficient, the accounts payable application should be electronically linked to the organization's bank to enable electronic payment of suppliers.

To facilitate a tightly controlled procure-to-pay process, the procurement application could also be considered a core application in some instances. It depends solely on the organization as to whether the procurement function should be automated and integrated with the accounts payable application. If the transaction volume exists, the procurement application should be considered a core application since it enables a greater level of control through purchase order and supplier invoice matching and automated integration with accounts payable.

Accounts Receivable

Perhaps more important than controlling disbursements is the control and collection of cash from sales and other revenue-generating activities. This process should be as automated as possible, utilizing *electronic data interchange* (EDI) as well as electronic bank transfers and lockboxes. Cash flow is important to every organization, and the accounts receivable module should facilitate the monitoring and customer collection of aged receivables. Basic reporting, such as the invoice register, aging, and cash application, are standard across many packages.

Fixed Assets

Perhaps the least glamorous of the core financial applications is fixed assets. This application calculates depreciation, which will be expensed on a periodic basis. The capture of fixed assets should be automated by tightly integrating fixed assets processes with purchasing and accounts payable—as assets are purchased, the information gathered during the procurement and payment processes flows directly to the fixed assets register. It is important to note that the function of capturing asset information, such as make, model, serial number, location, and employee assignment, can be performed using self-service applications.

Financial Reporting

Each of the previously listed applications will contain some form of standard reporting functionality, such as trial balances and account details in the case of the general ledger, or transactional reports for the other applications. Depending on the organization, enhanced reporting capabilities may be required to generate formal financial statements, such as income statements and balance sheets. Although financial reporting is deemed a required function, the organization's requirements usually can be met with the core applications.

Second-Tier Applications

After considering the core applications, the *second-tier* applications are discussed here. These applications are commonly in place at larger organizations where cost reductions and efficiencies can be gained due to the volume of transactions.

Cash Management

With respect to payables and receivables, cash management can be added to automate the reconciliation of cash disbursements and receipts respectively. Cash management should be integrated electronically with the organization's bank to automatically perform reconciliations while the financial organization focuses on exception handling. Cash management should also provide functionality to manage liquidity, to control cash, and to spot potential fraudulent activities. Finally, it should provide direct access to expected cash flows and cash requirements as well as currency exposures, to help sustain liquidity and manage the use of cash resources.

Travel and Expense

Employee travel and expense management applications should be added where volume warrants. The self-service functionality should not only help increase employee compliance, but also help increase efficiency by allowing payables resources to focus only on performing reviews and approvals of employee expense claims. Rules can be set up in many software packages enabling exception reporting when employees violate corporate expense policies. Linkages to a corporate charge card can be added to the expense solution, further improving automation and efficiency by allowing employees to access and import their corporate charges directly into their expense reports.

Planning, Budgeting, and Forecasting

Planning, budgeting, and forecasting applications are considered tier-two applications since a limited amount of their basic functionality (e.g., budgeting) is contained in most general ledger software packages. By implementing a planning, budgeting, and forecasting application, the next functionality can be enabled:

- Communication of corporate goals to every level of the organization by allowing budgeting and forecasting across the organization using a consistent framework.
- Establishment of a logical link between the budget and day-to-day performance measurement mechanisms. This allows organizations to develop financial targets and measures of accountability with a single, consistent framework.
- Creation and evaluation of *what-if* scenarios.
- Reporting and analysis across multidimensional data elements to evaluate key information across these dimensions,

such as chart-of-account line items, financial data elements, business units, and time periods.

Credit and Collections

Although the basic credit-and-collections functionality is usually included in the accounts receivable application, a number of software vendors offer increased functionality in specific applications focusing on collections. The number of customers, the average value of each invoice, and the days-sales-outstanding (DSO) metric will help determine whether the organization should place additional emphasis on the collection of outstanding receivables.

Tax

Tax software can be integrated into financial systems to help facilitate compliance and automate the calculation and recovery of sales and use taxes. Tax is usually one of the largest line items on an organization's income statement and, as such, requires the same level of transparency and integrity as financial reporting. It is important to note that the installation and setup of tax reporting software should be completed by tax professionals due to the dynamic nature of the tax environment.

Payroll

Payroll is a fundamental business activity requiring compliance, accuracy, and strict financial controls. The payroll function can be either performed within the organization or outsourced, depending on the size of the organization, available benefits, and the complexity of its compensation plans. Integrated payroll applications will perform the necessary accounting and interface directly to the general ledger in the same manner as any other subledger. For organizations that choose to outsource their payroll function, the outsourcer will provide a *feed*, or file, containing all general ledger entries for each payroll.

Regardless of the method of payment, a payroll management system can assist in controlling the resource costs and helping ensure the workforce is paid on time and according to the organization's compensation rules. It is also important to mention that most payroll applications are dependent on employee data, which is generally maintained in a separate human resource management application.

System Controls

Internal controls requirements (e.g., Sarbanes-Oxley section 404) and taxation compliance requirements are also complex. Proper compliance, therefore, is not simply a function of accounting software. These complex rules and procedures must be carried out by skilled finance professionals and may be reviewed and attested by auditors. The ability to track and determine user access is a key component in complying with regulatory requirements and facilitating corporate security. A number of applications provide real-time monitoring and proactive enforcement of crucial access policies based on out-of-the-box rules and rules you establish to support *segregation of duties* (SOD). These applications are designed to alert the organization to potential SOD conflicts before they arise. (See Chapter 9 for additional information on system controls and SOX requirements.)

Third-Tier Applications and Beyond

There are a large number of other applications that could be classified as belonging in the *third tier*. These applications satisfy unique requirements based on the particular organization (e.g., lease and real-estate management). A number of these applications usually can be integrated into automated financial systems through interfaces. Based on our experience, we discuss here the two most commonly implemented third-tier applications.

Project Accounting

The automated tracking of disbursements, resource costs, and revenue generation associated with a unique initiative is the core functionality of a project accounting application. It enables the assignment of a common *tag*, or marker, to a wide range of transaction types with reporting capabilities to provide actual results or variances against budgeted and actual amounts. Project accounting applications are most commonly seen in professional services and service organizations, in organizations with a large number of research and development projects, and in organizations that build assets. The project accounting application can be integrated with the payables and fixed assets applications to capitalize assets upon their completion. Conversely, project accounting can be integrated with accounts receivable to track the revenue generated from a particular project.

Treasury

Implementation of a treasury application can allow the organization to monitor and adjust currency and interest rate exposure while facilitating compliance with organizational risk policies. It also enables an efficient treasury operation through the automation and simplification of deal administration for debt, investments, foreign exchange, equities, and derivatives while enforcing internal security and limit controls.

Conclusion

This chapter presented a number of possible objectives for an organization implementing a financial system. It is important to keep in mind that a balance should be struck between lowering finance operational costs and at the same time not compromising the finance organization's ability to support the operational side of the business as well as serve its internal and external customers.

To support these objectives, the core, first-tier financial applications were presented as were a number of second- and third-tier applications that, depending on the size and requirements of the organization, could increase efficiency and lower costs of financial operations. The same concept, however, always applies: The finance organization must be able to support the business as well as its internal and external customers in a manner that is not only efficient but also facilitates the generation of revenue.

PART II

IT Hot Topics

CHAPTER 7

Shared Services and Financial Systems

Jessica Golden
Susan C. Hogan
Krista D. Mondschein

Creating Value through Financial Systems–Enabled Shared Services

Shared service centers (SSCs) are powerful enablers of enterprise benefits when effectively implemented and managed. SSCs can help consolidate processes, which can help reduce operations costs and improve quality. Although SSCs provide processing for back-office functions such as Finance, Human Resources, Information Technology (IT), and Procurement, the Finance process has historically been the first to move to an SSC and is where we see the deepest penetration. Together with financial systems, SSCs are the enablers that can allow Finance business leaders

---

Observations and conclusions presented in this chapter reflect the collective experience of the authors. The authors also used Deloitte Consulting LLP's 2009 Global Shared Services Survey of more than 260 executives worldwide as a source of research (Deloitte Consulting LLP, 2009).

to better focus on business support and analysis as opposed to data gathering and manipulation.

The focus of this chapter is to discuss the positive impact and opportunities that financial systems can have on shared service implementations and operations.

Key discussion topics include:

- Leveraging financial systems as a foundation to enable benefits when implementing and enhancing shared services
- Critical considerations for SSC and financial systems implementation
- Understanding the critical role of the financial executive in shared services implementations and operations

Financial Systems as a Foundation for Shared Services Benefits Realization

Shared services strategies are key enablers for enterprise transformation. Shared services can help companies dramatically improve back-office effectiveness and efficiencies, and financial systems are foundational to sustainable transformations. There are numerous important business benefits that SSCs can help organizations achieve, such as:

- Significant cost reduction (typically 15 to 25 percent) due to process improvement, economies of scale, working capital, and wage arbitrage
- Improved controls
- Improved back-office cost visibility and metrics
- Improved quality due to the SSC's focus on continuous improvement and creating a service-oriented culture

However, there is also a clear link between the extent of SSC benefits achieved and the state of existing financial systems. The economies of scale SSCs should achieve from consolidating business unit transaction processing are very often reduced when business units have different legacy systems and processes. Whereas the SSC can help to significantly enable process standardization, the maximum business benefit cannot be achieved if the financial systems are not consolidated and kept updated as well.

For example, Company A consolidated accounts payable (AP) for four business units. Each business unit had the same legacy system but different instances that had been locally customized over the years. The expected cost reduction (people support time) benefit from the SSC consolidation was limited until a single financial system was implemented. This was because the SSC had to maintain additional staff and capacity to manage the four different approaches and systems for AP processing. Without standardization on a single financial system, there was limited ability to level capacity among AP processors due to the level of training and specificity by business unit, resulting in suboptimization of the potential SSC benefit.

When a company is unable to consolidate legacy systems across the enterprise, an alternative is to build interfaces between the multiple legacy systems and the centralized system in the SSC. While this alternative may help minimize negative impacts to the people support time benefit described in the prior example, it has its own set of costs and complexities that also could impact the overall business benefit.

Another important role financial systems play in SSC benefit achievement is improving visibility into data across the enterprise. Common processes and reporting can enable increased customer confidence in the SSC, because both the customers and the SSC would then be looking at the same information and speaking the same language. With a consolidated platform, less time is spent on reconciling data from disparate systems; hence more time can be spent on value-added analysis of what the data really means to the business. Moreover, effective analysis of the customer data generated by an SSC can help a company to increase its understanding of its profitability drivers, to segment customers, and to guide targeted customer relationship management activities. Finally, better visibility into enterprise vendor data can enable a company to perform analysis of spend patterns and identify potential cost-saving opportunities through more effective management of vendor contracts.

More recently, financial systems have facilitated the SSC's goal to climb the value chain in terms of increasing the scope of value-added services provided because customers can become more confident in the SSC's ability to perform against service levels. A key driver behind this increasing confidence is better financial systems that provide visibility into the SSC, which allows customers to validate accuracy and confirm desired results.

In addition, Deloitte's 2009 Global Shared Services Survey reported that SSCs are increasingly expanding their process scope, with 57 percent of respondents indicating a plan to increase scope of analytical processes. This represents a 21 percent increase since the 2007 release of the survey, which is consistent with our experience and potentially due to improved capabilities in financial systems and tools as well as increasing SSC operations maturity.

SSC and Financial Systems Implementation Considerations

While some companies do move disparate legacy systems into SSCs or build interfaces to continue supporting them, implementation risks can be better managed by standardizing financial systems. The greater the level of standardization achieved, whether across the enterprise or across the business unit, the more implementation risks can be reduced. A single, integrated system also creates a foundation for moving processes and transfer of data and information between the business and shared services. Training of new resources can be simpler and more consistent and access to business-critical data can be made more accessible both within and outside of the SSC.

In developing a roadmap for an SSC implementation, special consideration should be given to understanding migration risks and their potential impacts on quickly achieving expected benefits. Two case examples are presented next, which illustrate the two most common approaches to creating shared services according to Deloitte's 2009 Global Shared Services Survey (see Figure 7.1), and the specific considerations in each case as a company moves through the phases of the implementation.

- **Case #1: Fix and Shift.** Move to shared services and make the technology and process changes at the same time (21 percent).

		Timing of Shift to SSC		
		Before technology change	During technology change	After technology change
Timing of Process Change	Prior to shift to SSC	4%	5%	6%
	During shift to SSC	5%	21%	3%
	After shift to SSC	31%	15%	10%

FIGURE 7.1 Sequencing Shared Services Shifts

Source: Deloitte Consulting LLP, Global Shared Services Survey, 2009.

- **Case #2: Lift and Shift.** Establish the SSC using the legacy technology environments and then make the technology and process changes (31 percent).

Scoping and Planning Assessment Phase: Program Roadmapping

- **Case #1.** The most efficient approach to roadmapping the implementation is to synchronize the SSC phases to the financial systems implementation phases for Scoping and Planning, Design, Build, Test, and Deploy. (See Chapter 3 for a detailed discussion of the systems implementation process.) The rationale is that the financial systems implementation program leadership, project management rigor, and change management are synergistic with the SSC implementation. Ramp-up of capacity in the SSC generally does not follow a "Day 1—Big Bang" approach but builds processing capacity incrementally as a proof of concept.
- **Case #2.** If the SSC is implemented before a financial systems implementation, additional time should be built into the roadmap to accommodate legacy process documentation, training on additional systems, and a longer-phased business case to benefits achievement per the previous section on SSC benefits.

Design, Build, and Test Phases

- **Case #1.** Design workshops for the financial systems and SSC should be conducted together, with a focus on end-to-end process design. Build and Test of technology components should include a focus on day-in-the-life testing to ensure that robust financial processes flow from business units, through the SSC, and back to the business units seamlessly. Metrics should be developed and built to measure the success of the end-to-end processing through the financial systems and SSCs. Reporting design should include reports specifically addressing the needs of the business units using the SSC as a service center.

- **Case #2.** Design and Build should focus on standardizing processes and consolidating legacy systems to the extent possible prior to implementation of new financial systems. The SSC design will need to also develop data warehousing and reporting mechanisms to provide the business units with visibility into the SSC's processing. As possible within the legacy systems environment, metrics and reports similar to Case #1 should be built. During Test, an environment reflecting the legacy systems should be created to ensure successful information flow between the SSC and business units.

Deploy Phase

- **Case #1.** Companies generally have two choices during a Case #1 implementation: "Big Bang," where financial systems and all SSC processes commence at the same time, and the more widely used technique of *piloting*, where SSC processes are ramped up at the SSC after the financial systems go-live. The process ramp-up needs to be tightly coordinated to be successful in a new single-instance financial systems world. Generally sequencing the implementation into waves, with each wave representing a set of processes, business segments, or locations, is recommended.

- **Case #2.** Companies have the option of all the approaches described in Case #1 plus transaction volume ramp-up. Determining the right approach should be based on an assessment of change management impact, systems access, speed to benefits, and risk mitigation. Piloting is the more conservative approach for Case #2 since a legacy systems environment has many more *breakpoints* in processes and

115

systems that cause complexity and issues. Piloting, therefore, creates a proof of concept in a more controlled environment.

Understanding the options described here and weighing the pros and cons are critical planning activities prior to the creation of an SSC transformation program.

Financial Executive's Role in Shared Services Implementations

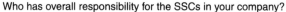

Large-scale SSC transformation initiatives fail without strong and visible support from senior leaders. Frequently, the main sponsor for shared services implementations is the chief financial officer (CFO) regardless of the processes being implemented, and especially so when pursuing finance shared services, because the CFO is usually responsible for the shared services organization. According to Deloitte's 2009 Global Shared Services Survey, the CFO is most frequently the executive responsible for SSCs (see Figure 7.2).

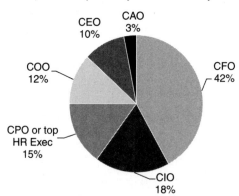

Who has overall responsibility for the SSCs in your company?

CAO 3%
CEO 10%
CFO 42%
COO 12%
CPO or top HR Exec 15%
CIO 18%

FIGURE 7.2 Ownership of the Shared Services Organization
Source: Deloitte Consulting LLP, Global Shared Services Survey, 2009.

Making Change Stick

Without strong leadership from the top, a typical issue after the SSC implementation is with business units internally rebuilding the processes that were previously moved into the SSC, creating duplicate work effort through these shadow organizations, and thereby increasing costs.

For example, one financial services institution created a captive offshore center in India that performed the majority of finance transaction processing for five business units, with significant planned benefits from consolidation and wage arbitrage. Within two years of the implementation, due to business changes and a variety of service issues related to technology challenges, three business units had begun to *build back* finance transaction processing activities. This, in effect, created duplicate workforces between the business units and the SSC, and cost the overall company. Because there was no strong leadership, a roadmap and funding had not been created to both enhance the SSC's capabilities and provide outstanding service, which would have eliminated the need for the business units to build shadow organizations.

Setting the Tone

A shared services organization will be more successful when it supports and aligns with the strategic direction of the organization. The tone and shape of that direction should be established early in the implementation and continually monitored. In addition, the SSC's benefit targets should be aligned with the organization's goals, from the initial implementation and going forward, and be flexible enough to change as the organization changes.

Conclusion

Shared services can enable important and material benefits for organizations. Potential benefits include cost reduction, process improvements, quality improvements, and improved risk and controls management.

To achieve the greatest benefit, an effective and consolidated financial system is a critical component of the SSC. While incremental benefits can be achieved without effective financial systems, an SSC strategy and roadmap should include a plan to enhance the technology environment. Managing and enforcing the SSC strategy and roadmap should be treated as an important role in the financial executive's agenda, to build initial and future success.

CHAPTER 8

Globalization Trends in Offshore Information Technology

Kalyana Sundaram

*O*ffshore or *remote delivery* of information technology (IT) tasks has been an effective practice for a number of years. This practice has matured into offshore-centric delivery of significant components of the entire development and support process. The U.S. demand for IT services is also driving the concept of specialized/focused IT work delivered offsite to many countries where the availability of IT talent and labor cost advantage make this economically viable. As a result, *offshore IT* is now multigeography; both the availability of IT talent and the labor cost advantage in these offshore locations are continuing to make offshore IT an essential consideration for businesses.

Strong growth in demand has fueled this trend. However, instead of just scaling into bigger and more geographically distributed delivery models, *offshoring* has morphed into something significantly different. The forces that shaped this transformation are different from the cost arbitrage that initially drove offshore IT.

In the technology industry, the current model of IT services is most commonly referred to as *global IT delivery*. Even though offshore IT was the genesis for global IT and continues to be

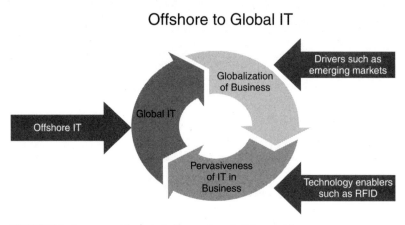

FIGURE 8.1 Business Trends Influencing Offshore IT

a big part of it, there are several other aspects to global IT that make it worthwhile to better understand its value. There are two key business trends that drive global IT. Not surprisingly, globalization of business is one of them. The increasing pervasiveness and criticality of IT to business is the other. It needs to be recognized that these two business trends are driven by factors unrelated to offshore IT. For example, the increased share of emerging markets in global demand is one of the drivers for globalization of business. Similarly, IT continues to be more pervasive in business due to advances in technology such as *radio frequency identification* (RFID). As shown in Figure 8.1, these three trends continue to evolve together and influence each other.

How Is Global IT Different from Offshore IT?

If offshore IT can be thought of as the outsourced manufacturing of component parts of a product or subassembly, then global IT is akin to the manufacturing/assembly of a large complex aircraft whose subassemblies were all designed, sourced, and produced in multiple (global) locations. Consider the critical decisions involved in the latter: Not only does each subassembly need to be sourced in a location best suited to produce it, but each location also offers a plethora of make, buy, or assembly choices for each component. The coordination required for matched design-production-assembly and the transportation of in-process work is enormous. Errors can cause cost escalations enough to wipe out the benefits of the entire production program.

Global IT, likewise, is the delivery of development and support services from a distributed network of definition, design, coding, testing, and deployment tasks performed in global locations. The locations are chosen so that the feasibility, cost, and quality levels in that location are best suited to performing that task. For example, the business analysts who would define the IT requirements need to be located in the same time zone as the users and need to be proficient in their language. The testing team, however, can be centrally located and serve both the development and support groups.

Unlike manufacturing, global IT is complicated by the need for extensive human interaction between the producers and consumers of IT services. Consider the case of the IT organization consolidating multiple global IT locations. This is not a simple exercise of determining where the best-quality deliverable is produced at the lowest cost and moving the production of all deliverables to that location. Instead, due consideration must be given to the level of understanding that exists between the business and IT in each location. This is because, unlike manufacturing, most of the requirements/specifications given to IT are understood, implied, or simply undocumented but considered acceptable because of the relationship or understanding. For example, if this understanding represents 50 percent of the requirements that are not documented, moving IT to a lower-cost location will likely lead to multiple iterations between business and IT, resulting in one or more of these factors: higher cost, reduced quality, and/or increased client dissatisfaction.

In the case of the aircraft, material, manufacturing, and handling/shipping costs are key considerations. In IT, the costs are primarily driven by time-zone delays, communication needs, related logistics, and variability in design and development.

This variability in design is another important concept to understand and keep in mind when moving to global IT. We described earlier how relationships/comfort can make undocumented requirements acceptable. Likewise, in the transfers among designer, developers, and testers, prior experience in delivering as a team can make up for shortcuts in documentation. In the long run, this can make the define-design-code-test teams more monolithic and could limit options while sourcing a specific person/team from outside the group. This tended to happen in the early days of offshore IT, when the deliverables from offshore coders were error-prone because they could not make sense out of design specifications from the "other group." Large IT organizations set up centers of excellence (COEs) as a way out of this dilemma. These centers house both local and global resources that specialize in specific business or IT domains, such as testing.

A key to reducing this variability and hence lost productivity is through standardization and reuse. *Standardization* stipulates what is considered as the minimum acceptable in documentation and often mandates the use of templates that specify required and optional sections. *Reuse* enables reduced effort in the creation of standard components that go into standardized deliverables while lowering delivery risk and increasing predictability. A related benefit is the better returns from mining and reuse of IT assets (which includes practices and methods). In the current economic environment, every increase in returns from any type of assets is immensely valuable.

How Globalization of Business Has Influenced Global IT

Globalization can be defined as the improvement of production and sales operations by sourcing, producing, distributing, and selling goods and services globally, or direct investment by foreign businesses in many developing economies. Global expansion led to a huge explosion in the volume and frequency of information collection, monitoring, and dissemination, which directly drives IT growth. In most kinds of business, at a very minimum, most employees at each new global location need a networked computer and a mobile device, which require IT support to set up and operate.

As these distributed IT operations continue to increase, companies are simultaneously trying to reduce their costs and improve their productivity. Otherwise, these global IT locations will likely become unviable for their businesses to consume their services.

Tax and regulatory services are good examples of globalized business spurring global IT. As companies extend operations to global locations, they need to comply with local tax laws and regulatory requirements. While these services can also be sourced locally, economies of scale often require the company to operate centralized tax services while engaging local specialists. This requires the capture, storage, and transmission of information around additional operational parameters. As the demand for these requirements grows, enterprise software packages have begun to incorporate these in their integrated application suites. This has in turn increased the demand for *cross-functional* global IT—tax specialists who can implement multilocation tax strategies.

Globalization can also lead to an increase in demand for different types of IT services since the configuration of the end-to-end transaction (business process) varies by geography. For example, in the United States, where printers are relatively inexpensive, the online travel-booking transaction ends with the user printing a boarding pass at home. In other countries, where the majority of consumers may not own or have access to printers, the service provider might offer, for a nominal fee, to have a courier deliver the ticket to the user within 24 hours. The fleet of couriers and print locations within a large city owned by the service provider will then be connected by a mobile network to optimize routing and transportation costs. Such *hybrid transactions*, with modifications, possibly can be replicated in different businesses with better results or may even enable businesses that were until now considered economically unviable.

How Pervasive IT Influenced Global IT

In large manufacturing plants, punch-card systems have long since been replaced by IT-intensive access cards or even more sophisticated biometric systems. For mobile workers who commute among plants, compatibility across these locations is a new requirement. So now the security function has to be IT literate and needs IT support, and the sourcing function needs to locate biometric access systems that are compatible in global locations. Additionally, the IT help desk and support functions need to be trained to handle these technologies.

From a very different, cost-based approach, many of the back-office functions in accounting and procurement have been sourced in low-cost locations. Because these functions are already IT enabled, they require IT support, and often at an advanced level. Consider, for example, the online auctioning for procurement of commodity goods and services. These applications are complex and require real-time capability, high-bandwidth networks, and security as well as frequent setting up with modifications. The supporting IT functions necessarily have to be in all locations with centralized monitoring and gathering of business intelligence.

How Global IT Continues to Drive Changes in Globalized Business

As IT increasingly moves to a utility status, it will tend to be provided from the location that offers the most effective combination of cost, quality, and reliability. The main determinants for successful global IT appear to be consistency in development and delivery processes.

IT firms from offshore countries have grown over the years. Acquisitions in the United States and other demand-heavy nations seem to be helping them move up the value chain. They seek to identify new opportunities where they can serve IT-enabled business at lower price points. The "IT business" is definitely changing.

An example from the financial services industry illustrates this mutual influence even better. Until a few years ago, fund transfer services from the United States to most foreign countries were not easily available, nor were they affordable. Today, there is a wide variety of such services available for many different countries from both organized financial institutions and others. This growth has been at least partly due to the increased demand for transfers from the increased number of IT professionals commuting to work among these countries. Speed, cost, and reliability of these transfers would have been impossible to achieve but for advances in Internet commerce and security. And because IT is essential for these remote transactions, it has become more pervasive in the financial services business.

A last and more striking example is from the IT–auto industry collaboration. A few years ago, the IT unit of an Indian business conglomerate started a dialogue around collaborative research with its client, which was in the automotive industry. Success with offshore IT made the client willing to try offshore research. Several years later, this design collaboration and indigenous low-cost manufacturing expertise have come together to deliver one of the world's lowest-cost autos.

As they mature, emerging technologies such as *cloud computing* will also positively influence the growth of global IT. At its simplest form, cloud computing could be interpreted as *on-demand* application and data storage services with custom interfaces to multiple applications. For example, online (application not owned or hosted by user) vendors enable downloads from multiple financial institutions (integration to multiple applications) and produce analysis reports (business intelligence and data not owned/hosted by user) on demand. Consider the possibility of an array of tax accountants, certified/trained in U.S. income tax laws, working on such applications to generate tax returns for U.S. consumers. For little or no investment in software, these people can be in any corner of the world and run a viable if seasonal business.

Conclusion

It is worth a financial executive's time to pay attention to offshore IT. (Just consider the number of *Fortune* companies whose strategic relationships include at least one offshore IT provider.) Additionally, global IT needs to be on the radar. Just as offshore IT led to significant offshoring in other services, financial executives should look at the influence of global IT on other business services. This may lead to fundamental redesign in how services are organized and delivered.

CHAPTER 9

Security, Controls, and Privacy

David Deckter

Jeffrey Fisher

S ecurity, controls, and privacy considerations are of para-
mount importance in financial system implementations.
With increasing scrutiny and regulatory oversight, ranging from
Sarbanes-Oxley 302 and 404 to numerous state and federal mandates, regarding the controls that should be in place to protect
the confidentiality of information, companies are feeling greater
pressure on getting these safeguards right. At the same time, they
are feeling great pressure to reduce or contain costs, especially
for risk and compliance management, which is often seen as
adding limited value. It is in light of these two opposing forces,
increased requirements and pressure to reduce costs, that we
explore security, controls, and privacy in financial systems.

Impact of Sarbanes-Oxley on Financial Systems Implementations

Most corporate professionals have knowledge of, or have been
impacted by, the Sarbanes-Oxley Act of 2002 (SOX) through
their involvement in the business world. Through this involvement, it is clear that SOX has had a profound impact on many

public companies. Prior to SOX, strong internal controls found within public companies most often were the result of: management reacting to, and trying to prevent, internal or external audit comments; the prevention of fraud; or management implementing specific internal control–focused departments. Once SOX was signed into law, management was required to take ownership of designing and implementing strong internal controls, as the penalty for noncompliance with SOX could result in significant fines and imprisonment.

From an information technology (IT) perspective, having a greater ownership and focus on internal controls, combined with knowledge of the SOX regulatory requirements, altered the processes and time frame surrounding a financial systems implementation in many ways. The following are five of the most prevalent impacts we have observed.

1. **More holistic view of the "system" implemented.** Companies now are looking through a much broader lens when asked to implement a system. Companies have a new appreciation for what constitutes a financial system. In the past, it was often believed that a financial system was merely one in which an accounting entry was created. In today's environment, companies realize many financial systems do not produce an accounting entry directly to the general ledger but can still have a significant impact on what entries get made. A good example of this is a typical purchasing system, which holds contract prices and directly impacts the disbursement and product costing entries that are subsequently made to the general ledger. Additionally, in planning an implementation of an enterprise resource planning (ERP) solution, companies today are also much more focused on how controls related to the operating system, database, and network layers of technology may be impacted. There is also a much closer linkage between business and IT departments

to keep manual and programmed controls operating in unison.

2. **Greater involvement of stakeholders.** Whereas well-designed system implementations have always had a planning phase, the extent to which stakeholders' input on internal control matters is being sought has dramatically increased. Companies are striving to incorporate controls as part of the implementation and not as an afterthought. Prior to SOX, it was rare for companies to consistently seek internal and external audit teams' involvement during the planning phase of a financial system's implementation; the overall feeling was that the audit teams would document issues observed in an audit report, which would be negatively portrayed throughout the company. Moreover, since SOX requires management to make an assertion as to the effectiveness of its own internal controls, if companies do not address their internal control requirements properly during implementation, they may have to self-report their internal control weaknesses, depending on likelihood and magnitude.

3. **Increased time to implement financial systems.** Since management has quarterly and annual requirements under SOX section 302 to certify that it has (1) evaluated the effectiveness of internal controls and (2) reported any significant changes to internal controls, many companies have made a decision to limit or eliminate financial systems implementations during the last three months of the fiscal year (commonly referred to as *Q4*). Since this leaves only nine months in any year to implement a financial system, many projects are taking longer to implement than in the pre-SOX era.

4. **Expanded focus on "auditability."** Since financial systems are included in the potential SOX testing scope for management and the external auditors, there continues to be a

greater appreciation for, and movement toward, maintaining evidence that a control is functioning effectively. For example, when application users can make changes to data outside of the application, companies are now more focused on tightly restricting such access and logging and monitoring all changes for validity and accuracy.

5. **Greater focus on implementing preventive controls.** As companies continually move to lessen their compliance costs, they are realizing that implementing preventive controls during system implementation can result in sizable cost savings and provide increased value over time.

Financial Executive's Role in the Security, Controls, and Privacy Area

The role of financial executives is one that continually evolves with time, industry, and the size of the company as they are asked to play crucial roles in strategic, operational, compliance, and, of course, financial aspects of the business. Moreover, in its purest form, one may say that the role of a financial executive is to manage financial risks. Today's financial executive has more of a risk-based focus than ever before. It is through this definition that one can establish a linkage to security, internal controls, and privacy as each could pose financial risk if not properly addressed.

- **Internal controls.** The financial executive has a key role in the corporate governance of the company. She sets the tone at the top and is a pillar of the control environment. She provides the necessary leadership and accountability to establish an organization designed to facilitate proper internal control and a process to support public attestations by the chief financial officer and chief executive officer (for public companies).

■ **Security.** Security is a fairly broad universe and, as such, the focus of a financial executive is primarily on the security aspects of financial reporting. This is where it becomes more challenging as security is often seen as an expense. Therefore, it is vitally important for a financial executive to be a visible advocate and champion of internal control and security-related projects where a strong value proposition exists as this can further convey a strong tone at the top.

■ **Privacy.** The financial executive's role is limited in this area; however, as it relates to providing direction on privacy and data protection, he still needs to be involved as it may impact financial reporting. A data breach could have an impact because of the potential fines for a breach, potential lawsuits, increased costs of credit reporting, and/or loss of shareholder value due to negative press affecting his company's brand reputation. The financial executive needs to work with the leadership team and the chief privacy officer to understand risks associated with a data breach so that they can plan for potential financial impacts.

Security, Control, and Privacy Safeguard Design

The first step in balancing the pressures to reduce costs while addressing increasing regulatory pressures on security, controls, and privacy is the design of the safeguards. The financial system in particular is considered by many organizations to be a crown jewel asset and therefore is one of the most frequently reviewed systems. Consequently, it is imperative to get the right fit of safeguards designed early, with supporting documentation captured throughout the process from inception to implementation. The primary activities and tasks to consider in designing financial system security, controls, and privacy safeguards are outlined here:

Activity 1—Requirements Analysis

- Identify internal and external mandates:
  - Internal policies and standards
  - Laws and regulations
  - Common practices
  - Industry standards
- Harmonize the requirements, removing overlap and inconsistencies.
- Key considerations while performing the requirements analysis:
  - Retain the context of the requirement to avoid over-controlling for different data types (e.g., payments card industry requirements applied to all data types may increase costs).
  - Include both control activities and test procedures when harmonizing to avoid potential confusion downstream during the assurance process.

Activity 2—Characterization and Modeling

- Define the financial "system":
  - People
  - Process
  - Technology
- Decompose the system into subsystems:
  - Presentation
  - Data integration
  - Business rules
  - Database
  - Data warehouse
  - Reporting
- Model the expected data flow.
- Define boundary conditions with other systems and organizations.
- Key considerations when characterizing and modeling the financial system environment:

TABLE 9.1 Conceptual Applicability Matrix

	Web Presentation Layer	Data Integration	Business Rules Engine	Database
Requirement 1—Access	X—applies	X—applies	X—applies	
Requirement 2—Logging	X—applies	X—applies	X—applies	X—applies
Requirement 3—Encryption	X—applies	X—applies		X—applies
Requirement 4—Segregation of Duties			X—applies	X—applies
Requirement 5—Other	X—applies	X—applies		

- Include vendors and business relationships involved in the supply chain that may access the financial system.
- Include both internal and external access mechanisms as well as future or planned access mechanisms (e.g., access through mobile devices by remote workforce).

Activity 3—Risk Assessment

- Develop an applicability matrix that combines the harmonized requirements with the operating environment defined in the prior two activities. (See Table 9.1 for a conceptual example of an applicability matrix.)
- Perform a risk assessment for each subsystem.
- Key considerations when performing the risk assessment:
  - Include confidentiality, integrity, and availability impacts.
  - Use a *risk management methodology* that is standards based, and use a common rating scale for the organization that includes impact and likelihood thresholds.

Activity 4—Risk Treatment
- Determine desired risk levels.
- Identify safeguards already in place at an organizational or functional level that can mitigate the risks.
- Identify other potential safeguards to be added.
- Based on the new/existing safeguards, establish the residual risk rating.
- Document the risk treatment results.
- Key consideration when performing risk treatment:
  - Include acquisition and development costs as well as ongoing support and maintenance costs that account for any changes in culture or broader implications when performing cost-benefit analysis of safeguard selection.

Controls Automation

Financial systems security, control, and privacy safeguard design often includes automated controls. Automated tools can help enhance security, controls, and privacy safeguards and, in many cases, help reduce the costs associated with control execution and control testing. The dual benefit of improved quality and lower costs has led many organizations, both large and small, to automate controls. The following areas are common targets for control automation.

- **Transaction-level control monitoring.** The automated review of system transactions based on business rules and organizational policy. A common example is the approval of a purchase order under a certain threshold. Transaction-level control monitoring is an excellent technique for automation due to the large volume of transactions, complexity of the business rules, impracticality of timely human review of the numerous transactions, and the desire to proactively prevent inappropriate actions rather than identify them after the fact. We have seen this automated control used in many industries and specifically in financial services companies to help in antifraud, anti–money laundering, and other operational risk–detection scenarios.

- **Segregation of duties.** The automated maintenance of access control roles and business rules for keeping users from having rights that can undermine the integrity of business processes and their related roles. A common example is separating the privilege rights for creating a purchase order, creating a supplier, and submitting payment through the accounts payable process. Segregation of duties is an excellent technique for automation due to the large volume of roles and access transactions, coupled with the complexity of the segregation rights in financial systems. We have seen this automated control employed in many industries, and it has been particularly useful in helping healthcare payors and providers address some of their unique industry challenges around access control.

- **User provisioning automation.** The automated assignment of rights and roles to users based on their job code, function, or organization. A common example is to automatically allow new employees access to e-mail and the organization's intranet site, and rights to enter time into a project- or time-tracking system. User provisioning automation is an excellent technique for automation due to the high frequency of administrative errors, coupled with the large amount of time it takes to set up and administer initial access manually. We have seen this automated control in many industries, and it has been a common technique in the oil and gas industry to offset rising onshore and offshore personnel costs.

- **Data leakage prevention.** The protection of sensitive information from being sent outside the organization's electronic perimeter. A common example is *intellectual property* (IP) associated with the pricing of goods being leaked through supply chain vendors to competitors. Data leakage prevention is an emerging technique for automation due to the complexity of managing the problem proactively. We have seen this automated control used in many industries, and it has been acutely effective in the aerospace and defense industry as well as the pharmaceutical industry in protecting their sensitive IP across the supply chain.

- **Event monitoring.** The automated review of events, security related or otherwise, and the analysis, correlation, escalation, and alerts based on the events. A common example is failed logon attempts or failed privilege escalation within the financial system. Event monitoring is a common technique for automation due to the high volume of events to monitor, complexity of the problem, and high cost of manual monitoring. We have seen this automated control employed in many industries, and it has been targeted for reducing resource costs and enabling companies to do more with less during lean times.

- **E-mail encryption.** The automatic encryption of messages being sent that contain sensitive or protected information. A common example is automatically encrypting e-mails containing payroll and employee benefit details to an outsourced payroll provider. Automatically encrypting e-mails is a popular technique due to the high frequency with which e-mail is used, the likelihood sensitive or regulated information will be contained in e-mails, and the high risk to the organization should unauthorized parties view that information. We have seen this automated control used in many industries, and it has been used effectively in the healthcare payor and provider space as electronic medical records and other information-intensive activities become more commonplace.

Ways to Test Controls

Assurance that the security, controls, and privacy safeguards are operating effectively is vital to the integrity of the financial system. Although there are no silver-bullet easy answers, there are several ways to test security, controls, and privacy to facilitate "clean" audits and Sarbanes-Oxley compliance. Some of these methods include:

- **Collaborative approach.** Business, IT, and audit representatives review the design before implementation and agree to the efficacy of the safeguard to avoid second-guessing during future audits.
- **Thorough documentation.** Integrated control plans are created that capture the *as-is* controls, including risk assessment and risk treatment decision making.
- **Test procedures.** Detailed test procedures are developed to avoid ambiguous or high-level criteria being interpreted inconsistently during an audit.
- **Self-assessment.** Business and/or IT representatives perform self-assessments of the environment prior to each audit to confirm that operating effectiveness is as expected.
- **Transparency to requirements.** Clear linkage between requirements (i.e., mandates) and the controls in place to address those requirements is maintained.
- **Compliance calendar.** A 365-day view of the assessments, audits, and reviews for the various operating environments is maintained, enabling a more coordinated and better-prepared environment for each audit.

Bob Kellner, Senior Vice President, Office of Enterprise Risk Management, has found a way to use automated tools to ready U.S. Bank for reviews. According to Kellner, "Use of automated tools allows the bank to demonstrate that their risk management practices are informed, results in more controlled risk assessments, drives convergence, and is a classic administrative relief, thereby freeing up time to actually manage and analyze risk as opposed to compiling the data." We have seen this trend in many industries, and it is likely to continue as organizations look to find ways to improve the quality and consistency of their risk and compliance programs while reducing costs.

Conclusion

Robust financial systems security, control, and privacy safeguards are needed to help address the expanding standard of care required by today's regulatory environment. The increased requirements coupled with increased complexity and costs associated with compliance have placed a substantial burden on businesses. There are techniques, however, starting with improved control design and increased coordination among key stakeholders, ranging from the chief financial officer, chief information officer, and chief information security officer, to the chief privacy officer, that can help ease the burden. Other techniques, such as the strategic use of automated controls and enhanced management processes, can further reduce the stress and help reduce or contain the costs associated with risk and compliance management. It takes all of the elements, working in tandem, to establish and maintain effective financial systems risk and compliance management.

CHAPTER 10

What Is IFRS and Why Is It Relevant to the CFO Now?

Colin M. Hartnett
James J. Taylor

International Financial Reporting Standards (IFRS) comprise a single set of accounting standards that is rapidly gaining acceptance by the financial reporting bodies of countries around the world, including the United States. IFRS is focused on the objectives of transparency and reduced complexity. Potential benefits of IFRS include reduced accounting and reporting complexity, greater transparency of financial performance, and increased comparability of financial performance. This has helped spread global acceptance of IFRS, particularly among investors wanting a more common basis of comparison for and clearer insight into corporate performance. However, the benefits of a conversion to IFRS come with the costs of transition. A reporting basis change to IFRS can impact a company's financial reporting, tax, information systems, business processes, and policies. It may require retraining the accounting staff to think very differently about the accounting treatment of many key transactions.

Clearly, there is much to consider with a transition to IFRS, and the U.S. Securities and Exchange Commission (SEC) has put forth a proposed roadmap for companies considering this transition. This roadmap covers a proposed transitional period from 2014 to 2016. This chapter will briefly discuss this roadmap and what it may mean for U.S. public companies. It also discusses the potential benefits and costs and the process of conversion to IFRS as a financial accounting and reporting standard for U.S. companies. It leverages experience gained both in the United States and in Europe, but these lessons learned are likely applicable for any company converting to IFRS.

History and Specifics of IFRS

IFRS dates back to 1973, when the International Accounting Standards Committee (IASC) was formed to develop standards that would provide for common accounting approaches across national boundaries. In July 2000, in response to growing international concerns about investor risk as a result of a number of very large corporate failures, and "to bring about convergence between national accounting standards and practices and high-quality global accounting standards,"[1] the IASC was restructured and strengthened to become the International Accounting Standards Board (IASB). The new IASB is "organized under an independent Foundation named the International Accounting Standards Committee Foundation (IASCF). That Foundation is a not-for-profit corporation created under the laws of the State of Delaware, United States of America, on 8 March 2001."[2] The following are components of the new structure:

- International Accounting Standards Board—has sole responsibility for establishing International Financial Reporting Standards.

- IASC Foundation—oversees the work of the IASB, its structure, and its strategy, and has fundraising responsibility.
- International Financial Reporting Interpretations Committee (IFRIC)—develops interpretations for approval by the IASB.
- Standards Advisory Council (SAC)—advises the IASB and the IASCF.
- Working groups—expert task forces for individual agenda projects.

Figure 10.1 provides an overview of the new IASB.

While much more can be written about the new IASB structure and operating model, what is relevant to our treatment of IFRS is the new IASB structure that provides a standing body with the sole responsibility of creating International Financial Accounting Standards. This board consists of 16 members who are selected based on geography of the countries they represent. The specifics of the selection criteria are described next.

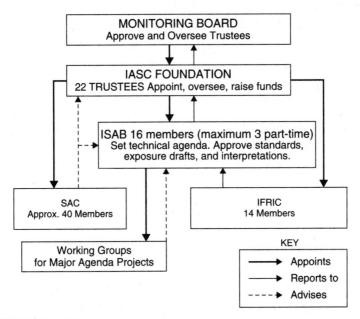

FIGURE 10.1 IASB Structure

There is a geographic mix of IASB members (effective February 1, 2009) that ensures a broad international diversity. By July 2012, there normally will be:

- Four members from the Asia/Oceania region
- Four members from Europe
- Four members from North America
- One member from Africa
- One member from South America
- Two members appointed from any area, subject to maintaining overall geographical balance

The background mix of IASB members includes an "appropriate mix of recent practical experience among auditors, preparers, users and academics."[3]

Since 2000, the SEC has worked with the IASB to determine a course of convergence for U.S. generally accepted accounting principles (GAAP) and IFRS. The SEC's objectives have consistently been to establish a financial reporting standard that enhances investor transparency and fairly and consistently states the financial performance of publicly traded companies. Since 2006, it has been apparent that in addition to supporting convergence of U.S. GAAP and IFRS, the SEC might also consider IFRS as a reporting basis for U.S. SEC registrants. In August 2008, the SEC published a proposed roadmap for IFRS adoption and transition that runs from 2014 to 2016. At the time of this writing, the SEC is evaluating its next steps with respect to this roadmap. However, it is clear that the SEC believes that there should be a single set of globally accepted, high-quality financial accounting and reporting standards. The August 2008 U.S. SEC Roadmap is discussed in more detail later in this chapter.

Concurrent with the SEC's objectives of IFRS convergence, IFRS has been gaining acceptance on a worldwide basis. As of this writing, IFRS-based standards have been accepted as a required or optional financial reporting basis by most of the countries in Europe, South America, and Australia; many in Asia; and several in Africa and the Middle East. Several more major economies have announced plans or proposed roadmaps for acceptance, including Canada (2009–2011 transition), Japan (2015–2016 transition), India (2011 transition), and Brazil (2010 transition).

As mentioned earlier, IFRS is focused on the objectives of transparency and reduced complexity. As of this writing, 8 International Financial Reporting Standards and 28 International Accounting Standards are in effect. These standards provide an overall set of guidelines for financial accounting and reporting. The following are the International Financial Reporting Standards and International Accounting Standards (IAS) in effect as of this writing.

IFRS

- IFRS 1 First-time Adoption of International Financial Reporting Standards
- IFRS 2 Share-based Payment
- IFRS 3 Business Combinations
- IFRS 4 Insurance Contracts
- IFRS 5 Non-current Assets Held for Sale and Discontinued Operations
- IFRS 6 Exploration for and Evaluation of Mineral Assets
- IFRS 7 Financial Instruments: Disclosures
- IFRS 8 Operating Segments

IAS

- IAS 1 Presentation of Financial Statements
- IAS 2 Inventories

- IAS 7 Statement of Cash Flows
- IAS 8 Accounting Policies, Changes in Accounting Estimates and Errors
- IAS 10 Events after the Reporting Period
- IAS 11 Construction Contracts
- IAS 12 Income Taxes
- IAS 16 Property, Plant, and Equipment
- IAS 17 Leases
- IAS 18 Revenue
- IAS 19 Employee Benefits
- IAS 20 Accounting for Government Grants and Disclosure of Government Assistance
- IAS 21 The Effects of Changes in Foreign Exchange Rates
- IAS 23 Borrowing Costs
- IAS 24 Related Party Disclosures
- IAS 26 Accounting and Reporting by Retirement Benefit Plans
- IAS 27 Consolidated and Separate Financial Statements
- IAS 28 Investments in Associates
- IAS 29 Financial Reporting in Hyperinflationary Economies
- IAS 31 Interests in Joint Ventures
- IAS 33 Earnings per Share
- IAS 34 Interim Financial Reporting
- IAS 36 Impairment of Assets
- IAS 37 Provisions, Contingent Liabilities and Contingent Assets
- IAS 38 Intangible Assets
- IAS 39 Financial Instruments: Recognition and Measurement
- IAS 40 Investment Property
- IAS 41 Agriculture

Detailed information on IAS/IFRS can be obtained through the IASB web site.[4]

Some Key Differences between IFRS and U.S. GAAP

Some of the key differences between IFRS and U.S. GAAP arise from the aforementioned differences in approach. These differences are numerous and, in many cases, can have material financial statement impact. The highest-impact key differences in the authors' experience are summarized in Table 10.1.[5] However, it is important to note that depending on a company's use and interpretation of U.S. GAAP, there can be many differences between it and IFRS.

Potential Benefits of Reporting under IFRS

Moving to IFRS can have long-term benefits for U.S. companies, and there are potential synergies with other activities the company may be involved with during the journey to IFRS. The key benefits, as mentioned earlier, are improved transparency and comparability of corporate financial information to investors, which could lead to greater availability of capital from global markets.

Depending on the initial financial accounting and reporting environment within a company, there may be cost savings from elimination of multiple GAAP reporting bases and moving to a single, globally accepted IFRS basis. The synergy opportunities available during the transition can include streamlining financial processes, enhancing financial controls, and contributing to the business case for upgraded financial performance management or enterprise resource planning (ERP) systems.

Potential Costs or Cons of Reporting under IFRS

Switching accounting basis to IFRS can be expensive from a people, process, and technology perspective. As stated earlier in this

TABLE 10.1 Key Differences between U.S. GAAP and IFRS

Topic	U.S. GAAP	IFRS
Fixed Asset Componentization (PP&E)	An item of property, plant, and equipment (PP&E) composed of significant parts is generally depreciated over a weighted-average useful life for the item as a whole. A component approach is permitted but not required.	IFRS requires that each "part of an item of PP&E with a cost that is significant in relation to the total cost of the item shall be depreciated separately." The determination of whether the cost of an item is significant should consider at a minimum: ■ The cost allocated to the component relative to the total cost of the PP&E ■ How componentizing and not componentizing affect depreciation expense differently
Research and Development	With the exception of certain Web site development and software development costs, research and development costs are expensed as incurred.	Under IAS 38, costs incurred during the development phase of an internal project are capitalized when the technical and economic feasibility of a project can be demonstrated and certain prescribed conditions are satisfied.

Topic	U.S. GAAP	IFRS
		Certain research and development costs related to rights to products acquired from third parties are capitalized as intangible assets.
Inventory—Use of last in, first out (LIFO) Method	U.S. GAAP allows the use of either first in, first out (FIFO), LIFO, or weighted-average cost method.	IFRS specifically indicates that the use of the LIFO method is prohibited.
Impairment of Assets	An asset is impaired when an entity will not be able to recover that asset's balance sheet carrying value, either through using it or selling it. Under Financial Accounting Standard 144: ■ Impairment loss is measured using a two-step approach. ■ Impairment losses are accounted for in the income statement.	Under IFRS, IAS 36, Impairment of Assets: ■ There is single-step approach to impairment; a charge may be recognized earlier than under U.S. GAAP. ■ There is the concept of recoverable amount. ■ There is a process to track reversals of impairment (except goodwill).
Pensions—Prior Service Costs	Under Statement of Financial Accounting Standards 87, prior service costs related to benefits that have vested are generally	Under IAS 19, the vested portion of prior service costs is recognized immediately in the statement of operations while the remaining costs

TABLE 10.1 (Continued)

Topic	U.S. GAAP	IFRS
	amortized over the remaining service period.	are recognized on a straight-line basis over the vesting period.
Pensions—Expected Return on Plan Assets	U.S. GAAP allows for the use of either fair value or a smoothed (market-related) value of assets for purposes of determining the expected return on assets in profit and loss. Any investment gains and losses that have not been reflected in the market-related value of assets are not subject to amortization in the gain/loss amortization calculations. The market-related fair value recognizes market movements over a period of up to five years. The funded status shown on the balance sheet is determined based on the fair value of plan assets and not	IFRS requires that both the measurement of plan assets and expected return on plan assets must be based on fair value.

Topic	U.S. GAAP	IFRS
	the smoothed market-related value.	
Share-based Compensation— Graded Vesting	Under SFAS 123(R), for awards with only service conditions and graded vesting, an accounting policy choice exists to recognize compensation cost (1) on a straight-line basis for each separately vesting portion of the award or (2) on a straight-line basis for the entire award (based on the last separately vesting portion of the award).	Under IFRS, the compensation charge for a graded vesting plan is recognized on an accelerated basis to reflect the vesting as it occurs (i.e., each tranche is treated as a separate award with a separate vesting period).

chapter, IFRS is a fundamental shift from the detailed rules-based approaches of U.S. GAAP and other country-specific accounting principles. The costs of training a GAAP-experienced accounting staff should not be underestimated, and the learning curve for using IFRS as the company's primary accounting basis should be monitored carefully to ensure that staff are operating under IFRS. IFRS can also have a significant effect on a company's financial business processes, and can even affect its supply chain and human resource processes. Finally, accounting under

IFRS will likely require financial systems adjustments, potential upgrades, and data conversions. Many European Union–based companies found that significant changes to existing financial and ERP systems were required to complete a transformation to IFRS. Two key reasons for this were:

1. In several areas, IFRS impacts the accounting treatment of transactions posting to the company's general ledger system. For instance, asset componentization changes attributable to IAS 16, Property, Plant, and Equipment, can require a company to change the definition of a specific asset in its fixed-asset subledger system and then assign an appropriate depreciation method to each asset classification.

2. The continued business requirement for financial transaction transparency. Over the past 20 years, companies have likely spent billions of dollars on implementing standardized supply chain, financial, and human resource processes in ERP systems that provide financial transparency into each transaction as it is conceived and completed. While IFRS can be treated as a statutory reporting requirement and handled entirely through adjustments to an IFRS-specific general ledger book of records, the transparency to the source subledger transactions is lost in this approach. This approach represents a reasonable avenue for transition to IFRS, but it cannot satisfy the requirements met by an integrated IFRS-based ERP system.

As we have seen from the discussion of inventory valuation, switching to IFRS can have short-term negative financial and tax impacts for companies using LIFO. One company the authors worked with had calculated that switching from LIFO to FIFO or average cost under IFRS would cost them several hundred millions of dollars in income tax. For that reason, they were waiting to proceed with IFRS pending the SEC's roadmap direction and relief on this one standard. Other companies' gains versus costs of IFRS are difficult to predict without an assessment of their current financial reporting status. To determine the potential costs of an IFRS conversion, the authors would recommend a thorough IFRS assessment as described later in this chapter.

The Decision to Move to IFRS

For U.S. companies considering a transition to IFRS, there is much to consider with regard to making the decision to move forward. As discussed earlier, a conversion to IFRS can have many impacts, and is best tackled when the organization can focus on addressing the associated people, process, and technology efforts. By the same token, there may be synergies with other activities, such as an ERP or performance management system implementation, financial restructuring, and mergers and acquisitions. By all means, all of the major departments of an organization, including Operations, Finance, Information Technology, Tax, Legal, Internal Audit, and Human Resources and Benefits, should consider providing input to the decision and timing of an IFRS conversion. It is also a decision that should be discussed with the company's Audit Committee and Board of Directors, and the company should keep its external audit firm apprised of the process. With so many departments and parties to coordinate around an IFRS decision, a prudent step is for the organization to perform an assessment of the potential impacts of the IFRS conversion and develop a conversion strategy and plan so that the effort can be adequately funded, staffed, and managed. The assessment phase of an IFRS conversion project is discussed in detail in the next section.

With respect to the timing of the IFRS conversion for U.S. companies, the SEC IFRS Roadmap proposes a period of time during which companies can convert. While discussion of the roadmap has somewhat of a shelf life, it is included in this text because of timeliness and importance for so many U.S. companies.

According to the proposed SEC Roadmap, the adoption of IFRS would be from 2014 to 2016. One of the first major decisions a company will likely make to convert to IFRS is the approach it will use to satisfy the dual reporting requirements. The SEC Roadmap specifies that the filing in the year of adoption will require companies to have three years of comparative data in the first year they file under IFRS guidelines. This requires companies to use a *dual-reporting* solution to maintain two sets of financial information, U.S. GAAP and IFRS, for two years prior to their first adoption year. For example, if a company's first filing year is 2016, it would need to include in its filing audited IFRS financial data for 2014, 2015, and 2016. However, the company's primary accounting method would remain U.S. GAAP and be reported to the SEC as U.S. GAAP through the fourth quarter of 2016.[6]

In addition to the 2016 Roadmap requirement for IFRS conversion, the Roadmap also indicates:

> *IFRS filings would begin for large accelerated filers for fiscal years ending on or after December 15, 2014. Accelerated filers would begin IFRS filings for years ending on or after December 15, 2015. Non-accelerated filers, including smaller reporting companies, would begin IFRS filings for years ending on or after December 15, 2016. In each instance, this would allow the filer to begin its books and records and internal accounting controls with respect to IFRS reporting for all three years of audited financial statements that would be required in its first year of IFRS reporting (e.g., 2012 to 2014 for large accelerated filers, 2013 to 2015 for accelerated filers, and 2014 to 2016 for non-accelerated filers).[7]*

See Table 10.2.

TABLE 10.2 SEC Filer IFRS Transition Date

SEC Filer Status	Adoption Date	Begin Dual Reporting	IFRS Transition
	Companies with fiscal year ending on or after December 15	Begin dual reporting at the start of fiscal year	Transition to IFRS as primary accounting standards at start of fiscal year
Large Accelerated Filers	2014	2012	2014
Accelerated Filers	2015	2013	2015
Non-Accelerated Filers	2016	2014	2017

Source: Securities and Exchange Commission, 17 CFR Parts 210, 229, 230, 240, 244, and 249 [Release Nos. 33-8982; 34-58960; File No. S7-27-08], RIN 3235-AJ93, "Roadmap for the Potential Use of Financial Statements Prepared in Accordance with International Financial Reporting Standards by U.S. Issuers."

IFRS Conversion Project Approach

How do you move forward once the decision has been made to convert to IFRS? What IAS board standards apply to your business, and how do these impact your current operations? At this point, the *IFRS conversion project* can be viewed as a large-scale business transformation that may impact a majority of the business. The approach to the project can be framed in the same way as any finance transformation project that involves gathering requirements, developing solutions, evaluating systems and infrastructure, testing processes and systems, implementing solutions, and providing postproduction support.

As shown in Figure 10.2, a typical IFRS conversion project includes three phases.

	Phase 1: Assess	Phase 2: Convert	Phase 3: Sustain
	Create a roadmap for implementation of sustainable reporting under IFRS.	Enable processes and infrastructure to accomplish conversion to reporting under IFRS.	Develop a sustainable "business as usual" IFRS reporting process..
Policy and Process		Evaluate impact on financial policies and procedures, ensuring policies are updated, documented, and monitored for compliance.	
Governance and Controls		Create or update governance framework for IFRS. Evaluate impact on risk management and interal controls, design future-state control environment to ensure reporting accuracy and timeliness, and develop an approach for maintaining and updating control framework.	
Organization and People		Determine impacts to organization and people. Create or revise learning strategy, communication plan, and change management. Execute change management and learning across the organization.	
Information Technology		Analyze impact across the system infrastructure. Design future-state technical environment, ensuring new data requirements are satisfied, multiledger support is enabled, analysis models are developed and consistently used, and reporting applications are updated for compliance.	
Tax		Analyze tax opportunities and impact of the IFRS adoption strategy to optimize the global effective tax rate. Evaluate applicability of IFRS for local tax reporting. Understand and implement operational changes to tax department.	

FIGURE 10.2 IFRS Conversion Project Approach

Source: Deloitte Development LLC.

1. **Assessment.** Assess the impacts of the planned conversion.
2. **Conversion.** Implement and convert to IFRS accounting.
3. **Sustain.** Sustain changes and maintain compliance with the new accounting standards.

Phase 1: Assessment

The assessment phase is part of the strategic decision-making process and allows you to quantify the impact of the IFRS conversion on the company. This process allows you to gain early insight into the conversion implications and positions you to develop a roadmap and timeline for adoption. This also allows you to bring together the multifunctional areas of technical accounting, regulatory capital, tax, processes and key controls, systems architecture, and organization and changes needed to assess the impacts.

ASSESS TECHNICAL ACCOUNTING IMPACTS   Impacts from the conversion to IFRS vary from company to company based on their size, industry, and sector. Accounting personnel should evaluate technical accounting and financial reporting requirements to determine the appropriate IFRS accounting treatment. Differences between IFRS and U.S. GAAP accounting and impacts on statutory requirements and consolidated reporting should be documented. Once the technical accounting portion of the impact assessment has been completed, the team can then start to identify other significant changes required to tax accounting, processes and controls, and systems and infrastructure and organizational change issues that should be addressed prior to the conversion.

ASSESS TAX IMPACTS   As U.S. GAAP converges with IFRS, tax accounting and reporting will also be affected. Tax accounting methods and one-time tax adjustments may be impacted by the conversion. Intraperiod tax-allocation rules should be reviewed for compatibility with new IFRS changes. Revisions to *fair value* accounting may impact how the tax department will track book versus tax-basis differences. Additional considerations should be reviewed, such as the impact on tax processes, controls, systems, first-time application issues, and tax planning.

ASSESS SUPPORTING PROCESSES, SYSTEMS, AND INFRASTRUCTURE

Accounting requirements are the foundation on which financial and accounting processes, systems, and infrastructure of a company are built. All pieces of a business rely on these accounting structures. The assessment should also focus on the other aspects, including:

- Analyzing the impact on processes and controls related to financial reporting and consolidation
- Reviewing the organization's current and future operating model and the impact on control structures
- Understanding IFRS conversion impacts on financial applications and technical infrastructure
- Identifying IFRS-specific requirements and remediation projects to solve any gaps in existing systems
- Assessing impacts on planned or in-process projects

ASSESS ORGANIZATIONAL CHANGE IMPACTS

Performing an organizational assessment allows a company to analyze current roles and responsibilities and provides a structure to identify required training for any new skills or changing roles required to support IFRS. An organizational assessment can also help a company develop a change management and communication strategy and focus efforts on areas that will be most impacted. Reward strategies should be considered to confirm retention of key workforce segments and appropriately applied to existing talent.

DEVELOP IFRS ROADMAP   Once the assessment has been completed and the results have been reviewed, the team can begin to develop the IFRS roadmap. A business case and implementation roadmap are key first steps for IFRS adoption. The foundation prepared during the assessment will be direct inputs to formulate a strategic business case for the conversion to IFRS.

Prepare the Business Case   The business case is used to formulate the IFRS implementation plan for the company. It can also help to build consensus among stakeholders and gain approval from project sponsors. A strategic approach should be taken while preparing the business case in order to identify opportunities for simplification, standardization, and reduction of costs relating to statutory reporting and global reporting. The business case allows the company to examine its ability to maintain flexibility and competitiveness in the capital markets and to prepare for future expansion into foreign markets. Additionally, the business case should identify interdependencies with other transformation initiatives, issues, and risks associated with the conversion, strategy, and approach for converting to IFRS, the timeline for the project, and the organization of the project team.

Develop the Transition Approach   Up to now, the focus has been on the assessment and impacts of transitioning to the IFRS environment. One of the next major questions to be answered is the method by which IFRS dual reporting will be performed. The main focus of dual reporting is to capture three years of comparative data in both U.S. GAAP and IFRS while maintaining U.S. GAAP accounting standards. A solution to this is to implement a reporting system that maps U.S. GAAP results to IFRS. In the coming years, the focus will likely switch from capturing IFRS data for comparative reporting to transitioning the primary accounting standards from U.S. GAAP to IFRS and transitioning the subledger, general ledger, and consolidation systems. This also should be considered in the IFRS business case as a step toward implementing IFRS-compliant accounting systems in the year after the first IFRS filing.

Develop a Timeline to Support a Strategic IFRS Implementation Plan   In planning an IFRS conversion timeline, take into consideration the transition, reporting, and conversion dates established for U.S. registrants by the SEC. Figure 10.3 shows the timeline of the SEC Roadmap for transition to IFRS. January 1, 2012, is the first comparative transition year for companies that will adopt IFRS in 2014.

The size and scope of an IFRS conversion has been compared to the previous Year 2000 and Sarbanes-Oxley initiatives. Although IFRS has far-reaching impacts as did those initiatives, it is fundamentally different because of the complexity of the impacts and changes required. Unlike Year 2000 and Sarbanes-Oxley, where many companies delayed transitioning until the last minute, financial executives will likely need to allow additional time to address the impacts and changes required to accounting policies, processes, and systems. Financial executives will likely need to get their IFRS conversion projects started and begin the road to adoption 18 to 24 months in advance of the first comparative year in order to make a successful transition to dual reporting. Put another way, given the proposed U.S. SEC Roadmap, a reasonable transition period is three to five years from the beginning of preparations to completed transition. This could also provide adequate time to communicate the changes to stakeholders and perform organizational change management and training.

Form a Multidisciplinary Project Team   One common misconception about the IFRS conversion is that it is only an accounting issue and will be handled by the finance department. The reality,

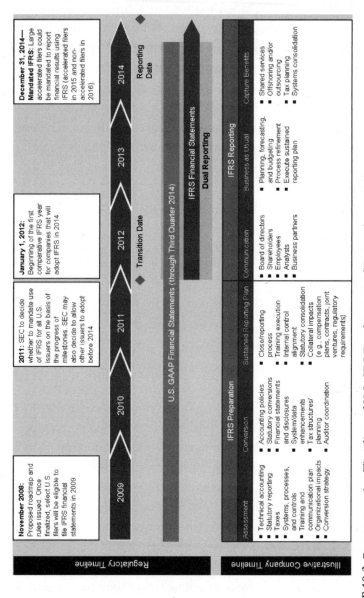

FIGURE 10.3 Representative Timeline of U.S. SEC Roadmap as of December 2008

Source: Deloitte Development LLC.

159

as revealed during the assessment phase, is that the entire company will likely be impacted and should be included in the transition process. The chief financial officer (CFO) should consider including representatives from all aspects of the business when building the project team. For example, a typical IFRS conversion project team could include resources from accounting, tax, internal audit, information technology (IT), and organizational change. It is also important to take the same approach when creating a steering committee, and include strong leadership resources from those same business areas, such as:

> Chief Financial Officer
> Chief Accountant
> Controller
> Accounting Policy Director
> Treasurer
> Director of Tax
> Legal Counsel
> Chief Information Officer
> IT Enterprise Application Director
> HR Director

DESIGN IFRS FUTURE-STATE ENVIRONMENT   An IFRS conversion is a significant shift that might impact all areas of a business. Therefore, it provides an opportunity for an organization to design a future environment, not only for IFRS but for the business as a whole. During the future-state design, a strategic review of policies, procedures, operations, systems, and infrastructure supporting the accounting organization should be considered. A key is to look at the overall business landscape and business plan to design a proactive future state rather than simply reacting to the current issue at hand. Areas to focus on while designing the future-state business processes include:

Accounting Processes and Controls

- Accounting treatment of specific transactions processed by each subledger across all business units (both integrated and interfaced) under IFRS guidelines
- Journal entries required for closing the subledgers and general ledger modules during month-end
- Subsidiary and parent consolidation processes for IFRS mapping and eliminating journal entries
- Additional business controls to reconcile key accounts and verify the IFRS mappings and accuracy of reporting under IFRS

IT Systems to Support IFRS

- Technical architecture to support both the dual-reporting solution and ERP systems
- Solutions for chart of accounts, consolidation, general ledger, and subledger systems
- Dual-reporting process and report formats between IFRS and GAAP
- Changes required to upstream and downstream system interfaces related to configuration, data, and other causes
- Cutover to IFRS as the primary accounting method in subledger, general ledger, and consolidation systems

DEVELOP CHANGE MANAGEMENT PROGRAM   Impacts to accounting and systems from the IFRS conversion can be identified and defined during the assessment based on current operations. However, impacts to people in the organization are not always so clear-cut. A potential risk to an effective transition to IFRS may be resistance from employees. Therefore, assessments should also highlight impacts to the people who are working in the company. As with any large-scale transformation project, a comprehensive change management program should be considered that evaluates current skill sets and operating models and develops a detailed training plan and program for deployment. Communication and awareness programs across all subsidiaries may help gain trust among employees and align executives with the change. Assembling teams and steering committees composed of business representatives will likely provide strong support for the IFRS program.

Phase 2: Conversion

The conversion phase is focused on the implementation and transition of the business processes and systems to support the IFRS conversion. This phase is very similar to any transformation project that contains business, process, and technology components. Transitioning into this phase will require formation of teams, detailed planning, mobilization, and execution of the project activities. During the project, teams will be focused on building prototypes, conducting business process tests, executing conversion and system tests, calculating adjustments, and finally deploying the IFRS solution. Key activities and outcomes from the conversion phase include:

Initiating IFRS Accounting

- Calculate and book financial adjustments resulting from transition to IFRS standards.
- Deploy new accounting policies, processes, and procedures.

Converting IT Systems

- Cut over to dual-reporting solution.
- Implement IFRS-compliant reports.
- Deploy IT systems and tools.
- Configure, test, and deploy final solution.
- Stabilize production changes.

Change Management

- Provide executive alignment and coaching.
- Communicate messages about the transition.
- Train employees on new methods, processes, and tools.

This phase is important to the success of the IFRS project because it is where the actual work to convert the business, people, and technology to support IFRS takes place. For companies reporting in the United States under the proposed U.S. SEC Roadmap, the conversion phase includes two major milestones: The first is concerned with implementing a dual-reporting solution to capture three years of audited financial results according to both GAAP and IFRS standards, and the second is focused on the final transition to IFRS standards and discontinued maintenance of U.S. GAAP reporting capability for the company.

The initial thinking about both milestones of the conversion to IFRS as proposed in the U.S. SEC Roadmap provides a number of options for transitioning systems, including:

- Determining the migration path provided by software vendor
- Implementing new financial/ERP systems
- Converting data into a new general and subledger structure

In the coming years, additional research and guidance will be developed regarding the transition to IFRS under the proposed U.S. SEC Roadmap.

In the next section, we will focus on the first milestone of the IFRS conversion phase, which outlines potential approaches for the dual-reporting solution.

DUAL-REPORTING SOLUTION OVERVIEW An important decision during the planning phase will be which IFRS dual-reporting alternative best supports the business. Dual-reporting requirements go into effect as early as 2012 and will likely have a significant impact on the project approach from the start. There are several alternatives available that utilize either a general ledger or consolidation approach to meet the IFRS requirements. Several criteria should be evaluated in order to determine the ideal solution for reporting, including differences identified during the assessment phase, current ERP systems, IT architecture, and investment required to implement.

This section provides an overview of the common general ledger and consolidation solutions available and considerations that should be taken into account when evaluating the dual-reporting options.

General Ledger   The dual-reporting solutions can be met with one of three different general ledger–level options:

1. **Single ledger.** Support dual reporting in a single ledger by expanding the chart of accounts (COA).

   This approach uses the concept of a single ledger to maintain U.S. GAAP transactions, IFRS adjusting entries, and dual reporting with possible vertical and/or horizontal expansion of the COA structure (adding new values to support IFRS adjustments). This is a simple option to adopt and can be maintained through account ranges set up to support dual reporting.

2. **Mirror ledger.** Create a separate ledger based on U.S. GAAP transactions that includes IFRS adjustments.

   This approach uses two ledgers: the primary U.S. GAAP ledger to record balances and a secondary, mirror ledger copied from the primary for IFRS-adjusting entries. Dual reporting is performed from each U.S. GAAP and IFRS ledger. This option supports additional detail in the secondary mirror ledger and can be considered where COA and currency are the same.

3. **Adjustment ledger.** Create a separate ledger used exclusively for IFRS adjustments.

This approach uses three ledgers. The primary ledger is U.S. GAAP, a secondary ledger is used for IFRS-adjusting entries, and a third, reporting, ledger is used for consolidations. Dual reporting is performed in both the primary U.S. GAAP ledger and the consolidated reporting ledger for IFRS.

Consolidation Ledger When considering the appropriate solution to enable the consolidation of IFRS results in an existing financial consolidation or financial management system, there are three likely solutions:

1. **Expanded dimensionality.** Utilizing a combination of a custom dimension and an alternative reporting hierarchy.

This approach integrates the dual-reporting requirement into a single application and single scenario by creating a custom dimension and alternative reporting hierarchy with IFRS-specific accounts. It requires one consolidation to aggregate the results for both U.S. GAAP and IFRS purposes. This option integrates the dual-reporting requirement with the existing close process.

2. **IFRS-focused scenario.** Utilizing a completely separate scenario within the existing applications to run IFRS consolidations.

This approach provides a completely separate scenario within the existing application to run IFRS consolidations. It utilizes existing metadata and minimizes application maintenance. This option allows for the flexibility to perform your IFRS consolidation after U.S. GAAP results are completed.

3. **IFRS-specific application.** Utilizing a completely separate and dedicated application to run IFRS consolidations.

This approach enables dual reporting but is not directly tied to the normal close-related activities of the U.S. GAAP application. This option allows for a high degree of customization in the IFRS environment but can lead to additional maintenance challenges.

It is important to recognize that each solution addresses the process required to enable dual-reporting functionality. In making the decision, the combined impact of the solution on an organization should be considered before deciding it is the optimal choice. The final decision will depend on several factors, including the complexity of the existing environment, the current close process, and the amount of change required to implement the solution.

Phase 3: Sustain

Once the actual implementation and cutover to IFRS have been completed, the project team will begin activities associated with stabilization of the new processes, procedures, and systems during a postdeployment support period. This phase is focused on the next issues.

Monitoring Compliance

- Review accounting transactions to ensure they are being booked properly.
- Review month-end results to validate that reports are generating the proper accounting information.
- Monitor compliance with new reporting standards.
- Prepare mock quarter-end and year-end financial statements and audit IFRS-compliant reports.

Implementing Continuous Improvement Program

- Facilitate knowledge transfer to accounting staff and end users of reports.
- Review status, productivity, and issues to identify areas of improvement and educational opportunities.
- Implement changes to improve reporting processes.

Just as the conversion phase is important to the success of the IFRS project, the sustain phase is important to maintaining the compliance of the company in its filings with the SEC. It is likely that sizable compliance efforts will need to be performed, focused on sustaining the organization during the first month on the new systems, the first quarter-end closing, and the first year-end closing and reporting cycle.

Conclusion

International Financial Reporting Standards have emerged to provide a uniform, transparent view of corporate performance. While IFRS is not yet the accounting standard of all major economies, it is already the most broadly accepted financial reporting basis in the world, and the SEC's proposed IFRS Roadmap may mark a clear path to acceptance in the United States. IFRS appears to be a natural next step in the evolution of accounting standards, and it is one that the financial executive should have on the radar screen throughout the next five to ten years.

For U.S. companies evaluating the transition to IFRS, there are many factors to consider. The basic principles of IFRS are different from U.S. GAAP in a number of respects, and the decision to convert likely requires a multifunction evaluation of these differences. Once the decision to convert is made, a multiphase plan should be considered to confirm the company's

IFRS-accepted guidelines, establish targets, detail changes to accounting policies, adjust or upgrade systems, convert accounting data, train accounting staff, and communicate all of the changes to the organization and external stakeholders as appropriate. As with all change, planning and preparation are two of the most important ingredients of a successful IFRS transition.

Notes

1 www.iasplus.com/restruct/restruct.htm#old, Deloitte IAS website.

2 *Ibid.*

3 www.iasplus.com/restruct/restruct.htm.

4 www.iasb.org/Home.htm.

5 Deloitte Development LLC, © 2009.

6 Securities and Exchange Commission, 17 CFR Parts 210, 229, 230, 240, 244, and 249 [Release Nos. 33-8982; 34-58960; File No. S7-27-08], RIN 3235-AJ93, "Roadmap for the Potential Use of Financial Statements Prepared in Accordance with International Financial Reporting Standards by U.S. Issuers," p. 34, footnote 72.

7 *Ibid.*, "Implementation of the Mandatory Use of IFRS," p. 35, section 7.

CHAPTER 11

The Phenomenon of Software as a Service

Franscisca Wahjudi

A new software-delivery model is changing the foundation of the software industry. It is estimated that by 2012, businesses will be spending one-third of their application budget on applications as services, as opposed to on-premises applications. Despite its increasing popularity, *software as a service* (SaaS) remains an "unknown" to many financial executives. This chapter includes a brief review of SaaS and its potential value to an organization.

Background: What Is SaaS?

The idea of software as a service (SaaS) has been around for a while. If you have been using Google Gmail or Microsoft Hotmail, then you have experienced SaaS. Simply put, *SaaS* can be defined as a software-distribution model in which applications are hosted by a vendor and made available to customers over the Internet. SaaS vendors manage the daily operations and provide maintenance and support to their customers, usually for a subscription fee based on the usage metrics. This concept appeals to finance and information technology (IT) executives as it allows them to "rent" an application without getting locked into purchasing the software or investing in the infrastructure.

In contrast to the on-premises software, SaaS is based on a multitenant architecture. This means that SaaS customers share a single, common infrastructure and code base that is centrally maintained. Each customer's deployment occupies a virtual partition that stores the data that defines each organization's business rules, unique fields, and interfaces to other systems. Within this virtual partition, an end user can still customize his experience without impacting other customers. The multi-tenancy approach can lead to cost savings by consolidating IT resources into a single operation and facilitates seamless updates and upgrades to the application.

The Value Proposition of SaaS

While the SaaS market shows a strong growth of adoption in the high-tech industry, financial executives should understand the underlying value proposition of this delivery model prior to jumping on the SaaS bandwagon. Here are some of the benefits:

- **Accelerated deployment timeline and lower up-front cost.** Since the software is delivered over the Internet, SaaS eliminates installation and setup at the customer's location. This enables the application to be deployed to users in a relatively short time frame and drastically reduces the up-front commitment of cost and resources.
- **Faster ROI.** As SaaS solutions offer lower up-front cost and a rapid deployment timeline, they can facilitate immediate business benefits. SaaS vendors address their reliability challenges through the use of state-of-the-art technology, and many offer service-level agreements (SLAs) for uptime. This means that expensive losses of productivity due to down-time can be avoided.

- **Reduced internal staffing requirements.** A shortage of skilled IT professionals within high-tech enterprise contributes to higher interest in SaaS adoption. Adopting SaaS shifts the burden of IT operations from the internal organization to the SaaS vendor. This can free up chief information officers (CIOs) and their staff to focus on innovation and strategic initiatives, such as business process improvement.
- **Ease of virtualization.** Most employees, but especially the new generation, demand more flexibility at work. They expect their employers to offer a wide array of web-enabled services to perform their job more effectively over a virtual corporate network. SaaS solutions can help simplify the mobilization of the enterprise applications, such as sales force automation and collaboration tools.
- **Greater agility.** As your company evolves through organic growth or acquisition, integrating and scaling enterprise applications can be complex and costly. SaaS solutions can free up IT resources to focus on the essential tasks of consolidating core business processes instead of spending significant resources on planning and building additional infrastructure to support the growth.
- **Rich user experience.** SaaS solutions generally incorporate the latest capabilities to deliver a superior application experience compared to the legacy on-premises applications.

Making the Right Decision: Is SaaS Right for Me?

The promise of addressing business challenges in a shorter time frame is encouraging financial executives to add SaaS solutions to their IT portfolio. However, to make the right decision, they should consider evaluating the viability of the SaaS solution as an alternative to an on-premises solution. Here are some factors to consider:

- **Uniqueness and complexity of business processes.** In general, SaaS solutions work best for non–mission-critical processes that are standard and not highly dependent on or integrated with other business functions and systems. As SaaS solutions are typically designed to serve multiple customers from a single, centralized *code base*, there are fewer options for complex customization. Thus, complex business processes that require a high degree of customization are less suitable for SaaS solutions.
- **Total cost of ownership (TCO).** Evaluating TCO is not simple but is necessary prior to making a decision between SaaS and traditional on-premises applications. To improve the accuracy of the cost comparison, the TCO model must include direct and indirect costs incurred throughout the life of the application. Other cost drivers, such as requirements for mobile and offline access and additional storage capacity beyond a preset limit for SaaS, should also be considered.
- **Legal considerations.** With the growing number of audit and compliance requirements, each organization should solicit agreement from the SaaS vendor to comply with global and local regulatory requirements. Include applicable control expectations in your service-level agreement with the SaaS vendor to help address audit concerns and better govern your service relationship.

Implications for IT Organizations

Adding SaaS to your IT portfolio can cause a shift in the IT organization's role and responsibilities. Financial executives should determine whether their IT organizations are prepared for the transition by considering the following implications:

- **Enterprise architecture.** The Enterprise Architecture group will play a key role in:

- Reviewing standards-based protocols for application interfaces between SaaS and legacy on-premises applications
- Developing framework for master data governance.
- Rationalizing IT portfolios to avoid redundancy.
- **Network connectivity.** Introducing the SaaS solution to your application portfolio could have an impact to the existing network capacity. This is especially true for global locations where the network may not be as sophisticated. In such cases, the Internet connectivity may require an upgrade to provide sufficient bandwidth for the user base to access the service.
- **Security and compliance.** Moving critical business data to SaaS vendors introduces a risk of data loss or exposure of sensitive information. The Security and Compliance staff must assess the data privacy and security needs and develop necessary standards.
- **IT governance.** IT managers will have to work very closely with business users to capture the real value of SaaS application. CIOs and business executives should provide the guidance to determine the application ownership and change management process.

Conclusion

In an increasingly challenging economic and competitive environment, corporate end users and executives are becoming more receptive to SaaS solutions to help them address their business needs. The transition to the SaaS delivery model requires companies to rethink and realign their roles and responsibilities. As an alternative model, SaaS adds another dimension to the technology-based decision-making framework. Instead of just evaluating a build-or-buy decision, the SaaS delivery model opens up another channel for the IT organization to pursue. In the future, the decision-making analysis will likely revolve around a build or buy or service to address business challenges.

CHAPTER 12

Investing in Product Information Management

Deborah Metzger

Overview

Implementing a *product information management* (PIM) solution is an important activity for any organization with a product master. As companies grow, so do the number of products and the underlying attributes, many of which are used to run upstream or downstream systems. Product data is used in part to track revenue, determine operating expense, assign capital expenditures, and summarize financial results. Therefore, it is of vital interest to financial executives. Product data is often presented externally to customers, suppliers, and distributors. Product data is exchanged via business-to-business (B2B) transactions. Product data may appear on customer-facing documents including invoices, purchase orders, and sales orders. As such, managing individual attributes and product number schemes, communicating internally and externally, and integrating new product data into an existing structure pose different and often costly challenges.

Implementation of a PIM system can provide a foundation and single location to standardize product data, enforce data governance, communicate with internal upstream and downstream systems, and simplify external communication with suppliers and customers. Integration of future product master data (e.g., via acquisition or other business event) into existing product-related data is often significantly less complex once a PIM system is in place.

This chapter will focus on catalysts for adopting a PIM system, implementation considerations, and return on investment considerations from a Finance point-of-view.

PIM Adaptation Catalysts

Multiple catalysts may lead to the eventual decision to implement a PIM system. Reviewing the next scenarios may assist you in developing your business case and subsequent measurement of your return on investment. Based on practical experience, one or more of these scenarios often exist, and are considered catalysts for eventual implementation of PIM.

1. **Heterogeneous product information exists in multiple systems.** Product data often exists in multiple systems, without a single reference point. Does your organization spend unnecessary time attempting to locate product information? Have you evaluated the cost associated with maintaining separate, diverse product information? Do you have similar or duplicate product data in multiple systems? There are various third-party tools that provide the capability to de-duplicate, classify, and standardize product data that is contained in multiple systems.

2. **New product data is introduced and maintained in a separate system.** New product information (NPI) is often managed separately from existing product data in transaction-based systems (e.g., sales and purchasing

systems). This separation of new product data from existing product data can introduce fragmented product attribute-level information across the various systems, along with the associated engineering drawings or marketing materials used to introduce the new product(s). Do you have a separate system for NPI? Have your suppliers or customers requested drawings and other product information that you cannot easily provide because it is contained in multiple locations? PIM vendors typically provide the capability to store various types of new product–related collateral, including attachment features that often follow the product and the associated drawings, or marketing materials through an enterprise resource planning (ERP) system.

3. **Merger and/or acquisition activity has introduced additional product master data.** Integration of new business units via merger or acquisition generally requires additional product data. Additional product data may be left as is, introducing more dissimilar, fragmented, and potentially duplicate product data. If your company is involved with a merger or acquisition, most likely you will face the issue of merging product masters, eliminating duplicate data, and/or developing standards for product data such that the new product information may be integrated with existing product information. Implementation of a PIM system can provide a single location from which to merge separate product masters.

4. **Lack of standardized product data.** Unlike customer data, product attributes are not easily classified in terms of standards. Although standards exist, they are not widely adopted, and only a handful of companies are participating in large-scale product-standardization efforts. For example, eCl@ss[1] has been adopted by some leading manufacturing and service companies in Europe as an international standard for product classifications and descriptions. This

is in contrast to customer data where generic-type standards, such as the U.S. Postal Code for addresses, have been widely applied and adopted. If your organization needs to adopt and enforce product-related standards, you will need to evaluate enforcing the standards using automation. For example, one PIM vendor may provide built-in standards capability; other vendors may require you to build your own automation.

5. **Multiple product attributes; no single reference or data dictionary.** Product attributes often exist in multiple systems. For example, one set of attributes may be used in purchasing, another in trade compliance, and still another in manufacturing. Individual product attributes often contain finance-related information, such as division codes, product line, cost center, or natural account (e.g., cost of goods sold). A product data dictionary often does not exist, and the same attribute could have different definitions depending on which system uses the attribute. Have you implemented a standard definition for individual product attributes? Do you have the ability to enforce the standard using any type of system, for example, rules-driven standards? Does your organization spend time searching for product data and managing fragmented product data, and lack the ability to easily search for product information using a data dictionary? Do you have challenges related to reporting revenue for a product or product line? Most PIM vendors provide a standard data dictionary that can be referenced and adopted for the purposes of implementing a common set of terms for product attributes.

PIM Implementation Considerations

PIM systems vary by vendor, the common thread being functionality to provide a single repository for product information. This chapter is designed to be system agnostic such that the princi-ples described may be applied once the organization decides to implement a PIM system. In practice, designing a single repository requires taking a somewhat methodical set of steps, each with the backing of a strong business sponsor. Standardiz-ing product data and implementing a PIM system is a challenging process. There are many vendors, each offering a unique list of positives and negatives for your organization to evaluate. As discussed earlier, product data is more complex than customer data, fewer standards exist, and any data issues may impact both internal and external parties. Key implementation considerations include these seven steps:

1. **Identify the PIM sponsor.** Selection of a sponsor for the PIM system is often the most important design prerequisite. Because product data crosses organization boundaries, fric-tion may occur if a single sponsor is not involved to make important ownership-type decisions. Establishing a sponsor for the PIM initiative can help expedite business case cre-ation, approvals, and eventual measurement of the return on investment.

2. **Develop a product data dictionary.** Product data often exists in multiple systems. Developing a common data dic-tionary to classify product attributes is a baseline design fundamental. Lack of a dictionary early in the design process will often result in the inability to convert data into the new PIM system.

3. **Establish the *system of record* (SOR) for product attributes.** Product attributes will likely continue to reside in multiple systems following the implementation of a PIM system. For example, product number often resides in mul-tiple systems. Product attributes may be classified in terms of which system owns them or creates them for use by other systems or business processes. Once a PIM system is

implemented, the SOR for product number will be the PIM system or central repository. If the product number continues to be created in multiple locations, the PIM system will likely lack the ability to enforce standards and governance. In general, the most important or key product-related attributes must be owned by the new PIM system. Finance attributes may be entered and used on the product. Often these finance attributes contained in PIM continue to have a system of record that is finance-centric (e.g., general ledger or accounts receivable).

4. **Classify product attributes according to internal and external standards.** Once the system of record has been determined, the many product attributes stored in the PIM need to be classified according to their usage. If a standard exists between your organization and your external suppliers, you may consider reclassification of your product attributes according to an industry standard. In many cases, an external standard does not exist; therefore, the organization should design PIM and classify product attributes according to an internal standard.

5. **Develop product hierarchical level classifications.** Once the individual attributes have been classified, usage of attributes within products for reporting or engineering purposes is often required. For example, a single product may be used in multiple systems. Grouping similar attributes can provide the capability to develop a product hierarchy. Hierarchies may vary depending on how they are used. Sales may require one type of product attribute grouping, whereas engineering requires a completely different view. Implementing a single product hierarchy may prove to be an impossible task. Consequently, if you need to classify your products into hierarchies, evaluate your PIM vendor's capability to use this feature. System capability within PIM

may be limited as compared to an external reporting tool or data warehouse to represent your product hierarchy.

6. **Develop product catalog(s).** Once your attributes have been classified, along with evaluation of product hierarchies, grouping the attributes into a catalog is an important implementation consideration. How many catalogs and how many attributes per catalog will be unique to the product within PIM? For example, you may elect to classify products into separate catalogs by division or organization. Alternatively, you may find that maintenance of separate catalogs cannot be cost justified or that your suppliers mandate a specific standard. Regardless of situation, implementation of a product catalog is a PIM design fundamental.

7. **Develop product data rules.** The last implementation consideration is to develop business rules. Standards are used to enforce similar, consistent product data across the enterprise. Rules are used to create the product attributes and/or enforce the data standard. For example, will the product number contain one segment or two segments? Does the number of segments depend on the vendor? Developing a vendor-specific rule is one method for enforcing consistent data in a product segment.

PIM Return on Investment

From our experience, implementation of PIM systems often requires a larger investment than originally planned and a corresponding extended duration to achieve return on investment (ROI) targets. This is due to the complex nature of product data as compared to other master data. Lack of standards for product attributes, variable data, and inconsistent use across multiple systems adds to the challenges associated with implementing a

PIM system. Failure to adopt standards and enforce consistent use of product data using PIM will prolong overall ROI. Once the PIM system is in place, establishing ongoing reviews against product data standards will assist in determining how rapidly the new PIM system has been adopted and ROI targets can be achieved.

There are multiple vendors that provide PIM solutions, most of which have been on the market for a short period of time. As the PIM vendor solutions evolve, the features and functionality that can be automated often reduce the need to invest in developing the capability separately. Once the PIM system has been implemented, product data standards established and enforced via governance, and the system adopted across the organization, the benefits in terms of ROI become measurable and tangible.

Conclusion

Implementing a product information management system can provide short- and long-term benefits. Finance has a vested interest in achieving accurate, high-quality product data. Although the initial cost of implementation may be high, once PIM is in place, a platform exists for faster adaptation of standards and rules, along with high-quality product data that is available in a single, trusted point of reference.

Note

[1] eCl@ss e.V., Cologne, Germany, "eCl@ss, International Standard for the Classification of Products and Services," www.eclass-online.com/.

CHAPTER 13

E-Commerce

Ryan C. Jones

E-commerce has rapidly grown in importance for businesses and consumers over the past several years. From the dot-com bubble of the late 1990s to a major economic growth engine today, e-commerce has been a large contributor to the growth of our global economy. Businesses and consumers alike are rapidly adopting e-commerce as a primary means to find information, compare products and pricing, and transact commerce in the virtual world.

For a finance executive, an understanding of e-commerce is essential, particularly as the e-commerce channel may be a material source of revenue and cost reduction for your organization. Additionally, you may need to provide financial oversight related to e-commerce investments, sales, reporting, and controls. Therefore, the purpose of this chapter is to provide an overview of e-commerce, its impacts on the business world, how it contributes to shareholder value, and how to calculate and measure financial results. So, whether yours is a pure-play e-commerce business or a traditional bricks-and-mortar business, this chapter contains something for you.

E-Commerce Defined

The term *e-commerce* involves the systems and processes that enable businesses and consumers to transact commerce electronically. E-commerce includes web sites (.com), mobile commerce, and electronic data interchange (EDI) media used to conduct business transactions. The terms *business-to-business* (B2B) and *business-to-consumer* (B2C) are often used to describe the nature of the e-commerce relationship. Additionally, a successful e-commerce operation requires tight integration between the business and technology teams. E-commerce operations are often run by the business team, with the technology platform being operated by the technology team.

E-Commerce Today

The origins of e-commerce began in the early 1970s, when Electronic Data Interchange (EDI) started to be used more widely for basic electronic business transactions. Since then, e-commerce has evolved to become a primary means by which consumers and businesses conduct transactions daily. Recently, e-commerce has been a major driver in breaking down many of the physical boundaries and traditional barriers to entering new markets. And because of e-commerce, smaller domestic companies are often able to compete with larger multinational organizations on a level playing field. Also, entering global markets in the online world has provided companies with new business opportunities by requiring less investment in physical infrastructure to enter local markets. In a very short time, e-commerce has changed the way consumers, competitors, and suppliers interact.

The growth and rapid adoption of broadband Internet access has greatly influenced *consumers* and business adoption of e-commerce. Markets once dominated by a few organizations have been opened up for *competition*, and smaller organizations are now able to establish virtual businesses that compete for the same share of the wallet that large bricks-and-mortar organizations have owned for years. For *suppliers*, e-commerce offers an opportunity for greater market penetration and sales volume, but it also puts pressure on margins as the transparency of pricing and quality has become greater. Also, the impact of e-commerce on *globalization* has been significant, as many businesses and consumers are using e-commerce as a means to conduct cross-border transactions and enter or operate in new markets. In short, e-commerce has provided a global reach to consumers and businesses that was once reserved only for large, multinational organizations.

Increasing Shareholder Value

E-commerce has become a means for competitive differentiation for an organization. However, although differentiation is important, it may not always increase shareholder value. Therefore, finance executives need to look for opportunities to increase value through e-commerce. One of your key responsibilities may be to provide oversight related to e-commerce investments and financial performance. So, understanding how to define and calculate the financial benefits of an e-commerce investment is important. Being familiar with the two primary shareholder value drivers related to e-commerce, described in the next sections, will also help.

Value Driver 1: Revenue Growth

E-commerce may be a critical source of revenue within your organization; therefore, understanding some of the trends that impact e-commerce revenues is an important first step.

The next list provides an overview of three e-commerce trends.

1. **Multichannel integration.** Non–e-commerce channels often have limitations related to reach, scalability, and customer influence, whereas the e-commerce channel often lacks the physical-world benefits. Therefore, over the past few years, many organizations have made greater efforts to align across channels within the organization to create a more consistent consumer experience and drive additional revenues. As a finance executive, being involved in the strategy and planning for a multichannel initiative is important input for revenue, cost, and budget planning.

2. **Online marketing.** The e-commerce channel is often able to scale marketing activities up or down with little incremental investment. Therefore, understanding your organization's strategy related to both internal and external marketing is important. For instance, many organizations are increasing e-commerce revenues by selling internal advertising space to third parties for profit, or by buying advertising space from third parties to drive sales to their site. So, it is important for the finance executive to understand the revenue models associated with these marketing and advertising programs, particularly as they become a greater portion of the e-commerce business.

3. **Entering new markets.** Entering a new market may require a significant investment in physical operations and the development of a local network for sales and distribution. Entering a market using e-commerce may be a lower-cost option, by setting up a dot-com presence and then serving the market from operations in another country. For instance, a company headquartered in the United States can open an e-commerce business in Japan in days as opposed to months. However, although leveraging e-commerce to enter a new

market may be enticing, make sure to research the local regulations to understand whether barriers to entry exist.

Value Driver 2: Cost Reduction

An organization may reduce current costs and/or avoid future costs by moving transactions to a lower-cost e-commerce channel or by reducing the long-term cost of ownership. The next bullet points provide a brief overview of each.

- **Reduce the cost of ownership.** The technology infrastructure, business processes, and people associated with running an e-commerce business may become costly and inefficient over time. Therefore, the decision to replatform or outsource outdated or inefficient e-commerce technologies or processes and realign the organization may become a means of reducing costs. A major consideration when replatforming, outsourcing, or reorganizing the e-commerce business is the business return for that effort. Forecasting the year-over-year cost savings and new asset accounting are two areas of focus for a finance team assessing cost of ownership.
- **Shift transactions to e-commerce.** The e-commerce benefit commonly called *shift* is achieved by moving a transaction from a higher-cost channel to a lower-cost e-commerce channel. The benefits from shift assume that a transaction performed using e-commerce is less expensive than using another channel, such as a call center. For instance, by moving the sale of products from a sales team to e-commerce, there is a cost savings related to not paying the sales team's commissions for the sales. There are industry benchmarks that may help assess the cost difference between channels for your organization, and can serve as a basis for the analysis.

Justifying the Investment

As with most corporate investments, an investment in e-commerce should be subject to a business case and return on investment (ROI) analysis, including the qualitative and quantitative benefits. The next five steps provide guidance on how to proceed with assessing a business case for e-commerce.

Step 1: Determine the Financial Goals

The financial goals should be measured by how e-commerce contributes to increasing shareholder value, by either increasing revenues or reducing costs. Basic ROI calculations can be used to forecast the financial benefits of e-commerce, and should be coupled with a qualitative assessment to provide context for the business benefits. After determining whether your focus is growing revenues, reducing costs, or both, the next step is to develop the business and financial hypothesis.

Step 2: Develop the Business Case Hypothesis

The business case hypothesis should serve as the qualitative framework used to either prove or disprove the value of the e-commerce to the organization. For instance, determining whether the focus of the business case is to penetrate a new customer segment or enter a new market is important to get the team focused and aligned on a core hypothesis. When developing a hypothesis focused on maximizing revenues, key areas of focus should be the size, growth, and competitive share of the market. Likewise, when focusing on a hypothesis related to cost reduction, the focus should be on either shift or cost of ownership. Either way, as a financial executive, you or your team will need to explore and better understand the causal relationships that impact both. After you determine the hypothesis, the next step is to perform the financial analysis.

Step 3: Gather the Right Data Points

When preparing to calculate the benefits, including relevant data points from both internal and external sources is a critical step. Some of the key data points you might wish to include as part of the business case are listed next.

- **Industry and competitive benchmarks.** Benchmarks provide a great measure on which to base your assumptions, particularly if your organization does not have the experience internally.
- **Consumer research.** Capturing the voice of the customer through primary or secondary research is often critical to establishing credibility for the business case.
- **Regulatory research.** Understanding the regulatory market and any barriers that may exist is critical, particularly when using e-commerce to enter a new market.
- **Market research.** The marketplace factors related to market growth, size, and readiness are important data points for forecasting future benefits.
- **Product research.** Knowing your product(s) and their e-commerce channel *fit* is critical, as some products are strong fits for e-commerce and others may not be.

Step 4: Calculate the Benefits

Using a consistent method to calculate ROI within the organization is advised, as it allows for greater transparency and comparability across investment opportunities. Common financial calculations used by finance teams to develop a financial business case and assess business opportunities are presented next.

- **Net present value (NPV).** Calculating the current value of an e-commerce investment is important when comparing other investment opportunities and hurdle rates internally. An NPV calculation gives profit and loss–based insight into the costs and revenues associated with an investment, and is a good tool for decision making. Forecasted revenues, costs, and the organization's cost of capital are critical input to an NPV calculation.
- **Payback period.** The payback period for an e-commerce investment is an important data point to assist finance executives in assessing an investment and determining when the investment will be recouped.
- **Financial statement impacts.** The income statement benefits of e-commerce are often greater revenues at the top line and reduced costs at the bottom line. The balance sheet benefits often include the addition of a new e-commerce asset, which is then amortized over the life of the asset. Therefore, an understanding of the impact of e-commerce on financial statements is important, as both the income statement and balance sheet would be impacted in varying degrees.

Step 5: Measure Results

After the budgets have been approved and the e-commerce investment has been made, the next step is to measure the results of the investment. Whether measuring website traffic, sales revenues, or cost efficiency, it is critical to establish the *key performance indicators* early and follow through on monitoring the investment to determine contribution to shareholder value. Developing the financial reports required to run the business is important, and ideally should be in place before Day 1 of operating the e-commerce platform.

Implementing Financial Controls for E-Commerce

As a financial executive, you are likely responsible for the financial controls of the business, particularly for systems such as e-commerce that may be material when it comes to revenues. Therefore, understanding the scope of financial controls required for an e-commerce system is the first step and one not to be taken lightly. For instance, the topics of pricing and order overrides should be of interest. The processes and systems used to establish or set pricing require pricing controls for both the e-commerce business processes and the systems involved. Controls related to who is able to set pricing and how pricing is set are critical to controlling the business. They are also important in areas such as customer service, where price overrides may be standard processes. Aside from financial controls being a good practice, financial legislation such as Sarbanes-Oxley requires these controls be put in place for the business. Therefore, as a financial executive, you need to understand the scope of impact that e-commerce has on financials, and review and validate that the appropriate controls are in place on both fronts. In addition to financial controls, finance executives must also provide oversight related to third-party vendors, which may include service, hardware, or software providers.

Conclusion

In summary, aligning e-commerce activities with shareholder value, evaluating business cases, measuring e-commerce results, and implementing financial controls are likely the responsibility of the finance executive. However, the degree to which you will be involved in each may differ. Therefore, we suggest you engage proactively with your e-commerce group to understand the scope of e-commerce within your organization and what it means to you.

CHAPTER 14

ERP: An Evolving Process

Amy Wolbeck

If your organization just spent millions on an *enterprise resource planning* (ERP) implementation, it should be getting all the anticipated benefits. Unfortunately, that frequently is not the case immediately after an implementation. There are a number of reasons this situation may occur: poor implementation process, "paving the cow path," bad data at cutover, and so on. Does this mean your organization should not do an ERP implementation? Of course not; ERP systems can give you the foundation to build on and continue to improve your business. You need to look at ERP as an *evolutionary* process to achieve the planned benefits and ultimately reduce the total cost of ownership (TCO).

Getting Started

After your system is stabilized, you should begin an assessment of the activities that are performed daily and determine whether they are value-added activities. When ERP systems and processes are not efficient, employees can end up spending the majority of their time focused on transactional activities. (See Figure 14.1—current state.) These activities, including entering

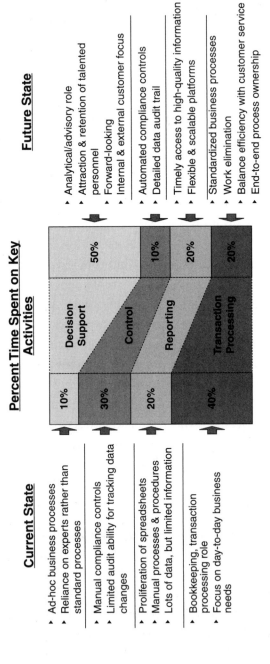

FIGURE 14.1 Time Spent on Key Activities

data, researching errors, and processing exceptions, take a significant amount of time. The results are that less time is focused on high-value-added activities such as analyzing the data and decision making. After you have identified any such activities, the next step is defining alternative options and solutions to reduce the wasted time and increase time spent on analyzing results. (See Figure 14.1—future state.)

There are several common reasons for a high number of transactional tasks being performed postimplementation, such as nonintegrated processes, lack of automation, poor system design, and unnecessary complexities added to data. In many cases, nonintegrated processes involve a significant number of handoffs within the process, which can cause redundant work, extended cycle times, and so on.

For example, let us take a contracts-to-cash scenario. Figure 14.2 represents a typical process within an organization. Each line indicates a touch point with different people within the contracts-to-cash process.

In this example, the contracting negotiator starts the process by negotiating the contract. The contract negotiator works with the contract administrator to get the contract input into the system. The administrator may need to work with the account analyst to make sure they have the correct information to put into the system for billing purposes. The billing analyst takes that data and generates invoices to the customer. Frequently, the contracting organization does not understand all the information that is critical to generating an invoice. The billing group then has to spend time researching to find the correct data. In many cases, there are questions that have to go back to the contracting organization to research answers and perform updates to the data so the biller can reprocess the invoice. Separate from both of these groups are the cash applications and collections organizations. If there is a discrepancy in the amount received from the invoice submitted, the cash applier has to spend time

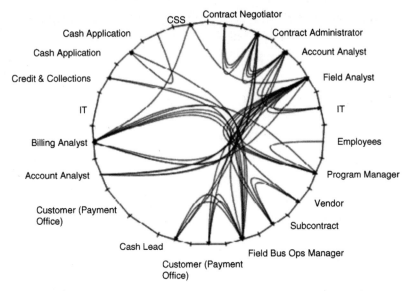

FIGURE 14.2 Functionally Oriented Process for Contracts to Cash

researching the issue. The issue may be understood and corrected by the biller, but this may have to go all the way back to the contracting organization to resolve. The end result is that the entire process may take far more time than is expected, which ultimately impacts cash flow. In addition, there is probably a need for more employees because of the time spent researching issues. All of these activities require significant time from your employees in assessing and researching issues and getting data corrected in the system.

You Have Identified the Problem; Now You Need to Define the Solution

A possible solution to address this problem is to align your processes by function (see Figure 14.3).

The characteristics of an integrated end-to-end process would include having accountability throughout the process for

Contracts to Cash

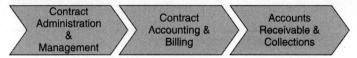

FIGURE 14.3 Integrated End-to-End Process

successful execution, improved understanding of the end-to-end process, faster error resolution, and reduced cycle times. If a contract administrator is put in charge of the process from contract to cash, he or she takes the responsibility of gathering the correct information because he or she is responsible for getting these invoices through the billing and cash application process. Therefore, less time will be required researching issues and more care will be taken throughout the process to ensure the data is correct.

So, how does this relate to your evolving ERP-based processes? You have identified the need to integrate your business process to reduce transactional activities. In addition, organizational changes most likely are required. These changes will cause a number of system changes in order to enable this streamlined process. You may decide to implement work flow in your system to streamline approval processes and handoffs. There will be security changes to allow different groups within the organization to perform activities. Data improvement will be required, so changes to the system to mark additional fields as necessary or validations on the data to ensure integrity at the entry point may be needed.

Now that you have identified opportunities for your organization to improve, you can define a *plan for implementation*. This plan does not need to be as aggressive as your initial ERP implementation. You can choose to address each issue in a separate mini-project or group similar issues into one project. In addition, it is imperative to track the benefits you identified in your assessment. As you implement these improvements, you will be able to realize more of the value of your ERP system and achieve a lower TCO.

Conclusion

When your organization implements an ERP system, consider this the beginning of a journey. Your first step should have been to make sure you do not make the typical mistakes during the implementation process, but even if you have already implemented, getting more value is still achievable. Recognizing the activities that do *not* provide value is key to identifying opportunities for improvement. You need to be willing to change from the way you have always done things and drive that change into your organization. This process needs to be business focused, not an IT project. Look at implementing ERP as an evolving process and understand that by continually evaluating your business processes, you will enable your company to achieve higher value from the ERP system.

PART III

Mergers, Acquisitions, Divestitures, and IT

Key IT-Related Questions Every Financial Executive Should Consider during a Merger, Acquisition, or Divestiture

Mark Walsh

There is a strong correlation between early and consistent information technology (IT) involvement in merger, acquisition, and divestiture (MA&D) transactions and transaction success.[1] In a recent analysis of major mergers, acquisitions, and divestitures, it was noted that in transactions where IT was involved in early due diligence and planning activities, transactions realized a higher likelihood of achieving an issue-free Day 1 and achieving or exceeding identified synergy capture targets. Despite this data, many companies often do not invite the chief information officer (CIO) or his or her team to the deal team until the diligence is completed, synergy numbers are calculated, integration timelines are developed, and transactions are announced.

Based on our experience and research, we believe there are a number of key IT-related questions every financial executive should consider asking before and during a merger, acquisition, or divestiture.

Before a Transaction Is Identified

Even before a decision has been made to pursue a specific transaction, there are a number of IT-related questions a financial executive can ask to evaluate and enhance the organization's chances for MA&D success:

1. **What is the role and perception of IT in your organization?**
   - **IT is integral to the business/IT is a key business partner.** If this is true, IT must (and likely will) be invited to the MA&D table early.
   - **IT is merely a back-office activity/IT is an afterthought.** If this is true, focused effort should be placed on assessing the importance of IT in future transactions. If IT will play a role of medium to high importance, concerted effort should be placed on pulling IT into the MA&D activities early.
2. **Given your anticipated MA&D activity, how important will IT be to transaction success?**
   - **High.** If IT is critical to your business or the target's business, or the planned integration/divestiture activities will be complex, IT should be a critical part of your deal team.
   - **Medium.** If the planned integration/divestiture activities will be of medium complexity or are unknown, IT should be a critical part of your deal team.
   - **Low.** Even if IT is not viewed as a key deal component, the IT team should be invited to participate in early diligence and planning activities to help identify any IT-related risks, costs, or issues.
3. **Is your IT organization prepared to successfully complete an IT due diligence effort?**
   - **People/training/experience.** Does your IT organization have an adequate number of trained resources with IT

diligence experience, capabilities, and skill sets? If the answer is no, it is a good idea to pursue some training for available resources and/or put plans in place to engage outside support to assist with IT diligence activities.

- **Diligence scope.** In situations where IT has been pulled to the table for IT diligence efforts, most teams include these basic areas:
  - IT-related risk
    - Business risk
    - Operational risk
    - Legal and regulatory risk
    - Delivery risk
    - Financial risk
    - People risk
  - IT scope
    - IT history
    - Innovation management
    - IT applications portfolio
    - IT projects
    - IT infrastructure
    - IT operations
    - Service portfolio/help desk
    - IT strategy/governance
    - IT organization
    - IT security and risk management
    - IT financial management

  All of these risk and scope items are important and relevant to the due diligence, but they really do not tell the whole story. As result, it is critical that IT teams dig deeper and focus on information that will be more useful for the deal team—the information that really matters, including:
  - Preliminary integration/divestiture planning (*blueprinting*)

- **Day 1/End State.** Completing initial integration/ divestiture planning during diligence that focuses on (1) what needs to be integrated on Day 1, (2) what needs to be completed by the End State, (3) how quickly the work can be completed, and (4) for what cost is critical. This planning should be completed across:
  - **IT organization**
  - **All functions (applications):** for example, Finance, Tax, Human Resources, Supply Chain, and so on.
  - **All towers (infrastructure):** for example, Data Centers, Voice and Data Network, Help Desk, and so on.
- **Key contracts and sourcing.** Often, existing contracts and outsourcing agreements can limit an organization's flexibility and speed or be costly to address. Identifying and addressing these issues early can help prevent last-minute negative surprises.
- **Preliminary synergy identification and capture planning (volume and timing).** In a recent survey of major mergers and acquisitions, it was noted that 60 to 70 percent of all revenue and cost synergies are directly driven by IT or are dependent on IT enabling them.[2] As a result, IT should play a key role in developing and validating initial synergy capture volume and timing estimates and make sure feasible assumptions are included in the valuation model.

4. **Is your IT organization prepared to successfully complete an integration or divestiture planning and execution effort?**
   - **People/training/experience.** Does your IT organization have an adequate number of trained resources

with IT integration/divestiture planning and execution experience, capabilities, and skill sets? If the answer is no, it is a good idea to pursue some training for available resources and/or put plans in place to engage outside support to assist with early IT planning and execution activities.

- **Process/playbook/guiding principles/roles and responsibilities.** Many companies anticipating MA&D activity develop functional MA&D playbooks, processes, and guiding principles to help them be prepared for when a transaction is identified. If your organization has not completed significant MA&D activity in the past or has limited/no MA&D materials, it may be prudent to initiate some preparation activities.

- **As-is technology footprint documentation (organization, applications, infrastructure, interfaces, contracts, etc.).** One consistent hurdle we find in integration/divestiture planning is a lack of as-is documentation of the technology footprint for both the buyer and the target. If the level of as-is documentation in your organization is not robust and complete, some early effort to develop pre-deal documentation can have a significant accelerator impact when a transaction is identified.

- **Data integrity.** Another hurdle consistently encountered in the MA&D space is data integrity issues. (See Chapter 21 for a discussion of data integrity.) Due to the very stringent data requirements for enterprise resource planning system integration and separation as well as the importance of data to today's business operations, data-related issues can have major negative impact on MA&D risk and timelines. Early pre-deal focus by the business and IT to improve data quality and data completeness can greatly reduce risk and improve MA&D transaction speed.

After a Transaction Is Identified

When the real action is about to begin, there are a number of additional IT-related questions a financial executive can ask to enhance the organization's chances for transaction success:

1. **What percent of anticipated synergy opportunities (revenue and cost) and Day 1 readiness activities are dependent on IT?**
   - **The MA&D IT mandate.** In many cases, functions such as Finance, Human Resources, Sales and Marketing, Treasury, and Tax cannot remove duplication, reduce staffing, and reduce costs without IT making applications and infrastructure changes. Likewise, supply chain organizations cannot optimize the combined supply chain without some help from IT. If this is the case with your transaction, heightened attention should be placed on IT early to help the IT team get the required traction and support from the business and deal team to be successful.
2. **How complex is the required IT integration/divestiture work? How aggressive is the timeline?**
   - **Impact to transaction-close timeline.** Due to the complexity of IT integration/divestiture activities, IT is often the long pole in the tent in MA&D transactions. If IT planning begins early, typically more options are available and integration timelines can be accelerated.
   - **Impact to overall synergy capture magnitude and timing.** As noted, IT is typically a key synergy enabler. Early IT planning not only can help accelerate synergy capture timelines, it also can help enable additional synergy capture opportunities and options to reduce synergy capture costs and risk.

Conclusion

Companies that place a strong, early, and consistent emphasis on IT and take deliberate steps to elevate IT as a key MA&D focus area can better position themselves to achieve a wide range of benefits, including:

- Faster deal closure
  - Faster execution time
  - Faster integration/divestiture
  - Rigorous and repeatable processes and tools
- Reduced cost
  - More efficient work completion
  - Less throwaway IT work
  - Quicker learning curve
  - Reduced internal and external staffing requirements based on standardized processes and focused methodology
- Enhanced credibility with key constituencies
  - Clear case to the Board of Directors, analysts, customers, employees, suppliers, and other constituents
- Improved flexibility and scalability to handle small, medium, and large transactions

Regardless of the size and complexity of an integration or divestiture, the IT team's speed and effectiveness is likely to have a big impact on whether the transaction ultimately achieves the expected results.

With billions of dollars at risk, asking a few IT-related questions can provide financial executives and their organizations with the information necessary to made solid decisions and better position mergers, acquisitions, and divestitures for success.

Notes

1. 2008 Deloitte Consulting LLP survey and analysis.
2. *Ibid.*

CHAPTER 16

The Importance of IT Due Diligence during a Merger or Acquisition

Pavel Krumkachev
Indira Gillingham
Shalva Nolen

D ue diligence is a major prerequisite of any merger and acquisition (M&A) deal and helps lay the foundation for post-merger integration success. Through a thorough process used to conduct due diligence, potential synergies and ease of integration can be determined, arming the post-merger integration teams with adequate knowledge to immediately begin planning once the deal is officially announced. One of the primary objectives in the due diligence phase is to accurately identify synergy targets with the goal of refining them as the M&A transaction moves forward. A secondary objective of due diligence is to analyze the information technology (IT) environment to gain insight into the effort and scope involved with integration.

Identifying and accomplishing these objectives is not a straightforward exercise. Lack of access to accurate and recent information as well as compressed time frames pose obstacles and impact the level of detail and accuracy of synergy estimates and IT integration effort analysis.

In this chapter, we will attempt to demystify the process of IT due diligence, explain its value, and provide practical advice on ways to effectively perform the due diligence exercise.

Why Bother with IT Due Diligence?

To answer this question, one needs to look no further than the reasons that most large M&A transactions fail. In many cases, insufficient information about a merger partner is the primary reason for failed M&A transactions. Insufficient pre-deal information is responsible for a large number of merger failures and results in costly surprises, unmet synergy targets, and integration budget overruns.

Information technology is both an enabler of merger synergies and a significant source of cost rationalization. IT also generally contributes the highest out-of-pocket cost to achieve post-merger integration. Gaps in IT due diligence can result in Day 1 delays, significant integration cost increases, and regulatory and compliance issues. IT merger integration difficulties can also dramatically impact employee productivity as well as revenue and profitability. Consequently, IT needs to be one of the primary focus areas of any due diligence effort, and the IT function needs to be evaluated both as an enabler of synergies and as an opportunity for cost reduction.

Role of the Chief Information Officer

Most chief information officers (CIOs) involved in merger integration efforts are forced to work reactively, presented with integration timeframes and synergy targets that were established without their involvement. Not including an experienced IT executive as part of a pre-deal *due diligence team* is an unfortunate situation that usually results in many complexities and an IT integration being misunderstood and underestimated. For instance, during the course of a recent acquisition we know of, a CIO had been informed of a pending acquisition literally days before the transaction closed. By that point, purchase agreements, transition services agreements, and asset-transfer agreements had all been finalized. The merger team had failed to include enterprise application licenses as part of the purchase agreement—a mistake identified by the CIO once the deal had already closed. This oversight resulted in tens of millions of dollars in extra merger costs and significantly lowered the value of the acquisition.

While being critical in the effort to correctly estimate merger integration costs, IT executives can also be extremely valuable in helping identify additional synergy opportunities. A CIO can help transaction leadership understand the nuts and bolts of the acquirer's information technology landscape and can quickly identify redundant systems, infrastructure, and staff, which can be rationalized in a combined company.

Looking under the Hood: Your IT Due Diligence Checklist

Because the goal of IT due diligence is to identify any areas of IT that could affect the overall success of the deal and determine how to effectively manage the risk, it is important to make sure that no key areas are overlooked. Using a checklist is one way to keep track. The key areas for IT due diligence are applications, infrastructure, organization, suppliers, operations, and culture. Within these areas, items to consider including in an IT due diligence checklist are shown in Table 16.1.

TABLE 16.1 IT Due Diligence Checklist

IT Area	Checklist Item
Applications	■ Enterprise applications
	■ ERP (enterprise resource planning)
	■ Finance and accounting
	■ CRM (customer relationship management)
	■ SCM (supply chain management)
	■ BI (business intelligence)
	■ ECM (enterprise content management)
	■ BPM (business process management)
	■ PLM (product lifecycle management)
	■ HRMS (human resource management system)
	■ Specialized applications (industry specific)
	■ Proprietary
	■ Open source
	■ Office productivity applications
	■ E-mail and calendaring
	■ Collaboration software
	■ Office and personal productivity
	■ Hardware
	■ Mainframes
	■ Servers
	■ Storage
	■ End-user devices (e.g., desktops/laptops, phones, personal digital assistants [PDAs])
	■ Network and telecomm
	■ Data
	■ Voice
	■ Mobile service
Infrastructure	■ Infrastructure software
	■ Operating systems
	■ Application development
	■ Middleware
	■ Data management
	■ Storage management

IT Area	Checklist Item
	■ Security systems
	■ IT operations
	■ Compliance
	■ Databases
Organization	■ Size and structure
	■ Capabilities
	■ Tenure
	■ Training (IT staff and end users)
	■ Outsourcing
	■ Staff location
	■ Compensation
Suppliers/Vendor Management (Hardware, Software, & Services)	■ Vendor viability
	■ Licenses
	■ Terms and conditions
	■ Transfer or relicensing fees
	■ Contract termination fees
IT Culture	■ History
	■ Governance
	■ Mission
	■ Innovation
	■ Adaptability
	■ Compensation structure
	■ Communication
IT Operations	■ IT operating and capital budgets
	■ Security and risk management
	■ Disaster recovery and business continuity
	■ IT service portfolio (including the associated service-level agreements [SLAs])
	■ Current and planned project portfolio
	■ Help desk
	■ Desk side services
	■ Regulatory compliance
	■ Data center facilities

The checklist items need to be considered in terms of appropriateness, performance, security, availability, reliability, scalability, extendibility, and level of effort required to integrate. When evaluated in these terms, the checklist items should help provide an overall picture of the organization's current health and capabilities as well as the future (combined) IT organization's capabilities, capacity, effectiveness, strengths, and weaknesses. It is important for the IT due diligence evaluation to be as thorough and completely documented as possible because this information will be used for synergy identification as well as pre-merger and post-merger integration planning.

Properly evaluating issues related to the checklist items can help transaction leadership develop an understanding of the magnitude of the potential risk related to the IT function. Effectively managing this risk can lead to a faster and smoother integration and a higher likelihood of deal success.

How to Get the Data

Collecting the desired data for areas on the checklist in Table 16.1 can be challenging. The time available to perform IT due diligence is often short, and the information available is often limited, inaccurate, out of date, or undocumented (i.e., residing only in employees' heads).

The first step of the data collection process involves researching public information, such as company websites, proxy statements, 10-Ks/annual reports, and Forms 5500 (Annual Return/Report of Employee Benefit Plan). The next step involves understanding the information that has been provided, such as the offering memorandum and management presentation. Next, the due diligence team should identify and request any additional data that are needed. The due diligence team should then assess the data-room information and quickly determine what is relevant. The next step of the data collection process involves interviewing knowledgeable personnel, with a focus on strategic direction and key application, infrastructure, and organization issues. The due diligence team should also arrange a site visit, if possible. Finally, a competitive benchmark analysis should also be performed in order to understand how the IT function is doing in relation to that of the company's peers.

When dealing with very tight time frames, it is important quickly to prioritize your action steps based on the magnitude of the potential risk and not get mired in the details. Collecting and analyzing all of this information can be a challenging and time-consuming undertaking. Thus, IT due diligence should begin as early in the due diligence process as possible.

Beyond Cost Reduction: Identifying IT Synergies

As the due diligence team begins to interact with prospects to request documentation and set up interviews, a normal tendency is to launch into developing an understanding of the application and infrastructure footprints and resources supporting them. However, a heightened focus on identifying, refining, and validating IT synergy opportunities also should be emphasized in due diligence. Synergy identification should be exhaustive, beginning with each of the IT capability areas, to understand how IT environments can be optimized across people, process, and technology. During interviews, the due diligence team should attempt to structure questions focused on assessing complexity of IT systems and opportunities to accelerate synergies through early identification of areas to retire, rationalize, or optimize.

Accurate synergy identification also hinges on clearly documented assumptions. Ideally, the due diligence team should attempt to validate as many assumptions as possible and provide clear distinction between assumptions that are validated and those that are not. A big mistake for a due diligence team is to make inferences or assumptions without proper data to support them. Another pitfall during due diligence is not identifying resources with the right knowledge and expertise to validate the stated assumptions. It is recommended that assumptions be discussed with IT resources that are either targeted for being part of the execution team or have deep knowledge of the IT environment so they can understand and validate findings during the detailed and final due diligence steps to confirm that the estimates map to a realistic time frame for delivery.

Although it is difficult during due diligence to place any estimates on the level of integration required with limited information, the exercise to uncover synergies should also take into account the cost to achieve. Not only will this help in aligning any expectations between business and IT, but it will also begin to get the wheels turning in thinking through what it will take to integrate IT systems, processes, and people.

Accelerating Merger Integration Planning through Due Diligence

Accelerating merger integration planning is made more difficult because due diligence activities are associated with highly compressed time frames and limited information that may or may not be accurate. Poor due diligence could result in a higher cost to achieve integration and also diminish synergy value. However, using a structured framework for conducting the due diligence focused on understanding all IT capabilities can help accelerate the completion of post-merger integration planning. There are three important steps that the M&A team should consider taking to accelerate integration planning in the due diligence phase.

The first step to accelerating merger integration is forming the right team. The due diligence team should be comprised of individuals with broad knowledge of the IT organization, complemented by individuals with deep knowledge across the IT capabilities. While the team size may vary, identifying the right team is important because these individuals can synthesize data on the target's environment and understand implications of integration into the current environment. Additionally, maintaining continuity of the team into post-merger integration is valuable as these individuals can provide guidance to the broader team based on their historical knowledge, which can help accelerate discussions on deal structure, rationale, and timelines (these areas tend to occupy a lot of the up-front planning time to bring post-merger integration delivery teams up to speed).

Second, due diligence teams should make every attempt to understand business processes and not just the systems supporting them. It is not safe to assume that having a common set of systems implies simpler integration. However, while the systems may be the same, the underlying business processes, business rules, and configurations may be vastly different. Furthermore, interfaces to ancillary systems can create complex webs that need to be unwoven carefully. Differences in business processes and associated business rules and integration points drive integration complexity, which can increase not only the time frame for completion but also cost. For example, during a recent merger of two media companies we know of, it was not until integration planning that the Functional Team realized there was a big difference in how customers were tracked and when revenue was recognized. This realization had major implications for the assumption that integrating both systems would be fairly straightforward. While both companies used customer relationship management (CRM) systems from the same vendor, the degree of customization and integration to support business processes was very different. A break in that business process resulted in a cascading effect of disrupting the business flow and having an impact on their customers and suppliers. The lesson learned from this scenario is to pay attention to the degree of customization and complexity of the IT environment.

Third, while conducting due diligence, IT leadership should begin assessing capacity. Begin by evaluating the portfolio of projects to assess resource constraints from current and planned projects in IT that might create a resource conflict if the merger were to go through. Working with business sponsors, IT should evaluate projects that have not yet started to determine whether these projects can be placed on hold or deferred until after the integration. In-flight projects should be evaluated to understand constraints on and implications for the merger integration in terms of system, environment, and resource conflicts and what kind of shifting is possible to free up resources for the integration project. One way to free up resources is to identify backups to replace project leads and begin transitioning to them. The final category of projects is those nearing completion. This category should be evaluated to understand when these resources will become available and whether they have the right skills to support integration projects.

Due Diligence after the Close

While most of the due diligence effort happens before a transaction closes, it is essential for IT due diligence to be an *ongoing* process through Day 1 and the near-term merger integration. After the close, and once both companies are combined, IT teams get much more visibility into the true state of information technology at the combined company. All assumptions and key decisions made during the pre-deal due diligence need to be revisited and validated. Additionally, as teams from both companies engage in joint planning exercises, their respective capabilities and strengths become more apparent. This allows IT executives to validate their initial assumptions regarding the speed with which merger integration can be achieved.

Conclusion

Information technology has to be a key area of focus for any M&A due diligence effort. IT can serve both as a strong enabler of planned merger synergies and as a major area where these synergies are achieved. In order to be effective, however, IT due diligence needs to be comprehensive and broad in its scope. It also needs to be carried out by the right team, with deep knowledge of the current-state environment of the acquirer, experience in identifying IT-related merger synergies, and ability to correctly plan merger integration projects in ambiguous environments.

Done right, IT due diligence can go a long way in helping the combined organization achieve the expected success of the merger. It can also become a great accelerator and help companies jump-start their merger integration initiative planning activities.

CHAPTER 17

Ways to Enhance IT-Related Synergy Capture during a Merger, Acquisition, or Divestiture

Pavel Krumkachev

Colleen Chan

Varun Joshi

Brandon P. Patterson

Even though the merger and acquisition (M&A) deal-making heydays were from 2004 through 2007, many companies are still in the process of completing acquisitions and/or divestitures that were consummated in the recent past. Information technology (IT)–related synergies usually account for a substantial portion of the overall cost rationalization; therefore, being able to manage the IT synergy capture successfully can have significant impact on shareholder value.

Based on our collective experience from being involved with IT due diligence, pre-close planning, post-close execution, and synergy tracking activities, we have laid out what we believe are the key components that drive IT costs; ways companies can establish aggressive, but realistic, IT synergy targets; and ways companies can capture these synergies effectively early on.

Sources of IT Synergies

There are four components that drive IT synergies in association with a merger, acquisition, or divestiture:

1. IT operating model
2. IT organization structure
3. IT application portfolio
4. IT infrastructure

Through these four components, IT-related costs can be benchmarked, targets can be set, and synergies can be captured.

IT Operating Model

The IT operating model is a part of the larger, corporate operating model and defines the framework for the IT organization. It serves to align the IT organization and its activities, services, and processes required to support the achievement of the company's business goals and strategic vision.

Any major change, especially a merger, acquisition, or divestiture, should be accompanied by a review of the IT operating model to determine whether it will support the new business model and new size of the company. The IT operating model helps to define the future IT organization, service levels, processes, and standards to be implemented across the company based on the new business model.

Right-sizing the IT operating model, including the exploration of using outsourced service providers, gives the IT organization an opportunity to streamline its operations and to improve its value and effectiveness while rationalizing the IT infrastructure and application portfolio. This alignment of the IT operating model with the new company's business model can drive cost reduction and position the IT organization to help support the achievement of the business objectives defined in the corporate operating model.

Four different models under which a company may choose to operate are outlined later in this chapter. Each of these models represents significantly different IT requirements and will impact the overall IT operating model of the company.

IT Organization Structure

The IT organization is affected by a merger, acquisition, or divestiture as much as any organization within the company, if not more so. The IT organization has to achieve multiple objectives during the transition period, such as: (1) combining or separating the portfolio of IT applications and services; (2) right-sizing the eventual IT organization to achieve synergy target; and (3) supporting the business throughout the transition period. Given all the objectives and dependencies, the full capture of IT organization synergy targets is usually delayed until the post-M&A transition is complete.

Usually, mergers can achieve economies of scale as an acquired organization is assimilated into the parent organization. The combined productivity of the IT workforce from both entities will no longer be needed. Since the relationship between the services provided by IT and the workforce required to deliver those services is not linear, careful attention needs to be paid to resource levels.

In the case of a divestiture, the divesting entity can realize significant cost reduction in the IT organization as early as Day 1. In many cases, IT services will be provided by the parent company temporarily through *transition services agreements* (TSAs) until the divested entity has fully staffed its IT organization and built out its IT capabilities. If such services are required, the parent company may not be able to immediately transform its organization on Day 1, though the cost of supporting

223

such services will be compensated by the divested entity through TSAs. Therefore, it should still begin to realize synergies on Day 1.

IT Application Portfolio

In mergers and acquisitions, there will always be overlap of the business capabilities provided by each entity's application portfolio. The duplication of capabilities provides another opportunity to capture IT-related synergy through application rationalization.

The process of rationalizing application portfolios is slightly different for mergers and acquisitions than for divestiture. However, in all cases, application rationalization begins with creating an inventory of all applications in each company or business unit's portfolio, identifying the business services provided by those applications, and determining which applications are required to support the new business model. At this juncture, the process diverges depending on the type of transaction: mergers and acquisitions or divestiture.

In the case of a merger or acquisition, the common services for both entities can be combined, and overlapping applications can be decommissioned to reduce overall IT costs. Synergies can be realized by eliminating all costs associated with the decommissioned applications including software licenses and support contracts, hardware maintenance and support contracts, data center costs (floor space, electricity, HV/AC, fire protection, storage, backups, disaster recovery, etc.), and personnel costs associated with the administration of the application and its corresponding infrastructure components.

Combining back-office applications such as enterprise resource planning (ERP) systems, demand planning systems, e-mail, and self-service Human Resources applications can lead to significant reductions in operating costs, unlocking a value component of the merger or acquisition.

In the case of a divestiture, the IT-related synergies are most easily recognized by the divesting entity since all costs associated with supporting the entity being divested will be significantly reduced. Though in most cases the divested entity requires IT services to be provided by the parent for a limited period of time, the cost of providing the services should be recouped through the TSAs.

IT Infrastructure

The corporate IT infrastructure consists of the technical components required to support the many applications and services required by a company. These components include, but are not limited to:

- Data centers (including disaster-recovery sites)
- Network and network equipment (switches, routers, etc.)
- Computers (servers, PCs, laptops) and mobile devices
- Phone systems

As an example, data center consolidation is one way to enhance IT-related synergies as part of a merger or acquisition. As companies are combined, an opportunity exists to combine infrastructure components into a single data center or set of data centers. Server virtualization and virtual storage arrays provide the opportunity to use excess capacity of one entity to host the combined applications and services portfolio with a decrease in cost.

The same principle applies to the network required for the new entity. In the case of a merger or acquisition, the acquiring company's network should be built out to handle the additional capacity required by the combined organization. Once again, the total capacity required by the combined organization will be less than the sum of the parts.

Standardizing hardware (computers, mobile devices, etc.) and software used by employees provides another opportunity to realize cost saving. Standardization of these items can lead to reduced support costs and provide leverage with vendors to reduce the purchase price of equipment and services.

Divestitures do not provide the same opportunities to leverage economies of scale with respect to the IT infrastructure. The divesting entity should realize IT cost reductions as the business unit is removed from the parent company's infrastructure; however, the divested entity will incur costs associated with its own, separate infrastructure. The advantage for the divested entity is the opportunity to move to new, more efficient infrastructure components and leverage commoditized IT services offered by various outsourcing vendors, services that may not have been available when the original infrastructure was created.

IT infrastructure synergies typically will have significant up-front costs associated with achieving a reduced run-rate. Care should be taken to do a cost-benefit analysis of where it makes sense to conduct a cost-rationalization exercise on the infrastructure components. This should be kept in line with the IT operating model and the business strategic direction.

Benchmarks to Establish IT Synergy Targets

Once a deal is announced, as part of the deal rationale, potential revenue and cost synergy targets are communicated to the markets. As opposed to revenue synergies, which are more often than not based on expectations of market share growth, the cost synergies provide a tangible metric to the investor community to assess the potential value of the deal. This creates some pressure on the teams involved in the deal execution during the pre-close planning phase of a merger or divestiture to come up with ways to identify synergies to meet those targets.

In our experience, effective and early use of benchmarking can greatly assist in confirming whether the externally communicated cost synergies are realistic and provide a comparative measure for external stakeholders to independently evaluate the deal value. IT usually accounts for a significant portion of operating cost and thus is a prime target for achieving overall cost synergies of a deal.

Companies should benchmark IT costs early in the pre-deal due diligence phase (see Chapter 16 for more details on IT due diligence). During due diligence, benchmarking is mostly restricted to publicly available data on the target, but it can provide a quick, back-of-the-envelope calculation for directional guidance on cost takeout. This can then be followed up in the pre-close planning phase with a detailed bottom-up analysis based on budget data (e.g., line of business and overall IT budget) to identify cost categories that are out of line with benchmarks.

Typical benefits from benchmarking IT costs in an M&A situation include:

- Visibility into the overall technology spend in comparison with industry and functional peers
- An understanding of true costs, performance, and quality of IT services
- Identification of IT strengths, problems, and opportunities
- Identification of any gaps in the overall business/IT alignment, which manifests itself in redundant or ineffective IT spend

Benchmarking should be used in a slightly different context in a divestiture as opposed to a merger. Whereas in a merger, it helps to compare the IT cost structure of the combined company against industry and functional peers, in a divestiture, benchmarking can help both the parent company as well as the carved-out entity in different ways. For the parent company, the shedding of *noncore* business units and an increased focus on the areas of core competency can provide a natural incentive to re-baseline its overall cost structure. Understanding how the IT costs compare against industry and functional peers can provide quantifiable targets for comparison. For the carved-out entity, benchmarking can help in the structuring of TSAs. Often the carved-out entity's business applications and IT infrastructure are so intertwined with the parent that it has to rely on TSAs for an interim period until its own IT capabilities are built out. Having tangible benchmarks against which to compare the cost of IT services can help limit the subjectivity in the TSA cost calculation. Benchmarked data can provide the carved-out entity with a starting point to determine the cost of services in structuring TSAs.

There are two types of benchmarking that can be conducted to identify IT cost synergies:

1. **Industry benchmarking.** This type of benchmarking compares a company's cost structure against industry peers. Thus, it can provide insight into the competitive landscape to drive prioritization/urgency of potential IT cost reduction efforts.
2. **Functional benchmarking.** In functional benchmarking, a company's IT cost structure is compared against other companies sharing a similar technology footprint and usage profile—irrespective of industry.

The combined view obtained from both industry and functional benchmarking is the most comprehensive and actionable way to identify IT cost synergies. At a minimum, industry benchmarking should be utilized to provide directional guidance for the cost reduction effort. Depending on availability of raw data against which to run benchmark comparisons and the aggressiveness of the cost reduction initiative, functional benchmarking should be employed.

The variances from benchmarked data should be mapped to the four drivers of IT costs (IT operating model, organization structure, application portfolio, and infrastructure) to better understand the reasons behind the variances from the benchmark. A company's unique business strategy or market position might necessitate spend at levels higher than industry or functional peers. These nuances should get highlighted when the variances are collectively diagnosed against the IT cost drivers.

Benchmarking IT costs can provide a top-down view of the potential cost synergies from a transaction. The top-down view should always be rationalized against bottom-up calculations, which should take into account the specific situation of the company. Actionable synergy targets and initiatives should be developed only after both of the views are analyzed.

Begin Early and Build Momentum

More often than not, IT rationalization and synergy capture efforts are not planned until after the merger is closed. In our experience, delay often leads to scope surprises, cost overruns, and reactive decision making. IT synergy capture should be an integral part of the whole M&A lifecycle, from target screening and due diligence, to pre-close planning and post-close initiative implementation.

Target Screening

During this stage of the acquisition, it is important to assess the magnitude of IT rationalization and cost reduction opportunities. This is particularly critical if the intent of a merger is to realize economies of scale and enhance profitability through cost reduction. The IT merger planning team should look at the degree of overlap between IT applications, infrastructure, and organizations at the acquirer and the target. They should also produce a complete assessment of how much and how quickly savings can be realized by combining the two companies. That being said, it is often impossible to get any accurate data during the target-screening process. The merger team usually has to rely exclusively on publicly available information in order to make their assessments. As stated in the previous section, we suggest leveraging industry-specific IT benchmarks, which can be a directional-correct indicator of how much the combined company should spend on IT costs and how much synergy can be realized if the merger goes forward.

Due Diligence

As discussed in Chapter 16, it is hard to overlook the importance of pre-merger due diligence. The definition of success for most mergers is developed at this stage, and the probability of a merger being successful is often directly proportional to the amount of time and effort invested in up-front due diligence. This is especially true within the IT function, which often gets overlooked during the due diligence processes, resulting in expensive surprises, integration delays, and failure to achieve planned merger synergies.

It is very important to quickly and effectively evaluate potential acquisition targets. Focused due diligence teams need to look at all parts of a business and leave no stone unturned before making their recommendations on value of an acquisition. It is not atypical for an initial value of a target to either increase or drop substantially after due diligence is performed. In fact, a very large percentage of potential transactions never move forward once the true cost structures and expected synergies are evaluated. This alone underscores the importance of performing a focused and exhaustive due diligence exercise prior to closing an M&A transaction.

Having IT experts on your due diligence team is not optional. Even a small oversight in evaluating a target's IT landscape can result in significant barriers to achieving merger synergies. For instance, a proprietary custom-built application, at the core of a target's business, may take months, if not years, to unravel and combine with an acquirer's own systems in order to realize cost savings. Unless this is known up front, millions of dollars in potential synergies could be delayed or forgone. Conversely, additional IT synergy opportunities (e.g., from licensing costs of similar applications) may be identified during the due diligence period, greatly enhancing the value of an acquisition.

Pre-Close Planning

Depending on the operating model being proposed for the merger, IT can become either an enabler of synergy capture or one of the primary sources of planned synergies. Generally, most mergers fall into one of four *future-state operating models*, each with its own set of IT implications, as shown in Figure 17.1.

These four operating models illustrate the spectrum of scenarios, where IT can become either an enabler of synergy capture or a primary source of synergies. For instance, in Model 2 (Combination), the business may wish to achieve revenue-related synergies by combining the sales channels of both merging companies. In this case, IT will focus primarily on consolidating and integrating synergy-specific applications (e.g., dealer systems and web sales channels). Thus, IT becomes an enabler of synergy capture without which the business objectives might not be met. Conversely, in Model 1 (Consolidation), IT-related cost savings may be a significant portion of planned

Company A   *Company B*

Model 1: Consolidation—Convert one organization to the same process and systems of the other. The business imperative of this model is to realize cost saving synergies, standardize global processes, and improve control and visibility over business operations.

IT Implications:

- Data migration from target's systems into acquirer's systems (or vice versa), except for highly unique systems
- Consolidation of ERP and non-ERP applications
- Significant economies from application and infrastructure rationalization
- Single IT organization

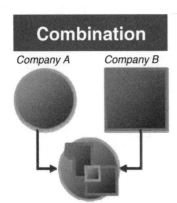

Model 2: Combination—Combine only "synergy-centric" processes and applications (e.g., sales channels). The business imperative of this model is to open new distribution channels, open new market segments, capture revenue synergies, and preserve the competitive advantages and uniqueness of each company.

IT Implications:

- Complex decisions about which systems to keep and which to abandon

FIGURE 17.1 Common Future-State Operating Models

- Data migration from abandoned applications
- Significant application integration effort
- Significant economies from application and infrastructure rationalization

Transformation

Company A   Company B

Model 3: Transformation—
Transform both organizations into a new whole by leveraging superior components of each. The business imperative of this model is to capture operational efficiencies, develop a new business model, and realize cost synergies.

IT Implications:

- Complex decisions for overlapping shared services functions and applications
- Significant work to integrate surviving back-office systems to operational and customer-facing systems
- Large up-front IT transformation effort
- IT organization structure and physical location needing to be determined

FIGURE 17.1 (*Continued*)

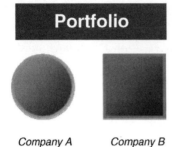

Company A   Company B

Model 4: Portfolio—Support each company as individual entity with unique capabilities and cultures. The business imperative of this model is to achieve purchasing economies of scale and preserve competitive advantages and uniqueness of each organization.

IT Implications:

- Low IT migration and integration effort
- Use of high-level processes and systems for financials' consolidation
- Some benefits from purchasing economies and standard risk management/security policies
- IT organizations staying essentially the same

FIGURE 17.1 (*Continued*)

cost synergies after the merger. Rapid consolidation of IT staff, applications, and infrastructure under this model is, therefore, the key to successful synergy capture.

It should be noted that these four models are not mutually exclusive. An organization may choose to implement different models throughout the transition period. For example, an organization may choose to implement a Combination model in the short term but eventually achieve the Transformation model (Model 3), or an organization may initially implement the Portfolio model (Model 4) and then decide to convert to one of the first three models based on a changing marketplace. Hence, IT organizations should be a step ahead in terms of architecting the appropriate model to support both the immediate as well as near-term business direction while planning cost reduction initiatives.

Post-Close Synergy Capture

The real work to capture merger-related synergies begins after the deal is closed. Here, quick and rigorous execution of post-merger integration projects defines the eventual success of the deal. In our experience, the speed with which these initiatives are completed is often more important than trying to fulfill all requirements and build an architecturally elegant solution. A no-frills version delivered 6 months after deal close will go much further in helping the business realize expected synergies than a souped-up version delivered 18 months later. Keeping this in mind, merger integration teams need to focus on minimizing IT solution requirements to just the *must haves* and for each new requirement to ask themselves whether it will improve or accelerate synergy capture.

Post-merger integration is also a great opportunity to look for additional IT synergies that previously had not been considered. More accurate information is now available to the combined team, and better decisions can be made about redundant systems, infrastructure, contracts, and people. Additionally, in the process of achieving revenue-related synergies, companies find new opportunities to cut IT costs through consolidation and system renewal. Thus, by addressing both cost and revenue objectives, the value of the merger can be greatly enhanced.

Conclusion

Information technology is a significant operating cost for all companies. It is imperative to establish realistic and appropriate targets for IT cost reduction prior to deal close; to begin IT combination or carve-out planning early; and to manage scope carefully with the objective to complete the transition in the shortest amount of time and enable a company to capture IT synergies per plan. These guidelines will in turn provide a much higher return for any deals into which a company may enter.

CHAPTER 18

Ways to Reduce IT-Related Costs during a Merger, Acquisition, or Divestiture

Asish Ramchandran

Given the unique market dynamics in place today, companies with strong balance sheets are acquiring organizations with reduced valuations. At the same time, in an attempt to free up cash flow, larger multinationals are shedding or divesting nonstrategic business units. We cannot recall a more fluid period in the history of the world financial markets. Every organization is being scrutinized via the contrasting lenses of public expectation and government regulation compliance.

Yet there is a significant disparity between the stated goals of a merger, acquisition, and divestiture-type transaction and the reality of the actual synergy and objectives being achieved. This is due in part to a dramatic increase in dependence on information technology (IT) to enable a large percentage of total synergies for most deals. IT synergies are tied to direct IT cost reductions and indirect reductions as a result of IT enabling streamlining measures to help reduce the total cost of operations in the enterprise.

However, from our experience, in merger and acquisition (M&A) transactions, the IT function is rarely engaged before the base target screening is completed. Typically, the deal is devised and structured by corporate development, legal, and interested business units. This results in development of valuation models that do not accurately comprehend the cost of the technical complexity being inherited. This gap in the transaction sequence makes it difficult for significant synergies to be realized from IT unless aggressive corrective measures are pursued.

While it is not expected that the deal makers will engage the IT function through every stage of the transaction, there are some techniques that can be applied that can help significantly reduce the IT-related costs of a merger, acquisition, or divestiture deal. The key to the techniques that can be applied is to understand the business rationale for a deal and the underlying transaction philosophies that may be applied to achieve IT cost reductions during a transaction.

This chapter lays out the fundamental transaction philosophies by deal types for a merger/acquisition or divestiture transaction and outlines a comprehensive approach for companies to consider as they pursue IT-enabled cost reduction activities. Considerations are discussed for several transaction philosophy constructs with the goal of systematically removing non–value-added costs from the very front end of the transaction planning process through the execution and synergy realization period.

Approach

Most organizations approach cost reductions reactively, when they are in the midst of a transaction with a bias toward headcount reduction and labor arbitrage. By approaching cost reduction strategically and systematically after laying out the fundamental drivers of a merger, acquisition, or divestiture trans-action, an organization would be better able to convert the IT cost reduction activity from being transitional and micro-focused to permanent and comprehensive. Figure 18.1 lays out the sequence that will be described further in this section.

Transaction Categories

IT cost reduction opportunities should be reviewed within the context of the following deal categories.

MERGERS AND ACQUISITIONS M&A involves the integration of two or more organizations into a single entity. Typically, the M&A deals are buyer or larger-entity driven. There are four basic integration philosophies:

1. **Assimilation.** The goal of this philosophy is to rapidly and efficiently convert the acquired entity into the strategy, structure, processes, and systems of the acquirer or parent organization. Significant resources are generally dedicated to IT consolidation efforts. This is the generally the easiest path toward achieving synergy targets and is generally reflected in aggressive market synergy expectations from IT that are mostly front-loaded in the synergy realization period.

2. **Transformation.** The goal of this philosophy is to syn-thesize disparate organizational and technology pieces into a new whole. The end result of the integration can look very different from the individual organizations. There is sig-nificant person, process, and technology impact requiring focused, detailed cross-functional planning in the pre-deal time frame and deliberate focus on execution. There is gen-erally a need for extensive use of internal and external resources. These transactions have complex change man-agement characteristics that will need to be very proactively

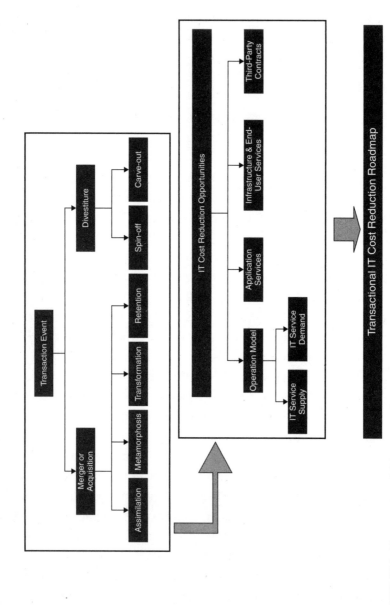

FIGURE 18.1 Transactional IT Cost Reduction Program

addressed. IT cost reductions are more back-loaded in the synergy realization period.

3. **Metamorphosis.** The goal of this philosophy is to select best processes, structures, and systems from each company to form an effective operating model. Objective benchmark-driven analysis is key to the selection process in the planning phase. There is increased functional friction that will need to be addressed via collaborative leadership techniques. There is a significant need for systems integration and increased internal resources dedicated to integrating operations. This is an excellent path toward achieving aggressive nonfinancial synergy targets. IT cost reduction in this case is spread across the value chain and evenly spread across the synergy realization period.

4. **Retention.** The goal of this philosophy is for the organizations to retain their unique capabilities. The transaction drivers are not synergy based. There is increased focus on consolidating contracts and financial reporting. The parent company operates as a holding company and uses a *portfolio* model. The governance is limited to stakeholder management. IT cost reduction is focused on leveraging IT economies of scale through IT process efficiency and increased productivity tools.

DIVESTITURES This type of transaction involves a sale of a business unit or product line to a private equity investment firm or private/public strategic buyer. Alternatively, the transaction could be structured as a spin-off of a stand-alone entity from the parent organization to be held as a wholly owned entity or publicly traded. Divestitures are typically seller driven in the near-term Day 1 scenario due to the level of integration with the seller's infrastructure and enabling functions.

1. **Carve out.** The goal of this philosophy is to separate a business unit or product line and sell to a buying entity. The typical driver is generally related to parent company's response to operating cost pressures or core competency focus realignment. The expectation is that the parent will get valuations via sale of selected units that will be value added to other organizations but do not support the internal business strategy. There is increased expectation on IT cost reduction in line with if not better than the reduction in company footprint.

2. **Spin off.** The goal of this philosophy is to stand up a separate entity that is intended to be publicly traded. *Spin-offs* are driven by interested parties when a segment or business unit consistently outperforms or underperforms against market expectations and/or is directionally different from the overall company performance and philosophy. The expectation around the spin-off of an entity is for the business unit's growth potential to be unleashed or to act as a catalyst and trigger incremental transformational efficiency. IT cost neutrality is the minimum expectation in spin-offs. The basic market expectation is that the IT performance will be better than industry benchmarks for the parent and the entity getting spun off.

IT Cost Reduction Levers

It is important to undertake an IT cost reduction initiative with a keen recognition and appreciation of the transaction type and philosophy. IT stakeholders must develop a meaningful understanding of the business goals that have prompted the transaction. This should form the basis for IT to direct its cost reduction efforts in line with increased strategic cost reduction areas. Sustained IT cost reduction should be the goal.

In general, IT cost is based on a series of *demand* and *supply* elements:

- Demand elements consist of consumption drivers determined by end users and the business (including application requirements, service needs, project requests, and license usage).
- Supply elements are generally driven by IT and include people, processes, and technology threads that are combined to provide the IT capacity and service levels necessary to meet the anticipated business demand.

While demand and supply elements are tightly interwoven in a cost reduction initiative, it is important to maintain these components as distinct elements to engage the appropriate business and IT stakeholders to assess and execute adjustments to both demand and supply levers.

Figure 18.2 outlines the components of the framework to use in the analysis of IT cost reduction opportunities including the cost categories and controllable levers.

The IT cost reduction process should be divided into two phases:

- **Phase I: Pre-Close Planning.** A pre-deal phase starts when the deal is announced. At this point, IT cost reduction should be put on the table as part of the pre-close planning or blueprinting workshops. This could be months before the actual close date. The goal should be to establish baseline targets by process, category, and functions. All the targets will also need an implementation plan for each of the cost drivers that will be reflected in the IT cost reduction roadmap.
- **Phase II: Post-Close execution.** Post-close phases require efficient execution, synergy-tracking tools, and governance

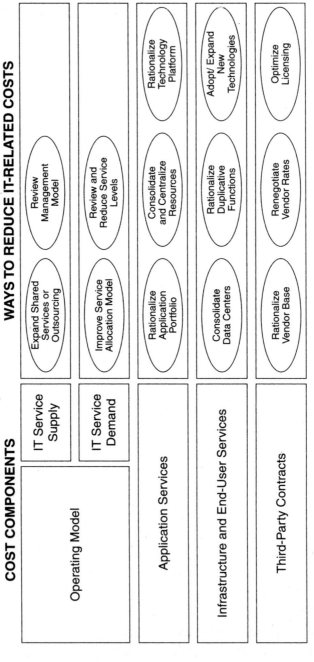

FIGURE 18.2 Transactional IT Cost Reduction Framework

structure for adjustments as necessary. The IT cost reduction roadmap is used to manage the program. IT cost savings identified during pre-close planning will feed into the synergy targets for IT. In order to be able to effectively execute and report against them, tangible initiatives and owners should be identified to the extent possible pre-close.

Transactional IT Cost Reduction Roadmap

The transactional IT cost reduction roadmap should be comprehensive in approach and driven by plans that are directionally bound by the top-down deal estimates but practically executed via bottom-up plans for each project/opportunity. This will help to align executive expectations with execution realities.

While the execution dashboard can be assessed on a milestone basis, the cross-functional dependencies must be carefully coordinated in order to drive cost out of the system permanently. A typical roadmap is structured as shown in Figure 18.3.

Cost Reduction during Merger or Acquisition

The relevant response to address supply-and-demand elements will be discussed in greater detail within this section. The objective should be to discern the most effective means by which to reduce IT-related costs, in a manner best suited to the nuances of the deal.

IT Operating Model: Demand Side

Demand-side cost reduction opportunities involve a fundamental evaluation of the way IT services are delivered to the business, end users, and customers and can be broken down into two primary elements: service allocation and service levels.

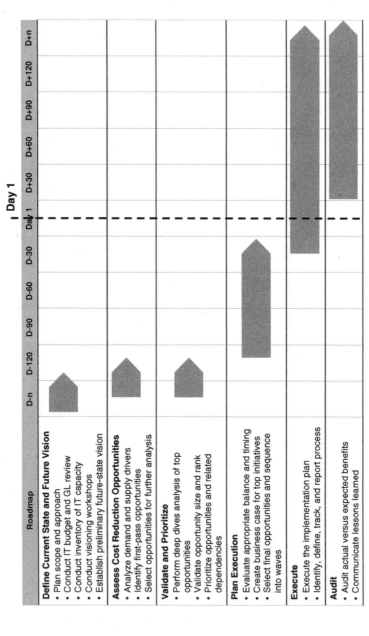

FIGURE 18.3 Sample Transactional IT Cost Reduction Roadmap

SERVICE ALLOCATION MODEL   The intent of addressing the model is to better align business consumption with actual costs. Merger, acquisition, and divestiture events typically require IT departments to provide and perform a detailed assessment of financial data and current allocations. This same data can be leveraged to improve the associated allocation methods and provide business with the transparency required to make effective investment decisions. The allocation categories appear in Figure 18.4, from least aligned (on left) to most aligned (on right).

ADJUST/REDUCE SERVICE LEVELS   The process of managing expectations around service levels usually goes hand in hand with a service-level review. A key step is to devise a common framework by which both entities' service levels can be reviewed. A periodic or event-triggered review of expected service levels can help bring down the total IT cost while only marginally adjusting service levels due to the continuous technology advances.

Private equity investors and other sophisticated M&A practitioners often require management to review and revise service levels as a part of the merger or acquisition process.

CONSIDERATIONS BY DEAL TYPE   The underlying business goals of the deal can influence the practical application of this cost reduction lever. Key considerations and critical success factors by deal types are illustrated in Figure 18.5.

IT Operating Model: Supply Side

Achieving IT cost reductions within the context of the *supply side* (people, processes, and technology) requires careful evaluation of the IT service model and its supporting management model. The decision process must be mindful of several factors—time

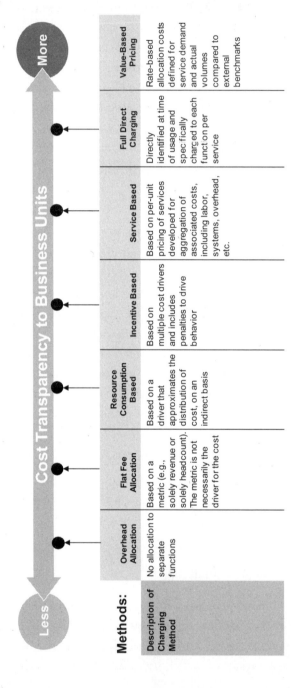

Cost Transparency to Business Units (Less → More)

Methods:

Description of Charging Method	Overhead Allocation	Flat Fee Allocation	Resource Consumption Based	Incentive Based	Service Based	Full Direct Charging	Value-Based Pricing
	No allocation to separate functions	Based on a metric (e.g., solely revenue or solely headcount). The metric is not necessarily the driver for the cost	Based on a driver that approximates the distribution of cost, on an indirect basis	Based on multiple cost drivers and includes penalties to drive behavior	Based on per-unit pricing of services developed for aggregation of associated costs, including labor, systems, overhead, etc.	Directly identified at time of usage and specfically charged to each funct on per service	Rate-based allocation costs defined for service demand and actual volumes compared to external benchmarks

FIGURE 18.4 IT Service Allocation Model

Operating Model—Demand Side

	Improve Service Allocation Model	Review and Reduce Service Levels		
Deal Type	**a. Assimilation**—Parent acquires and subsumes secondary organization.	**b. Metamorphosis**—Best components are integrated into a hybrid organization.	**c. Transformation**—New organization is established based on new end-state vision.	**d. Retention**—Merged entities retain individual IT operations.
Typical Approach Characteristics	• Parent's service allocation model and service levels are usually applied to secondary organization.	• Service allocation model and service levels are reviewed across organizations to determine most effective approach.	• Transformation-type deals provide the most viable environment to consider step-function improvements in service allocation model and service-level processes. • Mature service allocation models can be introduced as a part of the future-state vision.	• Service allocation model and service levels are typically retained by each organization. • While services are separate, common service allocation method may be adopted to streamline financial management.
Critical Success Factors	• Review any best practices in secondary organization before parent model and processes are applied.	• Strict enforcement of service-level reduction guidelines.	• Establish and execute against an end-state vision.	• If there are common business customers, steps should be taken to align service allocation models to improve long-term financial management.

FIGURE 18.5 IT Operating Model: Demand Side

horizon, costs, and organizational change and dynamics—in order for the effort to be successful.

OUTSOURCE/EXPAND SHARED SERVICES ORGANIZATION (SERVICE MODEL) The ideal future-state IT operating model will be dictated by the transaction type and the underlying objectives of the deal itself. Whether an acquisition is being undertaken with the *assimilation* or the *metamorphosis* approach, for example, will influence the decisions that need to be made around defining the final operating model best suited for the organization.

It is important to consider the short- and long-term time horizons and their balanced trade-offs when evaluating whether to outsource or further centralize the organization's IT functions. One of the key ways to reduce IT-related costs during a merger, acquisition, or divesture is to make and execute effective shared service and outsourcing decisions with short- and long-term cost reduction benefits.

Organizations sometimes shy away from making the deal and/or adopting necessary major shared service adoption or outsourcing decisions during a merger, acquisition, or divesture, fearful of causing too many short-term disruptions or driven by a desire to avoid incremental transition costs. This can be shortsighted, as the organization sacrifices (or trades off) its longer-term ability to benefit from laying a more stable foundation upon which to build.

While every situation is unique, an effective practice is generally to leverage the change environment (and associated budgets, finance, and business planning considerations) to drive through major operating model changes at the time of transaction. Often, writing off the merger-related expenses associated with establishing an outsourcing arrangement is greater than the cost of long-term amortization if those changes are undertaken over time.

250

Finally, from an organizational change perspective, experience has shown that enacting an outsourcing or shared service expansion can be more effectively positioned when the momentum and acceptance for change is at its strongest—and this is often in the weeks prior to and immediately after deal close.

MANAGEMENT MODEL   The complement to the immediacy of executing an outsourcing/shared service expansion is to take a phased approach after performing a detailed analysis that closely examines multiple management layers and cross-functional services (which can span IT project management to IT security). This model allows for the development and execution of a plan of action around the organization's application and infrastructure services that is closely linked to the required realignment processes and takes into account new reporting structures (organizational hierarchies).

Cost reduction in this category is made more difficult due to a framework comprised largely of subjective and hard-to-quantify characteristics for properly evaluating management. The pre-deal phase often provides the environment whereby management is put to the test. Final management decisions are often made soon after, but not before the deal closes. Regardless of the individuals who are hand-picked for key positions, it is critically important (from a cost reduction perspective) that the difficult decisions are not postponed and that discrete selections are made and executed upon completion of the transaction.

CONSIDERATIONS BY DEAL TYPE   The underlying business goals of the deal can greatly influence the practical application of this cost reduction lever. Key considerations and critical success factors by deal type are illustrated in Figure 18.6.

Operating Model—Supply Side	Expand Shared Services or outsourcing	Review Management Model		
Deal Type	**a. Assimilation**—Parent acquires and subsumes secondary organization.	**b. Metamorphosis**—Best components are integrated into a hybrid organization.	**c. Transformation**—New organization is established based on new end-state vision.	**d. Retention**—Merged entites retain individual IT operations.
Typical Approach Characteristics	• Parent's exiting operating model (outsourced or in-house) is typically adopted as the target state model in which secondary organization is integrated. • In this type of deal, parent tends not to change operating model. • If parent's IT functions are outsourced, the level and scale of change will be more significant for secondary organization.	• If one organization is outsourced and the other is in-house, the planning approach typically involves an analysis process to "objectively" assess respective models. However, analysis tends to support an implicit or explicit end-state strategy rather than the other way around.	• Outsourced solutions are often considered to stand up an end-state operating model that is distinct from the merged entities.	• Each individual entity tends to retain its existing operating model—in house or outsourced. • Certain common functions—such as help desk—may be integrated into a single outsourced provider.
Critical Success Factors	• If parent has outsourced functions, involve outsourced provider in early planning process. • Communicate strategy and rationale for strategy to secondary organization.	• Minimize the set of decision factors and associated analysis that will support the insourcing versus outsourcing decision—this will help ensure a targeted analysis process.	• Ensure sufficient back integration from selected solution back to current operations.	• Ensure that senior management makes an explicit decision to retain separate IT departments, and ensure that rationale for the decision is clear and logical.

FIGURE 18.6 IT Operating Model: Supply Side

Application Services

Cost reduction related to application services is typically driven around three focal areas: application rationalization, resource consolidation, and architecture standards.

RATIONALIZE APPLICATION PORTFOLIO Most organizations coming into a transaction have accumulated a variety of applications as a result of past acquisitions or business unit decisions. An M&A event provides a perfect trigger to streamline the application portfolio and align it to the required business capabilities to fuel future growth.

Cost reduction opportunities resulting from application rationalization are broad and can cover labor, software, hardware, third-party, and even facility savings. The process of analysis and execution should be tightly interwoven with other major initiatives, such as outsourcing or data center consolidation.

Given that the application portfolio most likely consists of hundreds of applications between the two merging organizations, the appropriate dispositioning of the applications should be approached by first grouping them into tiers. For example, the application portfolio can be broken down by broad functional categories:

- **Business facing.** Direct business function applications, such as sales force support, websites, and marketing applications
- **Enabling.** Indirect support function applications, including enterprise resource planning (ERP), financial, real estate, human resource, and other back-office applications

The scope of the cost reduction impact is typically greater for enabling applications as compared to business-facing applications. Within these categories, applications should be tiered based on a combination of importance and scale (e.g., Tier 1, Tier 2, Tier 3, etc.)

During pre-close planning, an effort should be made to disposition the Tier 1 applications and come up with the target state. Complex situations that may include competing ERP systems with similar-sized global footprints will require in-depth time-boxed blueprinting-based review and discussion, but these cases should be viewed as the exception rather than the norm. Most of the major application rationalization decisions should be made prior to the close of the deal, allowing the integration team to focus on consolidating legacy systems and "sunsetting" applications during the post-deal phase.

CONSOLIDATE/CENTRALIZE RESOURCES The current-state application landscape, support, and development model for the respective organizations needs to be measured against the future or target model and ties in closely with the application rationalization process. In order to effectively leverage this cost savings lever, the merging entities should profile their resource base against a common and agreed-upon set of capability profiles. Based on the significant offshoring component in many IT organizations, the capability profile must be linked with the location and compensation profile.

It goes without saying that any analysis related to personnel should be treated with utmost sensitivity, whether it is part of the pre-close phase or even after the deal has been successfully consummated.

It is critical to maintain a long-term perspective in reviewing this cost reduction lever. All too often, chief executive officers, chief financial officers, chief operating officers, and chief information officers focus on headcount rationalization as a method to meet short-term synergy targets, only to find that critical capabilities and knowledge have been eliminated, impacting critical business processes.

UPGRADE ARCHITECTURE STANDARDS   A major component of long-term cost management is upgrading architecture standards to consistently take advantage of improvements in programming and integration technologies. During a merger or acquisition, every organization should evaluate the respective entities' architectural standards and establish forward-looking standards for the merged entity.

CONSIDERATIONS BY DEAL TYPE   Based on the business goals of the deal, the application and impact of cost reduction levers can be very different; for example, in an assimilation-type deal, the focus will be on a transition to the primary organization's applications, application resources, and architectural standards. However, for a metamorphosis-type deal, the focus will be on selecting the right option across organizations, including potential hybrid options. Figure 18.7 shows key considerations and critical success factors by deal type.

Infrastructure and End-User Services

Cost reduction in infrastructure and end-user services is typically driven by three key elements to reduce costs during a merger or acquisition: consolidate data centers, rationalize duplicative functions, and adopt/expand new technologies.

CONSOLIDATE DATA CENTERS   Rationalization of the data center footprint is a key component of synergy savings during an acquisition. The scope of impact is usually dependent on the level of footprint overlap between the organizations and the level of excess capacity that can be leveraged to consolidate data centers. It is important to consider future data center growth requirements when implementing a data center consolidation strategy; short-term synergy targets should not be met at the expense of long-term cost management considerations.

Application Services	Rationalize Application Portfolio		Consolidate Centralize Resources		Rationalize Technology Platform
Deal Type	a. Assimilation—Parent organization acquires and subsumes secondary organization.	b. Metamorphosis—Best components are integrated into a hybrid organization.	c. Transformation—New organization is established based on new end-state vision.		d. Retention—Merged entities retain individual IT operations.
Typical Approach Characteristics	• Parent's organization transitions secondary organization to use of parent organization's applications.	• Detailed analysis and cost-benefit analysis or similar applications to select target application.	• Application portfolio is augmented by analysis of required application investments to support new business functions that will be added to support end-state vision.		• Individual entities maintain respective application portfolios, application resources, and architecture standards. • Elimination of obvious duplications of applications and associated resources.
Critical Success Factors	• Detailed analysis of secondary organization's application.	• Establishment of clear decision-making protocol for application categories—avoid decision-by-committee models.	• Balance cost reduction with targeted investment in new application capabilities.		• At minimum, perform basic application rationalization analysis —even in a retention-type deal, there are cost reduction opportunities.

FIGURE 18.7 Key Cost Reduction Considerations for Application Services

The implementation approach to data center consolidation during a merger or acquisition is the same as in a normal consolidation, except the level of change management will be higher. The unique aspects of the change management process will be aligning data center service level, support processes, and expectations across the respective organizations.

RATIONALIZE DUPLICATIVE FUNCTIONS Infrastructure and end-user service functions, especially highly commoditized functions, are prime targets for rationalization during a merger or acquisition. The execution of this cost reduction lever is linked to decisions on the operating model discussed earlier. Following are key infrastructure and end-user service functions to consider for rationalization.

- **Level 1 help desk.** The primary help desk is usually a key target for consolidation, especially if the function is outsourced across organizations. In order to minimize the impact on end-user experience, integration of the IT help desk is typically a requirement in most mergers.
- **Desktop and laptop support.** Desktop and laptop support functions should be integrated. However, the integration is usually predicated on centralization of financial responsibility for desktop and laptop assets.
- **Network monitoring.** This support function is a strong target for integration and rationalization of associated resources. Outsourcing/right-shoring strategies should be considered as a part of the transformation.

ADOPT/EXPAND NEW TECHNOLOGIES There is usually constant downward pressure on infrastructure service costs as a direct result of shifts and continued innovation in technology. Some technology changes are fairly easy to take advantage of as a part of normal operating procedures (e.g., storage *tiering* and reduction in storage costs); however, other technology shifts require major shifts in technology strategy, business processes, and investments to adopt.

It is precisely these technologies that should be the focus during a merger or acquisition. Companies should not shy away from innovation during a merger or acquisition, as these events often provide the required change window and one-time investments necessary to put in place the necessary technology that can significantly reduce the organization's future IT cost base.

Emerging technology options are usually driven by many urgent IT priorities and a desire by key stakeholders to:

- Reduce IT capital equipment spend.
- Lower implementation costs compared to on-premise solutions.
- Control the assets on the balance sheet.
- Optimize the required in-house IT resources.
- Treat cost as an operating expense (instead of as a capital expense).
- Gain flexibility and speed in implementations.
- Migrate internal IT focus away from pure infrastructure support to achieve improvements via deeper innovation.
- Allow greater ability to flexibly respond to the business as needs change.
- Reduce execution time frame while expanding flexibility in available options.
- Access readily available emerging technologies at a subsidized cost.

While many companies today are actively evaluating emerging market trends in response to the current dramatic economic downturn, they are not able to move forward aggressively. There is a mixed level of confidence with respect to adopting these emerging technologies as a viable alternative computing platform to their more traditional (and familiar) enterprise environments.

Business units are concerned about the ownership of data, associated controls, and increased complication around legal compliance and the like. Technical functions are concerned about scalability constraints, security gaps, reliability and availability of the infrastructure, and mitigation via backup, retention, and disaster recovery.

Some *software as a service* (SaaS) models incorporate Finance and Accounting business process outsourcing, but are not maturing rapidly due to the slow pace of adoption. (See Chapter 11 for a more complete discussion of SaaS.) SaaS support for large-enterprise supply chain/ERP is both technically and functionally immature.

Service-oriented architecture has addressed initial integration concerns, but many companies have already invested significantly in in-house ERP applications. In addition, the leading SaaS ERP vendors are not going to market aggressively enough to mute the value propositions being presented by the large ERP package players.

CONSIDERATIONS BY DEAL TYPE   Based on the business goals of the deal, the application and impact of cost reduction levers can be very different. Figure 18.8 shows key considerations and critical success factors by deal type.

Third-Party Contracts

Cost reduction in third-party contracts is typically driven by three key ways to reduce costs during a merger or acquisition: rationalize vendor base, renegotiate vendor rates, and optimize licensing.

Infrastructure and End-User Services	Consolidate Data Centers	Rationalize Duplicative Functions	Adopt/Expand New Technologies	
Deal Type	**a. Assimilation—** Parent acquires and subsumes secondary organization.	**b. Metamorphosis—** Best components are integrated into a hybrid organization.	**c. Transformation—** New organization is established based on new end-state vision.	**d. Retention—** Merged entities tend to retain individual IT operations.
Typical Approach Characteristics	• Secondary organization's data centers are shut down and services are transferred to parent data center.	• Two entities' data centers are merged into hybrid end-state footprint; typically, region-based approach is taken and a primary data center is selected in each region.	• Strategy is driven by end-state data center footprint that supports business goals— includes elimination of duplicate data centers and potential expansion in target regions.	• Individual entities tend to retain their individual data centers. • End-user (desktop support) functions are retained by business units. • Level 1 help desk tends to be integrated into single point of contact.
Critical Success Factors	• Ensure parent company's data centers have sufficient capacity to take over additional capacity.			

FIGURE 18.8 Key Cost Reduction Considerations for Infrastructure and End-User Services

RATIONALIZE VENDOR BASE   Reviewing and refreshing the vendor base is a critical step in any merger or acquisition initiative. The ability to reduce rates and renegotiate terms of engagement often depends on applying and executing against a real and viable threat of dropping vendors from the primary supplier list. The approach to a merger-related vendor rationalization program should be tiered based on importance and size of vendor relationships; negotiations should be staggered through progressively lower tiers and smaller vendors.

A key vendor base to assess during a merger or acquisition is the outsourcing service providers. Outsourcing agreements contractually provide an avenue to renegotiate the contract in the wake of a major change event. Scope, pricing, and future requirements of the deal should all be considered during the negotiation.

RENEGOTIATE VENDOR RATES   The greater economies of scale resulting from a merger or acquisition provide the impetus to demand higher volume discounts and preferential rates from vendors, especially key vendor relationships. This process should be closely tied with an overall benchmarking of market rates to provide a basis for comparison and negotiation.

OPTIMIZE LICENSING   This cost reduction opportunity is grouped under the third-party contract cost category and is interactively linked to demand reduction due to the cost reduction opportunities listed earlier. The organization should start with a pre-merger baseline of all major licenses and usage counts; headcount or service reduction initiatives should be tied to a systematic reduction in license volumes.

CONSIDERATIONS BY DEAL TYPE   Based on the business goals of the deal, the application and impact of cost reduction levers can be very different. Figure 18.9 shows key considerations and critical success factors by deal type.

Cost Reduction during Divesture

The techniques outlined here for cost reduction during divestiture are focused on the parent company and how the parent can effectively use the divestiture process to reduce its overall IT cost base. There are two key components to cost management during a divestiture:

1. **Reducing parent's IT cost base.** This requires offsetting the reduction in demand (resulting from the act of divestiture) with a parallel or greater reduction in the supply cost base.

2. **Negotiating and executing effective transition service agreements (TSAs).** This helps ensure the parent company effectively services the divested unit for a 3- to 36-month+ period.

REDUCING PARENT'S IT COST BASE   The levers for reducing the parent's IT cost base are more focused on the demand side of the equation to enable transformational shifts such as process-level sourcing decisions and evaluation of shared computing opportunities in tandem with application rationalization and data center consolidation. All of these activities are undertaken to recalibrate to the new and lower demand.

At a minimum, the post-divesture parent company should have a neutral IT cost basis. In general, the cost basis is expected to be lowered by the size of the IT demand being divested. This is not possible due to certain stranded fixed costs that cannot be eliminated. As a result, in order to achieve the expected IT cost reduction, the following three systematic measures have to be taken:

Third-Party Contracts

Deal Type	Rationalize Vendor Base	Renegotiate Vendor Rates	Optimize Licenses	
	a. Assimilation— Parent organization acquires and subsumes secondary organization.	**b. Metamorphosis—** Best components are integrated into a hybrid organization.	**c. Transformation—** New organization is established based on new end-state vision.	**d. Retention—** Merged entities retain individual IT operations.
Typical Approach Characteristics	• Parent organization's primary vendors are typically selected for future organization. • Secondary organization is transitioned off vendors that are not primary vendors for parent organization.	• Optimal vendor base is selected from across organizations.	• Vendor base is rationalized; however, select vendors may be added to fill new capability requirements associated with future-state vision.	• Vendor base is maintained to support both organizations. • Common rates are negotiated for shared vendors.
Critical Success Factors	• Establishment of a communication program to appropriately communicate with deselected vendors. • Effective management of vendor switching process.	• Clear decision criteria are established to ensure decision-making process is quick and effective; different decisions are assigned to individual resources rather than decision making by committee.	• Early identification of missing vendor capabilities.	• Execution of common contracts and rates, even if usage of contracts is independent.

FIGURE 18.9 Key Cost Reduction Considerations for Third-Party Contracts

1. Business will need to revalidate the expected services from IT given the new, smaller footprint of the organization.
2. The IT function should benchmark itself against the new, smaller anticipated baseline and publish the results to the executive team.
3. A detailed IT cost reduction roadmap driven by detailed guiding principles and a robust analytical framework must be developed as early as possible. An aggressively driven blueprinting exercise can help lay out the transition state and the future state of the organization.

Projects should be categorized (as depicted in Figure 18.10) into TSA-related projects, business-related projects, and separation-related projects.

Certain organizations have gone beyond lowering the cost base by the size of the IT demand being divested by using the divesture event to push through larger cost reduction initiatives that have met or could meet highest resistance if attempted during normal business conditions. Key among these is evaluating outsourcing by the entire process value chain versus applications or infrastructure aspects. Also, providing added cost transparency to the business unit helps the executive make effective foundational decisions such as degree of sourcing.

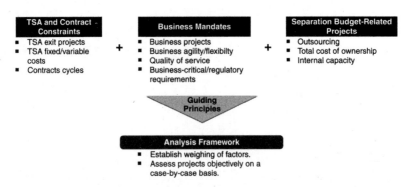

FIGURE 18.10 IT Project Analysis Framework

	Degree of Separation →			
	Limited	**Logical**	**Physical**	**Isolation**
Infrastructure	Shared	Shared	Shared/Separated	Separated
Applications	Shared	Shared/Separated	Separated	Separated
Data	Shared	Shared/Separated	Separated	Separated
IT Services	Shared	Shared	Shared	Shared/Separated
Access	Open	Constrained	Restricted	Very Limited

FIGURE 18.11 Degrees of Separation and Associated Impacts

The parent entity's IT organization should critically evaluate the degree of separation to be targeted (by infrastructure, applications, data, IT services, and access) while setting up the enabling environments for the entity being carved out or spun off. The degree of separation will impact the IT cost reduction mandates. Figure 18.11 lays out the impact by thread, depending on the degree of separation.

In general, the more separation completed up front, the less onerous the TSAs. However, the one-time restructuring costs will be higher.

Once the degree of separation is agreed on, the actual carve-out options by applications suites should be finalized. There are four basic carve-out options to consider:

1. **Transition.** Transfer ownership of appropriate portions of the application portfolio to "NewCo" (delete or vitiate sensitive master and transactional data according to scope of the divestiture). From a cost reduction perspective, this is beneficial since there is a direct drop to actual run rate of the parent organization.

2. **Data transfer.** Extract and transfer the required NewCo master and open transactional data to NewCo for loading, by NewCo, onto NewCo systems. This reduces required TSAs since the data has been replicated, but the stranded costs of a system that is not fully utilized will have to be borne by the parent until the system is retired.

3. **Copy and cleanse.** Copy the existing system onto a separate instance for NewCo; then delete or clean out sensitive non-NewCo master and transactional data according to scope of the carve-out. This eliminates the need for that system or function since the functionality has been replicated for the parent. This can be the fastest and least expensive solution if done with existing infrastructure in the parent's portfolio and can help reduce total cost of ownership and eliminate stranded costs for the parent.

4. **New implementation.** A new application is developed for NewCo with a focus on standard functionality. Data will still need to be extracted, transformed, and loaded for NewCo. This is time intensive but can help the parent reduce its cost footprint if done with existing infrastructure that is repurposed.

NEGOTIATING AND EXECUTING EFFECTIVE TSAS Before reviewing effective cost management or reduction techniques during a TSA, it must be noted as a general concept that TSAs should be avoided as much as possible if IT is not typically a service that the parent sells to third parties. Although a parent can put in place measures to cost-effectively manage a TSA, because it is not the parent's core business the company will always struggle to execute the service effectively.

Negotiating effective TSAs is built on a clear vision for how IT services will be delivered during the TSA period. Due to security requirements, it is rare that IT services are provided "as is" to the carved-out or stand-alone divested unit. Typically, some level of logical of physical separation has to be introduced. For standup of isolated application or environment instances, an outsourcing provider (e.g., Oracle on demand) can be considered versus building a new environment in-house.

For the parent organization, TSAs are a mechanism through which legally agreed-upon market rate–driven services can be provided to the entity being carved out or spun off while the parent focuses on bringing down the IT cost structure. In most cases, the scale-down of IT services and capacity is not immediate. TSAs afford a means by which some of these stranded costs can be shared by and accounted for in the interim state.

Conclusion

There are significant cost savings opportunities during a merger, acquisition, or divesture. Following are practices to consider for an effective execution:

1. Align IT cost reduction focus with the business strategy and integration or divestiture plan.
2. Plan for IT cost reduction in parallel with the integration or separation activities. Work to get IT cost reduction on the table as early as the target screening or due diligence phase.
3. Adopt a centralized management structure, and staff the management office with resources that are focused on identifying, tracking, and communicating the IT cost reduction initiatives.
4. Use desired end-state target company comparative benchmarking to develop top-down baseline targets for the potential IT cost savings.
5. Structure IT cost reduction in two phases: pre-close planning and post-close execution. The post-close phase would typically be long term with a one-to-three-year time horizon.
6. Build quantifiable cost reduction targets into the goals and objectives of the IT functional leads (i.e., application lead, infrastructure lead, governance lead, etc.).
7. Build in a safety factor since a percentage of synergy tends to evaporate.

IT cost reduction should be approached holistically and strategically in alignment with business goals in the context of mergers, acquisitions, or divestitures. The approach and segmentation described in this chapter should help an organization achieve permanent cost reduction potential and set it up for continued efficient IT operations.

CHAPTER 19

Effective Approaches for Managing IT during a Merger, Acquisition, or Divestiture

Anna Y. Lea Doyle

S o, you've got a merger, acquisition, and divestiture (MA&D) transaction facing you. As a result, you are probably wondering what the big deal is and how it is different from a typical information technology (IT) project. Well, there are three key differences that a financial executive should know about prior to launching the IT portion of the transaction:

1. New terminology
2. Faster pace
3. New challenges for IT

The IT department will face pressures from familiar and new angles. In this chapter, we will explore each of these differences and introduce new concepts for you to consider in your efforts to manage your MA&D deal from an IT perspective.

New Terminology

Mergers, acquisitions, and divestitures come with language that may be new to IT as well as to the rest of the organization.

Table 19.1 provides some of the key terms with which the IT area must be familiar.

There may be slight variations in the application of these terms from deal to deal; therefore, it is important to consult with your corporate development team to be aligned in the use of the MA&D terminology for your organization.

Faster Pace

MA&D deals typically move quickly through *due diligence* (identify risks, likely synergies, and high-level integration strategy and timeline), slow down through bid and negotiation processes, and then accelerate to deal close and Day 1. In the due diligence and preparation for deal close and Day 1, IT will be pressured to move fast with limited information and a high degree of hedging due to the unknowns. Integration and divestiture timelines require rapid formulation of the IT plans and ultimately execution. These types of transactions generally move much more rapidly than a traditional IT project.

Buying as much time as possible to give IT the runway necessary to prepare for Day 1 is vital. Some techniques include:

- Use a clean team (secured servers, paper files with monitored check-in and check-out procedures) in areas where data privacy and complying with complying with all legal regulations (Hart-Scott-Rodino Act, European Union Merger Regulations) that restrict data sharing prior to approval (e.g., customer data, products, pricing, intellectual property).
- Jump-start IT planning during pre-deal close.
- Focus on Day 1 *must-haves* (e.g., integration of e-mail, networks, telephony, calling cards, personal digital assistants, financial close processes and management reporting, and website rebranding) and address the nice-to-have items if time permits.

TABLE 19.1 Key Terms for MA&D Transactions

Term	Description
Day 0/Deal Close	*Day 0* is also referred to as *deal close* or *legal close*, whereby the acquirer is legally responsible for the acquired entity or assets.
Day 1	*Day 1* is a point in time when the target is declared as integrated into the acquirer (even if minimally). It is typically the next business day after the deal close. It is also common for organizations to close the deal, but declare a Day 1 event in the future (not integrated initially/stand-alone for a period of time). Day 1 is generally declared across the entire MA&D program.
TSA	*Transition service agreements (TSAs)* are temporary agreements generally for 12 to 24 months for services to be provided by the seller to the buyer. It is also common to have *reverse TSAs*, where the buyer needs to provide services back to the seller.
Clean Team	*Clean teams* are launched to protect sensitive information (e.g., price list, contracts, and customer names and terms) from openly being shared between the acquirer and target prior to the deal close (i.e., Day 0). They are somewhat like a brick wall through which information must be carefully passed. Information within the clean team/room is used by designated individuals (e.g., current employees, retirees, or consultants) to perform analysis (e.g., jump-start synergy or integration planning activities). The information exchange is monitored and tracked (check-in and check-out). If the deal does not move forward, all information in the clean room is destroyed or handled as defined in the nondisclosure agreement between the potential seller and buyer. Your legal team should prescribe the dos and don'ts of handling sensitive information.
End State/Day 2	Fully integrated into buyer or separated from parent (no TSA dependency between buyers and seller). Functions may reach *end state* (or *Day 2*) at different times.

- Clearly define the degree of integration across all functions by Day 1. IT will be relied on as the enabler of related functions success for Day 1 (e.g., payroll conversion, legal entity structure additions/changes, first financial close, enhanced management reporting, or changes to external-facing documents for logos, addresses, and tax identification numbers).
- *Adopt and go* as much as possible. Identify the most effective process or system of either party and go with it. Avoid tendencies to reengineer. The most complex situation is *transform and integrate* (new or changed processes and systems while integrating or divesting).
- Start with the end state in mind. Lay out IT integration plans on a path to achieve the integrated end state (e.g., IT locations of operation, enterprise resource planning solutions entirely integrated, data centers integrated with appropriate business continuity plans, integrated IT organization and IT service delivery model, and secured integrated network with appropriate data privacy and security controls).

Keeping ahead of the other functions and meeting management expectations can and will be challenging at times. The faster pace may introduce program risks and burnout. Include IT program management and IT employee retention on your IT speed radar. Even the best plans can be successfully executed only with a high-performing team all headed on the same integration or divestiture path.

New Challenges for IT

Many IT shops have a *systems development* (SD) methodology. For MA&D deals, parts of the SD methodology apply; however, many lack the MA&D-specific considerations (topics and faster pace). For example, the project management thread of the methodology is typically appropriate (IT project management office, governance, milestone and detail plans, monitoring issues, risks and actions). MA&D deals introduce challenges for IT that are not typically faced on regular IT projects, such as:

- Adjusting the IT operating model
- Achieving IT synergies
- Developing (or enhancing) MA&D capabilities
- Managing the IT employee experience
- Minimizing TSAs
- Preparing for Day 1 readiness

It is critical for IT to be aware of these areas and ensure they are addressed as part of the overall deal strategy.

Adjusting the IT Operating Model

Integrations or divestitures typically introduce a change in the required IT services or service levels. An IT operating model is a combination of the IT organization and capabilities, IT services, service levels, and service delivery locations, all within an affordable IT cost structure and based on business demand. When a merger or divestiture occurs, the existing IT operating model may need to be adjusted to fit the end-state requirements. For example, in a merger of a multinational target with significant regional operations, due consideration to the IT operating locations and the types of services to be provided at the locations may change (e.g., increase or decrease in demand and supply). In a divestiture, the IT services required by the business may be smaller or less demanding service-level agreements on service provision.

Revisiting the IT operating model should be addressed early in the deal cycle so it can influence the plans of any merger, acquisition, or divestiture. An integration or divestiture provides the opportunity for IT to determine whether the right IT services are being delivered at the required service level.

Achieving IT Synergies

IT will be expected to be one of the greatest contributors of synergies in integrations and divestitures alike. Furthermore, many other functions will require technology enablement to successfully integrate or separate while achieving synergy targets.

Ingredients for successful IT synergy programs include:

- Dedicate an IT synergy team with formal IT synergy planning and tracking.
- Develop a synergy plan linked to the IT budget (great motivator).
- Plan for synergy leakage (i.e., identify opportunities to exceed the synergy target by approximately 50 percent).
- Include key synergy initiatives on your overall IT milestone plan.

It will be vital to understand other functional integration and synergy plans (like Finance, Human Resources, Supply Chain) and the dependencies among them as well as on IT for success. Synergies should be planned as carefully as the integration or separation activities.

Developing MA&D Capabilities

Another consideration is whether you will become a serial or parallel acquirer. Do you have the team to lead multiple mergers, acquisitions, or divestitures? Do they understand the key trade-offs and the degree of integration desired by leadership?

Can they rapidly perform integrations or divestitures? At what point does the organization strain under the volume of MA&D deals?

There are additional factors at play when rapidly integrating/ divesting serial or parallel MA&D deals. Successful serial acquirers have key integration or separation capabilities, processes, or tools to manage and execute the serial or parallel deals based on deal scenarios (e.g., degree of integration, deal type—integration or separation, lines of business(es) impacted, and time to Day 1). Some organizations design and implement repeatable processes and procedures as well as define their core and extended team members with expertise in integration or separation activities.

To effectively manage IT within one MA&D deal is very strenuous, let alone many deals. An effective practice is to use a current MA&D deal to build your *IT playbook* of repeatable processes/procedures, tools, and checklists. Furthermore, it will be imperative that the playbook be a living instrument that captures lessons learned and additional procedures or tools along the way.

Managing the IT Employee Experience

Mergers, acquisitions, and divestitures are very stressful to the employee base. They wonder about such things as impact to pay and benefits; who will be their boss; changes to performance management; how to get assistance to payroll, IT, procurement questions; whether their laptop/desktop will come with them; and what happens to their data (electronic and paper).

An effective technique is to prepare a *Day 1 welcome guide* (for IT and the rest of the organization) addressing what will change, what is not changing, what is the new help desk number to call, who can be called to procure a new laptop, whether e-mail addresses change, and so on. The IT department may even be called on to implement a site on the intranet dedicated to the integration or divestiture (e.g., project news, progress, Day 1 communications). The key is to take the mystery out (where possible) and overcommunicate even if decisions have not been made.

Another consideration is keeping your IT integration or separation team motivated to stay focused on successfully achieving key milestones while keeping the lights on in support of day-to-day business activities. Consider the use of retention or bonus pay for your IT integration or separation team based on milestone achievement or contribution to the integration or separation. Since a lot of blood, sweat, and tears will go into the integration or separation on top of their daily responsibilities, your top performers will appreciate your acknowledgment of their dedication and stellar performance.

Minimizing TSAs

The development and management of TSAs is not a typical IT project consideration. Transition service agreements temporarily provide services between the buyer and seller until the service recipient no longer requires them. TSAs look and feel like a contract and require engaging with your legal or contract administration organizations. Furthermore, tax implications can arise based on the service provider location and service delivery location, so remember to get input from your tax department.

TSAs can allow time to determine the final solution and reduce risk associated with potential business disruption. It is important for the financial executive to keep in mind that TSAs will come with additional management requirements (track change orders or termination of service orders, service-level monitoring, invoicing or payment processes). Whether you are the provider of services to a buyer or the recipient of services as the buyer, it is often best to keep the number of TSAs to a minimum.

Readiness for Day 1

Day 1 readiness is about ensuring that key Day 1 must-haves for IT have been designed and tested, appropriate mock cutover and training was performed, support processes have been bolstered, and sign-off for approval to proceed has been achieved (*go now/go later*). Day 1 must-haves revolve around legal and regulatory compliance as well as maintaining business continuity (no business disruption).

Leading up to Day 1, regular tracking of these key items in the IT roadmap and informal assessments of readiness (go now/go later) should be performed in coordination with contingency planning around key failure points.

Some key considerations include:

- Global reach/global readiness for the transition (testing, new and interim policies and procedures such as help desk, break/fix services, provision of end-user training)
- Degree of change in processes impacting key stakeholders (customers, employees, and suppliers)
- Likelihood of failure

Day 1 readiness is about the proactive planning, scenario role-play, and support structures (special-purpose action teams, help line, etc.) to minimize business disruption due to the integration or separation activities. Readiness for Day 1 is like an insurance policy that is rarely used.

Conclusion

Most IT methodologies have approaches, processes, and tools that are table stakes for implementing systems. An MA&D deal builds on them and requires even further attention to detail, rapid decision making that sticks, alignment with business needs, and the IT recipe (playbook) for successful integration or separation projects.

CHAPTER 20

Ways to Use Mergers, Acquisitions, or Divestitures to Build Sustainable Information Technology Value

Peter J. Blatman
Joseph Joy

The "secret sauce" required to realize the expected business value from mergers, acquisitions, and divestitures can be described succinctly as *doing the right things, and doing them right*. With respect to information technology (IT), "doing the right things" is ensuring that all planned post-transaction IT initiatives are aligned with the business/synergy objectives of the transaction itself. "Doing them right" is executing these planned IT initiatives flawlessly by adhering to rigorous project management methodologies and staffing all projects in a cost-effective manner. When you stop to think about it, these are the things that financial and technology executives should be focused on *all the time*.

With this thought in mind:

- In what ways can financial executives, in collaboration with the chief information officers (CIOs), extend mergers and acquisitions (M&A) IT best practices beyond the microcosm of an individual merger, acquisition, or divestiture transaction and bring similar high levels of intensity, visibility, and focus to their full IT agendas, including measurement of return on investment and business value delivered?

- In what ways can IT organizations realize potential M&A-like benefits (e.g., synergy capture, cost reduction, and efficiency/effectiveness improvement) for all IT projects by adopting the well-established project management disciplines of focused planning, rapid execution, and benefits tracking to enable IT to become more agile and responsive to ever-changing business requirements?
- In what ways can financial executives work with the CIOs to use M&A and divestiture transactions as springboards for building sustainable, business-aligned IT capabilities that provide incremental, ongoing business value?

Based on our extensive M&A and divestiture consulting experience, we believe many of the typical tactical activities, decision criteria, and opportunities associated with M&A IT integration programs can be beneficially applied to business-as-usual IT agendas with a sharp focus on building sustainable IT-enabled business value. The $64,000 question is: Where do you start?

In order to harness the value of M&A best practices, financial executives and CIOs must, first and foremost, understand the critical role played by IT in achieving targeted M&A synergies and, moreover, how to leverage those synergies to deliver well-defined business value. Potential M&A synergies may vary by industry sector and the particulars of an individual transaction, but irrespective of the specific synergies anticipated, it is IT that most often makes the difference between rhetoric and results. Synergies are meaningless unless the source can be identified and worthless unless they add economic value by reducing

	Reduce Costs	Increase Market Share	Enter or Create New Markets
Shared Overhead	Eliminate duplicate IS roles and functions Reduce support costs through standardization		
Economies of Scale	Common technologies, platforms, and systems Combined IT procurement	State-of-the-art scheduling, forecasting, or yield management Global systems	Combined electronic delivery channel infrastructure
Cross-fertilization	Groupware, intranets, workflow	Customer database Data mining	Selling derivative information Channel innovation
Operational Integration	Integrated operational systems— for example, production, forecasting and logistics workflow engine	Order-entry or customer-facing systems Data warehouse Internet presence	Truly integrated products/services
Synthesis of Capabilities	Computer-assisted design IT technology transfer	Uncommitted product and customer models	Cross-industry business models Content/context/conduit

FIGURE 20.1 Sample IT M&A Synergy Enablers

costs, increasing market share, or supporting the creation of new markets, as shown in Figure 20.1.

During post-transaction integration activities, a company's focus should be squarely on achievement of these well-defined synergy targets and capture of associated business benefits. In supporting everyday business operations, the company is similarly challenged to control IT operating costs while identifying and exploiting opportunities for IT to help the business compete more efficiently and effectively. Absent the well-defined targets typically associated with an M&A or divestiture transaction, we believe a company's focus must be balanced across four primary dimensions of achievable IT-enabled business value, as depicted in Figure 20.2.

Furthermore, the relative emphasis given to each of these dimensions will require prioritization reflecting consideration of individual organizational characteristics, competitive landscape, and business cycle phase. For example, in a downturn economy, a company's focus will generally be skewed toward IT initiatives delivering *near-term economic impact* (e.g., IT-enabled cost reduction), whereas in a steady-state or growing economy,

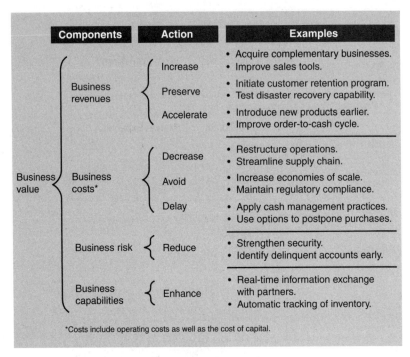

FIGURE 20.2 Dimensions of IT-Enabled Value
Source: Deloitte Consulting LLP.

the dominant focus will likely be skewed toward IT initiatives with *long-term strategic impact* (e.g., enhancement of business capabilities), as shown in Figure 20.3.

In much the same way that companies must understand how to employ IT to both achieve M&A synergies and leverage them to deliver targeted M&A business benefits (as discussed earlier in this chapter), they must similarly understand what *levers* are available to them to drive business value across the four dimensions of potential business benefits in the everyday environment. An analytical look at the *IT value chain* (shown in Figure 20.4) brings to light three key levers that companies must understand how and when to engage in order to be better positioned to maximize overall IT-enabled business results.

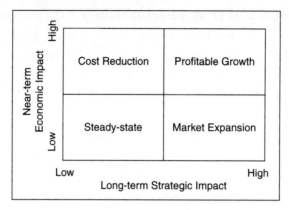

FIGURE 20.3 Business Cycle–Related IT Focus Objectives

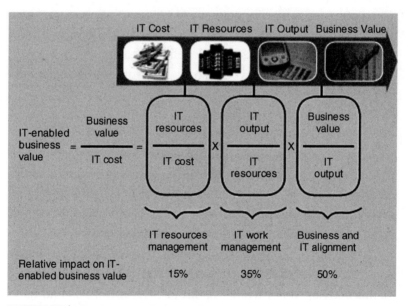

FIGURE 20.4 The IT Value Chain and IT Business Value Levers

Source: Deloitte Consulting LLP.

1. **Business and IT alignment.** Spending IT dollars only on initiatives with the *potential* (i.e., properly executed and resourced) to enable delivery of business benefits
2. **IT work management.** Applying rigorous IT program/ project management techniques to successfully deliver business-aligned IT initiatives
3. **IT resource management.** Securing and applying resources (both people and technology) to execute business-aligned IT initiatives in the most cost-effective manner

Engaging the *business and IT alignment lever* requires a clear understanding of what IT capabilities are required to enable the business capabilities that ultimately support overarching business goals and objectives. In an M&A situation, a company's focus must be on IT initiatives (e.g., rationalizing of applications) that will drive specific business benefits that align with the stated intent of the deal (e.g., revenue growth, market positioning, cost reduction).

In a business-as-usual scenario, companies must understand what IT initiatives are required to deliver the IT capabilities required to support both near-term and longer-term business goals. Development of comprehensive business-driven IT strategic plans and/or implementation of business-driven *project portfolio management* (PPM) systems are both well-established means of identifying goal-supporting IT initiatives.

Engaging the *IT work management lever* requires familiarity with effective best-practice program and project management methodologies, frameworks, and tools. Organizations that have grown through acquisition or have gone through multiple divestitures frequently develop *playbooks* that spell out, in detail, the sequencing and specifics of IT initiatives (e.g., IT organization rationalization) and the synchronization with business initiatives (e.g., business process integration) required to achieve stated transaction objectives.

In a business-as-usual scenario, financial executives and CIOs must be familiar with the appropriate set of program and project management methodologies and tools to be utilized across a range of everyday IT projects and activities (e.g., applications development, break-fixing, etc.). Many high-performance IT organizations have adopted the playbook concept and have installed the types of well-defined methodologies and tool sets used to execute post-merger integration IT initiatives. In addition, the separation of steady-state IT work from *interrupt-driven* IT work can increase overall IT work management efficiency.

Engaging the *IT resource management lever* requires an identification of both the skill sets and resources necessary to cost-effectively execute a set of defined IT initiatives. In an M&A environment, this may encompass reduction in indirect spending by pooling the purchasing power of both organizations to reduce hardware, software, and telecom costs and/or negotiating improved discounts for current third-party services. In divestiture situations, astute "buyers," as a condition of the transaction, may require "sellers" to provide current IT services via *transition services agreements* over a defined period of time to provide the buyer sufficient time to design and install an effective and efficient long-term IT services delivery capability.

In a business-as-usual scenario, economic downturns may provide an opportunity to renegotiate hardware, applications, and vendor services contracts. A simultaneous reexamination of the skills necessary to support the full range of IT development and support activities, and available third-party support options can yield insights into effective but less costly means of delivering IT services (e.g., moving applications support and/or help desk operations to more cost-effective offshore locations) while bringing into sharper focus those activities that require greater levels of business knowledge and skill to be better positioned to maximum business benefits (e.g., IT PPM and IT governance). For these higher-value, "measure twice, cut once" activities, such as IT strategic planning, an in-house support model might be more appropriate and effective.

Conclusion

Mergers, acquisitions, and divestitures are truly microcosms of the broader set of everyday IT planning and operational activities. They should be embraced by companies as opportunities to learn, adopt, and adapt well-honed IT planning techniques, efficient IT program and project management methodologies, and effective approaches to IT technology and people resource management to everyday IT initiatives.

In M&A and divestiture situations, CIOs usually have well-defined targets and must understand how to use IT to pragmatically achieve and leverage anticipated deal synergies to deliver business benefits. In everyday situations, CIOs need to establish appropriate targets balanced across revenue growth, overall cost reduction, risk reduction, and business capability enhancement, appropriately influenced by business cycle and other factors. CIOs need to further understand the IT levers of business and IT alignment, IT work management, and IT resource management available to them to achieve these targets and how to use them effectively to achieve targeted business benefits.

CHAPTER 21

Time-Tested Approaches to Maintaining Data Integrity during a Merger, Acquisition, or Divestiture

Sheri Fedokovitz
Jason McClain

An organization's data often plays a key role in a merger, acquisition, or divestiture. Whereas data is often one of the less visible assets of an organization, during a merger, acquisition, or divestiture, successful data integration or data separation can be a key contributor to the success or failure of the transaction.

Along with the process of integrating or separating an organization's data, the integrity or quality of the data plays an equally important role in the overall success or failure of the transaction. Data that lacks integrity or is of poor quality can present challenges to the integration or divestiture objectives. However, high-quality data can help expedite the integration or divestiture.

This chapter outlines the potential impact that data can have on a merger, acquisition, or divestiture along with some key areas that should be considered to address the potential impacts.

Potential Impacts of Poor-Quality Data

The business case for a merger and acquisition (M&A) event often includes assumptions or dependencies that rely on the successful integration or separation of an organization's data. These assumptions or dependencies often do not take into account the relative quality or integrity of the data. Data that lacks integrity or is of poor quality all too often derails the best-defined data integration or separation plans.

In addition to potential impacts to the business case, poor-quality data, or data that lacks integrity, can lead to unforeseen financial risk and potential loss of shareholder value. If the integrity of financial data is comprised, this may lead to the delay in timely communications of financial results to investors, which in turn could impact the organization's credit rating and access to capital.

The following are some examples that underscore the importance of maintaining the integrity of data during an M&A event.

Missed Timelines = Missed Planned Benefits

M&A events are often predicated on being able to achieve certain planned benefits within a predefined period of time. Often there are certain planned benefits that can be either directly or indirectly tied to an organization's data.

For example, a planned benefit may be to capitalize on the combined customer base within the first 90 days of an acquisition. In order to capitalize on the combined customer base, there is an assumption that both the acquired and the acquiring organization have customer data that can be efficiently integrated together. Inherent in this assumption is that both organizations' customer data is of sufficient quality and consistency to allow it to be integrated in a timely manner.

A common misstep in this process is that assumptions are made about the quality of the data without any quantitative analysis to back up the assumptions. Unfortunately, if the assumptions about the quality of the data are incorrect, there may be an adverse effect on the projected timelines and ultimately on the planned benefit.

Introduction of Data Integrity Problems

During the data integration process, an organization is vulnerable to many risks. In particular, organizations are vulnerable to increased financial risk due to the potential of introducing data integrity problems or furthering existing data-quality problems within key applications. While this risk exists for any data integration effort, it is more prevalent when integrating data that comes from an organization that has a different governance and control structure.

The following are examples of the financial risks an organization may face if poor-quality data is integrated into a new environment:

- Inability to produce reliable financial statements in a timely manner due to data-quality issues with key financial data
- Financial and other key decisions being made based on inaccurate data
- Potential compliance penalties related to customer interactions (e.g., e-mail, phone calls) that are inconsistent with a customer's preferences due to inaccurate opt-out data
- Loss of customer confidence due to disruptions (e.g., incorrect pricing or terms, inaccurate or missed shipments)

Time-Tested Approaches to Help Maintain the Integrity of the Data

There are several proven approaches that can contribute to maintaining the integrity of the data during an M&A event.

Execute an Assessment of Critical Data

While it is often not feasible to assess the integrity of a target organization's data prior to the formalization of an acquisition, it is important that an assessment of critical data be conducted immediately upon the commencement of the integration. The assessment should be focused on the key data domains in an effort to identify any data integrity issues that need to be addressed as part of the integration efforts. Planning for this assessment should be a part of the overall integration plan, as the output of the assessment can impact the strategy for data combination/separation.

For example, as part of a complex acquisition, a large telecommunications company performed a detailed data assessment of the customer data of the acquired company. In addition to clarifying the data integrity issues within the acquired customer data, this assessment also accomplished several other business objectives:

- Identified customer overlap between the existing and acquired customer bases
- Determined the most profitable relationships within the new combined organization
- Provided a framework for proposed customer base segmentation

The output of this assessment was used as key inputs into the overall business and IT integration plan.

Establish a Repeatable Data Integration or Separation Process for Key Data Domains

Based on an organization's industry and business characteristics, each organization has key data domains that contain valuable intellectual capital about the organization's business. These data domains may be an organization's customer data, product data, and/or another master data domain. Often these data domains play an important role in the planned benefits of an M&A event. As such, organizations should consider establishing a standardized and repeatable process for the integration or separation of this data for key data domains.

For example, a leading consumer business company, with a history of frequent acquisitions, assessed its ability to efficiently integrate newly obtained customer data with its existing customer data. The company determined that if it could accelerate the integration of an acquired organization's customer data, it could positively impact the success of the acquisition. In order to do so, the organization established a process to efficiently and effectively assess the quality of a potential target company's data. The results of the data-quality assessment were then utilized to customize a preestablished process to efficiently integrate the customer data into its existing customer base. By focusing on the development of a repeatable and efficient process, the company was able to significantly reduce the time needed to integrate the acquired organization's customer data. This resulted in the organization being able to efficiently capitalize on the combined customer base, thereby providing it with the ability to more rapidly capitalize on the integration and accelerate the achievement of its desired business benefits.

While no two integrations will be the same, the key is for organizations to have an established approach to facilitate the data integration or separation process.

Maintain Control of the Data

Due to the nature of M&A events, the timeline for certain data-related activities is often accelerated. As such, many times the need exists to introduce additional manual reporting processes, which in turn often lead to an increase in financial risk.

For example, a common challenge organizations face during an acquisition is related to the ability to report consolidated financial data on a timely basis. All too often, the need to report consolidated data occurs before the various financial systems are appropriately integrated. In these cases, organizations turn to manual-laden procedures to produce the necessary reporting. In this example, organizations should ensure that the necessary detective controls (e.g., enhanced quality assurance reviews of manual processes, robust reconciliations) are in place to help mitigate the increased risk introduced by manual procedures.

While certain manual processes may be necessary, it is important for the organization to understand, design, and implement the necessary financial controls associated with these processes to ensure that the manual processes do not introduce errors or other undesired consequences.

Conclusion

The approaches outlined in this chapter are intended not only to help ensure that the integrity of data is maintained during an M&A event but also to help mitigate the applicable risks associated with maintaining the integrity of the data. Approaches described, such as an assessment of critical data, established repeatable processes, and a robust control environment, can help achieve a successful and timely integration during a merger, acquisition, or divestiture.

Glossary

A

access mechanism The device or method by which logical or physical access is obtained.

account analyst A resource that executes transactional steps to enter data and performs analysis on the output of the data.

acquirer The company taking ownership of another company, also known as the *parent company*, upon completion of the acquisition.

acquisition A transaction where one company acquires another company.

assertion A declaration or statement, often without support.

audit comments Written correspondence from the auditors to management about results of the audit performed.

auditability The degree of evidence availability with regard to an audit.

automated controls Internal controls that are solely enforced by a technology system or device without human interaction. See also **internal controls**.

B

bandwidth Information-carrying capacity of an electronic network.

benchmarking The process of comparison in which one set of metrics comes from the entity being measured and the other set of metrics comes from averages for an industry, specific configuration, or other common attributes.

best-of-breed system A third-party system developed to solve a specific business problem that has gained acceptance in the marketplace.

billing analyst A resource that performs billing and reviews output of billing.

biometric systems Information technology access systems that store and use the unique physical characteristics of people, such as thumbprint, for identification and access.

bottom-up An approach in which plans are developed at the lowest levels of the corporation and rolled up to determine the outcome.

boundary conditions The existing state of the limits.

brand reputation The past experience associated with a brand, where *brand* is defined as the total meaning applied to a product, service, individual, or organization.

build phase During this phase, the project team will build the system based on the agreed-upon design through system configuration and development.

business analyst Member of a software development project team; understands business requirements and translates them into software specifications.

business case A document that provides a justification for a business investment, often used in terms of technology investments. Business cases can be built by identifying financial (hard-dollar) benefits and intangible benefits, including mitigation of risk.

business intelligence (BI) Software that enables users to obtain enterprise-wide information for reporting, analytics, data mining, benchmarking, business performance management, and predictive analytics in order to support business decision making.

business process integration Integration framework comprised of a collection of technologies and services that form a middleware to enable integration of systems and applications across the enterprise.

business process management Software that models an enterprise's human and machine tasks and the interactions between them as processes and can monitor these tasks in real time in order to trigger a unit of work or set off an alert when specified time limits are exceeded or a response is not received within a specified time.

C

CEO Chief executive officer.

CFO Chief financial officer.

change management Process of enabling change in an organization as a result of a system implementation.

characterization A written representation of something.

CIO Chief information officer—job title for the board-level head of information technology within an organization. The CIO typically reports to the chief operations officer or the chief executive officer.

clean team Clean teams are launched to protect sensitive information (e.g., price list, contracts, and customer names and terms) from being openly shared between the acquirer and target prior to the deal close (i.e., Day 0). They are somewhat like a brick wall through which information must be carefully passed. Information within the clean team/room is used by designated individuals (e.g., current employees, retirees, or consultants) to perform analysis (e.g., jump-start synergy or integration planning activities). The information exchange is monitored and tracked (check-in and check-out). If the deal does not move forward, all information in the clean room is destroyed or handled as defined in the nondisclosure agreement between the potential seller and buyer. Your legal team should prescribe the dos and don'ts of handling sensitive information.

cloud computing   A technology where the data and the application are stored remotely and made available to the user over the Internet on demand.

commercial off-the-shelf (COTS) system   A third-party system that solves a specific business problem and can be implemented without extensive customization.

configuration   Software packages can be adjusted (configured) to specific business needs through changes of parameters in the software application.

contract negotiator   A resource in the contracting organization that negotiates contracts with customers.

contracts-to-cash scenario   The business process that begins with the signing of a contract and concludes with receipt of cash.

control activities   The internal controls that a company has implemented. See also **internal controls**.

controls   See **internal controls**.

critical success factor (CSF)   An element that is necessary for an organization or project to achieve its mission.

crown jewel asset   An asset that is considered to possess the highest level of value.

customer relationship management   An integrated information system used to plan, schedule, and manage aspects of dealing with prospects and customers. The software supports the combination of policies, processes, and strategies implemented by an organization to track customer information and unify its customer interactions.

customization   A modification to a packaged (purchased) system, where technical code is written to enhance the features already available.

cutover rehearsal Commonly referred to as *mock cutover*, this is a dry run of all activities required to switch on the software application in the final production environment.

D

database An organized, searchable repository for the storage of electronic data.

data breach A failure of an obligation to protect against the release of secure data.

data mart A targeted repository of data to support reporting and analysis of a specific set of financial or operational data.

data room A secure, private room (physical or virtual) used in mergers and acquisitions or other transactions where confidential data about a company is disclosed to prospective buyers or investors during the due diligence process.

data warehouse A large, often enterprise-wide repository of data used for reporting and analysis. Data warehouses generally collect and manage data from a large number of operational and financial systems across an enterprise.

Day 0/deal close Also referred to as *legal close*. The day on which the acquirer is legally responsible for the acquired entity or assets.

Day 1/Day One The first day companies involved in a merger, acquisition, or divestiture are legally merged or separated. The day the transaction is closed (e.g., currency is transacted and the legal entity/assets transferred). Also, Day 1 is a point in time when the target is declared as integrated into the acquirer (even if minimally). It is typically the next business day after the deal close. It is also common for organizations to close the deal, but declare a Day 1 event in the future (not integrated initially/stand-alone for a period of time). Day 1 is generally declared across the entire merger, acquisition, or divestiture program.

deal rationale   Reasons behind the creation and pursuit of a merger, acquisition, or divestiture transaction.

deliverable   A work product completed within a project phase by members of a project thread; the defined output of one or more related IT tasks.

deployment phase   During the deployment phase of the project, the team will perform all activities to cut over to the new system and start monitoring the system operations.

design phase   The purpose of the design phase of the project is to create a to-be business process model with sign-off from all key stakeholders.

deskside services   A source of technical support for resolving user problems and completing tasks that cannot be completed remotely, such as setting up and configuring computers for new workers, scheduling software upgrades, moving workstations, and repairing hardware. The deskside services team is typically responsible for desktops, laptops, printers, personal digital assistants, and other peripherals.

dimension   A slice of data used in analysis and reporting. For example, in a report that shows sales by customer and product for the year ending December 2009, "customer," "product," and "time" would be the dimensions used.

disclosures   Periodic financial reports issued to shareholders and regulators, such as the 10-K annual report and the 10-Q quarterly earnings release.

distributed delivery   Process of delivering (technology) services from multiple locations in a coordinated manner.

divested entity   This company is the portion of the divesting entity being removed from the corporate portfolio.

divesting entity   Often referred to as the *parent company*, this is the company from which a business unit, division, or department is being removed from the corporate portfolio.

divesture   Disposition or sale of an asset by a company. A company will often divest an asset that is not performing well, is not vital to the company's core business, or is worth more to a potential buyer or as a separate entity than as part of the company.

download   Transfer application/data from a remote location.

due diligence   An investigation of financial, accounting, tax, cash flow, and operational matters in order to understand where value in the target company exists and to identify issues that should be considered pre- and post-acquisition. Also, the process of evaluating the target company to validate the deal value based on detailed review of all aspects of the business.

E

efficacy   Effectiveness.

electronic data interchange (EDI)   The structured transmission of data between organizations by electronic means. It is used to transfer electronic documents (e.g., accounts payable invoices) from one computer system to another using a standardized format.

encryption   To transform information from readable plain text to unreadable cipher text to prevent unintended recipients from reading the data.

end state/Day 2/Day Two   Fully integrated into buyer or separated from parent (no transition services agreement dependency between buyers and seller). Functions may reach end state (or Day 2) at different times.

enterprise content management (ECM)   An information system used to capture, manage, store, deliver, and preserve an organization's unstructured information, including converting to and from digital content as well as converting to and from traditional media such as paper. ECM encompasses the traditional domains of records management and document management.

enterprise resource planning (ERP)   Complex computer systems that manage financial and operational data and processes. ERP systems generally include a general ledger, subsystems such as accounts payable and accounts receivable, inventory and manufacturing, supply chain, and logistics applications. Also, an enterprise-wide computer system that manages and coordinates a business's resources, information, and functions from shared data stores.

external stakeholder   Any party that has a vested interest in the merger and acquisition transaction but is not an internal part of any of the businesses being merged, acquired, or divested.

F

financial consolidation   The aggregation of financial results on a legal entity basis, including elimination of equity interests and intercompany transactions, conversion to a common currency, and application of ownership percentages.

fit/gap   Evaluation of requirements against a software application in order to highlight functionality not covered by the software application.

function   A group of activities and processes that integrate to form an end-to-end business process.

functional benchmarking   Process of comparing a company's information technology cost structure to that of other companies sharing a similar technology landscape and usage profile, irrespective of industry.

functional specification   A document that describes the required business functionality of a software program.

G

general ledger   Accounting records for a business, which includes the group of accounts represented on the financial statements.

generally accepted accounting principles (GAAP) The standardized approach and guidelines for financial accounting used in any given jurisdiction. GAAP includes the conventions and rules accountants follow in recording and summarizing transactions and in the preparation of financial statements.

globalization Distribution of business processes of a firm in more than one location for economic benefits.

governance model A structure within a project team or organization that defines the escalation path of any issues and the resolution approach.

H

hard-coding A method of writing technical code where variables are static and not designed to be maintainable, unless code is directly updated.

help desk A source of technical support for hardware or software that is staffed by people who can solve technical problems directly or forward the problem to someone else. Help desk staff log problems and track them until solved.

hierarchy An organizational structure that defines the relationship between master data elements.

homegrown system A system developed internally by a company's information technology staff.

human resources management systems Software systems or modules that automate the human resources (HR) processes such as employee selection, evaluation, payroll, and tracking employee data (e.g., skills, accomplishments, salary, etc.). These systems are often integrated into enterprise resource planning systems where the company's HR information and financial information are linked through a common database.

I

IASB See **International Accounting Standards Board**.

implementation   Deploying a software solution in a company is accomplished through an iterative sequence of activities. These activities are bundled into an implementation project.

industry benchmarking   Process of comparing a company's cost structure to that of industry peers.

information technology plan   A strategic document that assesses a company's existing system and technology environment and outlines a roadmap to developing an optimized long-term system and technology environment.

infrastructure   The technical components and their connectivity comprise the technological infrastructure within an organization.

in-house   Refers to the production of some commodity or service using a company's own funds, staff, or resources.

integration test   A comprehensive test, usually a concatenation of string tests with the purpose of validating system functionality across multiple functional areas.

internal controls   A process, procedure, or system designed to help an organization meet specific goals or objectives.

International Accounting Standards Board (IASB)   Founded in 2001 as the successor to the International Accounting Standards Committee (IASC, founded in 1973), an organization responsible for developing the International Financial Reporting Standards (IFRS) and promoting the use and application of these standards.

Internet commerce   Conducting complete business transactions over the Internet.

IT application portfolio   The inventory of software applications in use by an organization and the purpose of said applications.

IT assets   Tangible deliverables created during the course of an IT project that can be used in other similar projects. Examples include design, software code, or a testing scenario.

IT development group   Members of the team who design and build software applications.

IT-enabled business   Business processes that are enabled through technology.

IT infrastructure   The technical components (e.g., servers, network, security, etc.) required to run the many applications and services used by a company.

IT-intensive access cards   Key cards that have electronic chips embedded in them for controlling whether someone can access a facility.

IT operating model   Defines the framework for how the IT organization will conduct its operations.

IT organizational structure   Defines the hierarchical reporting relationship of employees within the IT organization.

IT pervasiveness   The increasing dependence of many business processes on information technology as an enabler.

IT support group   Members of the team who perform troubleshooting and maintenance for software.

K

key performance indicators   Financial and nonfinancial metrics used by an organization to define and evaluate how successful it is, typically in terms of making progress toward its goals (e.g., increase sales order processing time by 20 percent).

L

lawsuit   A legal proceeding or action in a court of law involving a claim by one individual or party against another.

legacy system   Term used to describe the original financial system when implementing a new financial system.

legal entity   An artificial construct that the law treats for some purposes as if it were a person, such as an incorporated organization.

M

mandates Requirements that must be complied with by an organization.

manual controls Internal controls that require an element of human interaction. See also **internal controls**.

master data The set of codes and structures that identify and organize data, such as customer numbers, employee IDs, and general ledger account numbers.

merger A transaction where two or more companies join together to form a single entity.

merger and acquisition (M&A) Aspect of corporate strategy, corporate finance, and management dealing with the buying, selling, and combining of different companies that can aid, finance, or help a growing company in a given industry grow rapidly without having to create another business entity.

merger, acquisition, and divestiture (MA&D) The merger, acquisition, or divestiture of an entity.

methodology A logical sequence of tasks and activities that have deliverables as an end result. Implementation projects typically follow a predefined methodology.

middleware Software that connects software components or applications, functioning as a conversion or translation layer or a consolidator and integrator. Middleware enables one application to communicate with another that runs on a different platform or comes from a different vendor, and it allows multiple processes running on one or more machines to interact across a network.

modeling A plan or representation intended to show appearance or construction of something.

mutually exclusive In an option-oriented environment, selection of a particular option automatically excludes the other options.

N

network A system of interconnected devices that provides a means for data to be transmitted from point to point.

O

offline A process that is performed outside of using the system.

offshore Relocation by a company of a business process from one country to another; typically an operational process, such as manufacturing, or supporting process, such as accounting. Also, a location other than client/project site offering resources generally at a lower cost.

online A process that is performed within or on the system.

online auction An auction performed over the Internet.

operating system Commonly abbreviated OS or O/S, a computer's master control program that manages all other applications, handles input and output from attached hardware peripherals, and manages sharing of the computer's resources. Also, software that controls the functionality of computer hardware.

order-to-cash A standard set of financial processes covering activities from receiving and processing a customer order through the final receipt of cash.

outsourced manufacturing Contracting with sources external to a firm to deliver manufacturing services.

P

payments card industry requirements The standards set forth by VISA, MasterCard, American Express, and other credit/debit card companies to protect cardholders' account data.

performance test   The purpose of the performance test is to confirm that the production system will be able handle the anticipated volume of users and transactions.

playbooks   Documents that outline and describe a strategy for a certain organization or activity.

potential revenue   Projected cash inflow from a merger, acquisition, or divestiture after taxes.

preventive controls   Obstacles designed to prohibit a particular action from occurring.

procure-to-pay   A standard set of financial processes covering activities from procuring goods and services through the final payment for those goods and services.

product information management (PIM)   Processes and technologies focused on centrally managing information about products, with a focus on the data required to market and sell the products through one or more distribution channels. A central set of product data can be used to feed consistent, accurate, and up-to-date information to multiple output media such as websites, print catalogs, ERP systems, and electronic data feeds to trading partners. PIM systems generally need to support multiple geographic locations, multilingual data, and maintenance and modification of product information within a centralized catalog to provide consistently accurate information to multiple channels in a cost-effective manner.

product lifecycle management   The process of managing the entire lifecycle of a product from its initial conception, through the design and manufacture, to service and eventual disposal.

programmed controls   Internal controls that are enforced by a technology system or device. See also **internal controls**.

Project Management Institute (PMI)   The leading global association for the project management profession. PMI advocates project, program, and portfolio management that can enhance and accelerate organizational change.

Project Management Office The department responsible for managing the implementation project and delivering the solution in time and within budget.

project phase A grouping of different activities that are performed during a major stage of the project.

project portfolio management (PPM) Term used by project managers and project management (PM) organizations to describe methods for analyzing and collectively managing a group of current or proposed projects based on numerous key characteristics.

project thread A common theme of functional areas and a team that performs related activities during each project phase.

Q

QA environment Quality assurance (QA) is used to complete comprehensive systems tests prior to deployment to the productive environment.

R

radio frequency identification (RFID) The technology to tag and identify a firm's assets/inventory; uses devices that can read and respond to radio waves.

real-time capability Ability to receive and process data very rapidly with minimal or no time lapse between the event and processing of the data about the event.

right-sizing A process of reducing a company's workforce to match the expected workload from the business operations. (Formerly known as *downsizing, right-sizing* was created when *downsizing* was perceived as too negative.) Also refers to any process that makes the resources match the requirements.

ROI (return on investment)   Performance measure used to evaluate the efficiency of an investment or to compare the efficiency of a number of different investments.

S

safeguard   Something intended to serve as a defensive or protection mechanism.

Sarbanes-Oxley (SOX) Act of 2002   A 2002 act of Congress, authored by Paul Sarbanes and Michael Oxley, that mandates stricter corporate accounting policies and financial controls. U.S. legislation that sets new or revised standards for public companies and public accounting firms.

Sarbanes-Oxley 302   Section 302 of the Sarbanes-Oxley Act of 2002, which requires internal procedures to be designed to ensure accurate financial disclosure.

Sarbanes-Oxley 404   Section 404 of the Sarbanes-Oxley Act of 2002, which requires management and the external auditor to report on the adequacy of the company's internal control over financial reporting (ICFR).

scoping and planning   During the scoping and planning phase, the project team will perform initial planning and preparation activities.

server virtualization   A technique to share and dynamically allocate physical server resources to logical server partitions. Each partition appears to the end user as an individual physical resource, but is really a virtual representation of the combined and shared physical resources.

service-level agreement (SLA)   Defines response times and service commitments of a service organization for specific service activities.

shared services   The provision of a service by one part of an organization or group where that service previously had been found in more than one part of the organization or group.

shareholder value   The estimated worth that an owner is able to obtain from an investment in a company.

SOX   See **Sarbanes-Oxley Act of 2002**.

sponsor   A senior executive in the company who is responsible for championing the project.

stakeholders   Individuals who are affected by an organization's actions.

steering committee   A group of senior-level employees in an organization who support the project and can assist the project team in resolving issues and driving decisions.

stock-keeping unit (SKU)   A set of identifiers for goods and services offered by a company.

string test   A concatenation of several individual unit tests that are used to ensure that a specific system function works as intended within a broader business context.

subassembly   A (big) part of a manufactured product; often itself made from/consisting of a number of parts and components.

supply chain management   Software tools or modules used in the planning, scheduling, and control of supply chain transactions (spanning raw materials to finished goods from point of origin to point of consumption), managing supplier relationships, and controlling associated business processes.

synergy   Value-creating opportunities resulting from a merger or acquisition such as cost savings, revenue enhancements, and/or improved asset utilization. For example, a cost synergy is an opportunity for the combined organization to reduce expenses and a revenue synergy is an opportunity for the combined organization to generate more revenue than the pre-merger entities standing alone.

system   A combination of hardware, software, and data devices.

system development methodology   The structured approach to scoping, planning, designing, building, testing, and deploying a system.

systems integrator   A consulting firm specialized in deploying software solutions at businesses.

system of record (SOR)   An information storage system (commonly implemented on a computer system) that is the authoritative data source for a given data element or piece of information. The need to identify systems of record can become acute in organizations where management information systems have been built by taking output data from multiple-source systems, reprocessing this data, and then re-presenting the result for a new business use.

T

target   The organization or business being considered for acquisition.

target screening   An analysis of potential candidates for a merger or acquisition based on the strategic objectives of the would-be parent company.

technical specification   A document that describes the required technical details of a software program in order to meet the needs described in a functional specification.

testing phase   During the testing phase of the project, the system will go through a series of tests to validate the complete system.

test script   A guide to how to perform a system test. It typically contains detailed step-by-step instructions, data to be used, and the expected outcome for each step.

top-down   An approach in which the results are determined first (e.g., by industry or functional benchmarking) and the details of the methods and activities to achieve the desired results are determined second.

total cost of ownership (TCO) The total price in money, time, and resources of owning and using software, including hardware, software, services, and maintenance.

transactional data The set of records of individual business activities or events.

transactional tasks These tasks primarily include activities that create or transfer information and data.

transition services agreement (TSA) An agreement between the buyer and the seller where the seller provides interim services to the buyer until such time that the buyer can assume full operational responsibility for those business activities. Also, TSAs are temporary agreements generally for 12 to 24 months for services to be provided by the seller to the buyer. It is also common to have *reverse* TSAs, where the buyer needs to provide services back to the seller.

U

unit test A test of an isolated functionality within a software application.

user acceptance test (UAT) The focus during the user acceptance testing activities will be to confirm that the users can perform their business functions with the application that has been created and that all business requirements are met.

V

value-added activities Activities that generate a positive return on the investment of resources that cannot be eliminated without impairing a process.

value proposition The benefit received for the investment made.

virtual storage array A bank of hard disk drives housed in a common cabinet and managed by software to provide a single view of all disks in the cabinet as one large expanse of storage. The storage can be dynamically allocated through the management software with the physical disk attributes masked from the end user.

W

workaround Manual process designed around a system limitation. Because the system cannot automatically perform the task or output, personnel must either manually process or reformat information to achieve the optimal result.

workflow System process to manage the routing and approval of documents and transactions across multiple people and/or departments within an organization. Also, automating a business approval process that will notify the appropriate resources when activities/approvals need to be performed.

About the Author

Janice M. Roehl-Anderson is the principal in charge of Deloitte's Enterprise Applications practice in the Northern Pacific Region. As such, she is responsible for facilitating the delivery of all ERP-related services. Jan has managed the implementation of numerous enterprise resource planning, customer relationship management, and human resource management software packages. She has over 20 years of global systems-related experience in a variety of sectors, including consumer business, media and entertainment, communications, high-technology manufacturing, state and local government, and financial institutions. Additionally, she has extensive experience with global implementations and with mergers, acquisitions, and divestitures (MA&Ds) and is responsible for coordinating Deloitte's enterprise applications–related efforts on MA&D projects.

Prior to joining Deloitte, Jan spent 14 years with Ernst & Young, where she was responsible for managing the Denver office's software package implementation practice.

Jan has a Bachelor of Business degree from the University of Washington and an MBA from the University of Southern California in Accounting and Information Technology. She has co-authored over ten books for John Wiley & Sons and has passed the Certified Public Accounting exam.

Index